KING OF THE SLOTS

KING OF THE SLOTS

WILLIAM "SI" REDD

JACK HARPSTER

 PRAEGER

AN IMPRINT OF ABC-CLIO, LLC
Santa Barbara, California • Denver, Colorado • Oxford, England

Library of Congress Cataloging-in-Publication Data
Harpster, Jack, 1937–
  King of the slots : William "Si" Redd / Jack Harpster.
     p. cm.
  Includes bibliographical references and index.
  ISBN 978-0-313-38208-6 (alk. paper) — ISBN 978-0-313-38209-3 (ebook) 1.
Redd, William Si (William Silas), 1911-2003. 2. Gambling industry—United
States—History. 3. Slot machines—United States—History. 4. Businessmen—
United States—Biography. I. Title.
  HV6710.3.R43H37 2010
  338.7′61795092—dc22
  [B]
                                                        2010009420

ISBN: 978-0-313-38208-6
EISBN: 978-0-313-38209-3

14 13 12 11 10   1 2 3 4 5

This book is also available on the World Wide Web as an eBook.
Visit www.abc-clio.com for details.

Praeger
An Imprint of ABC-CLIO, LLC

ABC-CLIO, LLC
130 Cremona Drive, P.O. Box 1911
Santa Barbara, California 93116-1911

This book is printed on acid-free paper ∞
Manufactured in the United States of America

CONTENTS

ILLUSTRATIONS AND TABLES

ILLUSTRATIONS

TABLES

ACKNOWLEDGMENTS

There are a number of individuals and organizations that played an important role in telling this life story of William Silas "Si" Redd.

First and foremost, I owe a deep debt of gratitude to the family of Mr. Redd, his daughters Sherry Green and Vinnie Copeland, and his son-in-law Alan Green, all of Massachusetts. All three shared stories, photos, and recollections of this amazing man. They allowed me—even encouraged me—to tell the *whole* story of his life, the bad parts along with the good. Thanks to their spirit of generosity and honesty, I was able to write a book that pulled no punches in describing one of the twentieth century's most remarkable business geniuses.

During his lifetime, Mr. Redd graciously sat down with two university oral history interviewers and related his life story in his own words. I am indebted to the University of Southern Mississippi and the University of Nevada Oral History programs for capturing and preserving this important and often colorful information. Because Mr. Redd passed away in 2002, without these two outstanding programs it would not have been possible to see into the creative mind of this gaming legend.

Twenty-four friends, foes, employees, customers, competitors, and gaming industry observers of Mr. Redd also sat patiently for interviews and gave me firsthand knowledge about the "real" Si Redd, as they saw and understood him. Their names and relationships with him are all listed in the Bibliography, and I thank each and every one of them for their valuable contributions.

The Special Collections Department at the library of the University of Nevada–Reno and the Nevada Historical Society in Reno were also great helps in gathering information.

A story without pictures is like a gambler without hope—it just doesn't work. Thus I'd like to thank the individuals and organizations that allowed me to use the great photographs that accompany the story. These are the Redd family, Marshall Fey, Dale Rodesch, *Slot Tech* and *Always Jukin'* magazines, Las Vegas News Bureau, Nevada Historical Society, and Wayne Namerow.

Finally, for always being there when the phone rings or the doorbell chimes and I'm in the middle of a complex paragraph, I'd like to thank my assistant, Mary Louise Turtletaub.

CHAPTER 1

THE NESHOBA COUNTY FAIR

As he sat hunched over on the bench at the rear of the rude plank dais awaiting his turn at the lectern, seventeen-year-old William Silas "Si" Redd was probably more aware of the butterflies in his stomach than of the hundreds of his friends and neighbors who were crowding into the open-sided wooden pavilion where he would shortly begin his speech.

It was not yet 9:30 a.m. at the 1930 Neshoba County Fair, but already the hot, muggy air of a Mississippi August morning was beginning to crowd in on him. The last strains of music from the early morning concert by the Philadelphia String Band still echoed in his head as he saw the master of ceremonies rise to introduce him. As he nervously shuffled his notes in his lap, Si Redd probably did not waste a single thought on the colorful history of the organization that had invited him to speak.

* * * *

It had been another typically hot, muggy August day in 1889.[1] The officers of the local branch of an east central Mississippi chapter of the Grange—the nation's oldest and largest agricultural organization— smiled at one another as dozens of men, women, and children hurried across the field to where they stood. A large hand-painted sign hanging high over their heads, fluttering gently with each passing breeze, proclaimed it to be the Coldwater Community

Fair. The officers—all Neshoba County farmers themselves—were excited because they did not know if any of their friends and neighbors would even show up for their little party.

Their expectations were modest. They charged no admission fee, and they planned to keep the event open for only a few hours. There were some agricultural displays, a colorful palette of home-grown vegetables carefully arrayed on a wooden table, a few quilts and articles of handmade clothing hanging over ropes stretched from tree to tree, and a noisy assemblage of horses, mules, cows, hogs, and chickens. Naturally there was also homemade lemonade and freshly baked pies.

There were no rousing political speeches planned, no entertainment—save Miss Kate Spivey singing "Dixie"—and none of the scrumptious jars of put-up bread-and-butter pickles or plates of sweet, sticky BBQ that would become staples of the event in years to come. But it was a beginning, albeit a modest one; and the 100 or so folks who turned out had a grand time.

Within a few years this Coldwater Community Fair would become the Neshoba Fair, then the Annual Neshoba Fair, and finally the Annual Neshoba County Fair. As the name grew, so did the crowds, and by the turn of the century, thousands of rural folks would flock to the fairgrounds, located about eight miles southwest of Philadelphia, the county seat. The fair lasted two days, then three, and finally seven. Early on, some fairgoers began constructing slapdash little cabins where they camped for the duration of the event, while others slept in the back of the covered wagons they had arrived in. A crude hotel was built to house visitors, then a second one. A simple town square was built in the middle of the field, and a giant pavilion built in the center; a racetrack was put in, and people began to build more small cabins around the perimeter of the square. The Fair grew, the crowds got larger every year, and the town square with its mélange of cabins and huts became equal in size to many of the small rural Mississippi villages and crossroads from which it drew its attendees.

A tradition had begun in that field in 1889; and today, in the early years of the twenty-first century, the Neshoba County Fair is still going on stronger than ever, one of the top summer attractions in the entire nation.

One fairgoer summed up why the event has remained so popular with rural Mississippians for more than 120 years: "It's not really a fair; it's more like a reunion, a big homecoming."[2]

* * * *

The late 1920s and early 1930s were not a good time to be a Mississippian. Mississippi was the poorest state in the nation. The monetary chasm between the state's old wealth and the large majority of her poor citizens was huge, and devilish Jim Crow laws dealt with black citizens with a heavy hand. The Ku Klux Klan, in its second iteration since the end of the Civil War, had reached its peak, and it held sway throughout the state. The cotton crop had been sub-par for a couple of years due to a boll weevil infestation, and the threat of hurricanes and tornadoes kept folks throughout the state on constant edge. Finally, the Great Flood of 1927 left almost the entire western half of the state under water in one of the most powerful natural disasters of the twentieth century.

One of the state's greatest writers and poets in the first half of the century was William Alexander Percy. In his autobiography, he spoke eloquently of the disaster that took nearly 300 lives and washed 700,000 people out of their homes:

The 1927 flood was a torrent ten feet deep the size of Rhode Island; it was thirty-six hours coming and four months going; it was deep enough to drown a man, swift enough to upset a boat, and lasting enough to cancel a crop year . . . The South Delta became seventy-five hundred square miles of mill-race in which one hundred and twenty thousand human beings and one hundred thousand animals squirmed and bobbed.[3]

Then, of course, there was the Great Depression that first cast its ugly shadow over the state in late 1929. But any person who believed that all this misfortune would cancel, or even constrict, the Neshoba County Fair simply did not understand the psyche and the spirit of rural Mississippians. The 1930 Fair, the 39th annual, would go on as usual. It would be the first year a carnival company was commissioned to stage midway shows, rides, and entertainment; the first year for a brand new, giant livestock barn; and the first time a generator was in place to provide electric lighting to replace the kerosene lanterns and pine-knot torches that had always lighted up the grounds and cabins after dark.[4]

Si Redd was in his second year at Philadelphia High School in 1930. The town of Philadelphia was home to just under 1200 men, women, and children, some white, some black, and a few Choctaw Indians. It had no particular claim to fame in the early 1930s, and it wouldn't, in fact, until 1964 when three young civil rights workers were murdered outside the town jail by the violent White Knights of the Ku Klux Klan—an ugly incident that prompted the 1988 movie,

Mississippi Burning. "The troubles," as the folks in Philadelphia call it, is a chapter in the town's history that most longtime residents are still trying to put behind them.[5]

It was quite an honor for Redd to have been invited to be one of the speakers at the Fair, the prize, really, for his having won the high school debating club's annual competition. He would join well-known state and local politicians addressing the fairgoers who considered these speeches one of the highlights of the annual event. Redd was to deliver a brief history of the Neshoba County Education System. It was an assignment at which he must have excelled, because he was invited back the next year to present a brief history of the Fair itself. Many years later, Si Redd recalled that he had also been selected to introduce one of the main speakers at the Fair, but he wasn't sure which year it was.[6]

However, there can be little doubt that when young Redd made that speech on the history of the county's education system in 1930, his high school sweetheart Ivy Lee Oliphant was in the crowd cheering her boyfriend on. Without a doubt, his parents Marvin and Nannie Redd were there too, busting their buttons with pride at their son's accomplishment.

After his talk was over—and judged to be a rousing success—Si and Ivy would likely have spent the remainder of the five days hand-in-hand, enjoying the many shows, displays, and special events that would draw over 30,000 people to the Coldwater Fairgrounds that year. There was a greased-pig chase and home-churned butter tasting, trotter and pacer racing, a hot-air balloon ride, Angora goat shearing, a thrilling rodeo, baseball games, and crazy quilt displays. From the grandstand, Si and Ivy may have listened to the concert by Jack Bigelow and his Sorority Girl Band, and watched a daring aerialist show by the Romanoff Troupe.

There may have been a small arcade with a few coin-operated vending machines and musical contraptions on the midway. The pinball machine was still a few years in the future, but player pianos, crude jukeboxes, and machines vending soda pop into cups, or gum and gumballs, were already popular. If so, it's a safe bet that Si Redd spent some blissful time investing his pennies and listening to the whirring and clanging of the gears, springs, and levers of those mechanical marvels. These machines seemed to be in his blood, and they would play a major role in the young man's life for the next three-quarters of a century.

* * * *

William Silas "Si" Redd was born outside of Union, Mississippi, on November 16, 1911, the second of three children, to Marvin and Nannie Redd. Si's parents were definitely *not* part of the Magnolia State's aristocratic upper crust. They were sharecroppers, barely eking out a living from east central Mississippi's grudging red clay soil.[7]

The family lived in a small log cabin no bigger than an average garage.[8] The farm wasn't much larger. "Maybe thirty acres," Redd recalled, "fifteen of it in farmland and fifteen of it in the cows and the pastures." Recollecting another fact, he added through a scrunched grin, "Those pastures had a lot of bitter weeds, so when the cows ate bitter weeds, the milk was bitter."[9]

In addition to Si—so named after the biblical Silas by the old preacher who helped in his birth—his household consisted of his parents and siblings. Father Marvin, a second-generation Mississippian whose family originally hailed from South Carolina, came from a much

The Redd family as they appear in this 1911 photo. Marvin and Nannie Redd were sharecroppers, and Marvin was also a Pentecostal street preacher. They had two children at the time. Paul was almost two and William Silas was three months old. Daughter Marie would join the family a few years later. *Redd family photo.*

larger family. The 1900 Census lists him living in Neshoba County with his father, mother, five siblings, and an unidentified 22-year-old male. Si's mother Nannie—nee Eatman—was from Meridian, Mississippi, and had married Marvin in 1908. Si's siblings were older brother Paul, born in 1910, and younger sister Marie, who would be born four years after Si entered the world.[10]

Their small farm was not located in Union proper. "[It was] about fifteen miles back of the depot in Union," Redd said.[11] The old depot, torn down in the 1970s, was a whistle stop for the Meridian & Memphis Railway, its thirty-two miles of track connecting Union with Meridian. Through connections with other small railroads, Union's citizens, once isolated, were tied to the rest of the state and Mid South.[12]

One of Si Redd's earliest memories of life in rural Mississippi had to do with a regular Saturday night ritual for a lot of country folks: the weekly bath. The entire family would take a bath, one at a time, in a large old dented tin washtub. To save both soap and water, the family's turn did not come until after the weekly laundry was completed, leaving one to wonder how clean the last person out might have been.[13]

Union township is little more than a flyspeck on a map of east central Mississippi. The town straddles the boundary between Neshoba County to the north and Newton County to the south. Today, approximately 75 percent of Union's 2000 residents live on the Newton side of the boundary; in 1911, the total population was just under 700, both black and white, with most sharing one condition: poverty.

The Redd farm was north of the boundary, in Neshoba County, and it was in that county that Redd grew up. Despite having the smaller part of Union's population, Neshoba still claimed seniority over its southern counterpart. Neshoba County was carved out of the wilderness in 1833 from the territory ceded to the United States three years earlier by the Choctaw Nation through the Treaty of Dancing Rabbit Creek. The county's name means "grey wolf" in the Choctaw dialect, a Muskogean language that bears a striking similarity to the dialect of the nearby Chickasaw nation. Less than three years later, Newton County—named, it is said, after English mathematician Sir Isaac Newton—was created out of the southern half of Neshoba County. Today, Decatur is the Newton County seat, and the grandly named Philadelphia enjoys that distinction in Neshoba County.

There are two local legends about how Union township acquired its name. The first claims that because the small settlement is located on the boundary between Neshoba and Newton, it represents the symbolic joining of the two counties. The second legend says there were three congregations on the site in the beginning—Baptist, Presbyterian, and Methodist—but they shared one church building on alternating Sundays. So the area was initially named Union Church, but there happened to be another town in the state by the same name, so eventually "Church" was dropped from its name.[14]

Neshoba County is level along the river and creek bottoms, and the remainder of the land is hilly and undulating. Pine, oak, hickory, black walnut, and beech trees dot the landscape. The Pearl River and its tributary creeks provided plenty of fresh water for those living in the southern part of the county.[15] Farmers such as Marvin Redd, who tilled the clay soil in Neshoba and Newton counties in the early twentieth century, eyed with great envy their counterparts across the state. There, in the rich alluvial soil of the Mississippi River Delta, crops flourished. Despite the weaker soil, however, few east central Mississippi farm families went hungry. Early Newton County historian A. J. Brown described a cornucopia of local produce: "Corn, peas, potatoes, pumpkins, and everything necessary to live upon were made at home. The same was true as to bacon and other provisions, which could be raised in the county. There was a good deal of wheat made in the county too."[16] Naturally, everybody also grew cotton, the region's main cash crop, and most grew black-eyed peas, soybeans, pole beans, figs, and other fruit trees. Another local farmer working a plot near the Redd's farm agreed it was an adequate bounty, and added, "[We made] sorghum molasses . . . and hunted rabbits and squirrels."[17]

In an interview, Si once explained that in Mississippi sharecropping, the land's owner normally received 80 percent of the bounty, and the family working the soil got the other 20 percent. Quoting a neighbor, he said of the situation in which he was raised, "I don't mind being poor, but it sho' is inconvenient."[18]

Despite their poverty, the Redd family got by. But it was often in spite of—rather than because of—the family patriarch, because in addition to his farming, Marvin Redd was also a freelance Pentecostal street preacher. "My father would go on the street and preach," Redd recalled. "He would say that the Good Lord spoke to him and told him to spread the word. He never had an education . . . he was a jack-leg preacher."[19]

Warming up to his subject, Redd related how his father would leave the farming to Nannie and the children while he went out to preach. "One day he told my mother that the Lord had spoken to him," Redd grinned. When Nannie asked what the Lord had said, Marvin replied, "Well, he didn't actually speak, but He gave me a sign: the letters GPC written up in the sky. He was telling me to Go Preach Christ."

The long-suffering Nannie Redd looked him right in the eye and said, "Well, Marvin, maybe He was trying to tell you Go Plow the Corn."[20]

Marvin's faith was genuine and deep-seated; it was not just an excuse to get out from behind his mule and plow. He instilled his beliefs in his children too. "We were taught religion until it came out of our ears," Si recalled.[21] But he admitted that as he grew older, the faith took hold. He remembered his mother telling him about an incident when he was three or four months old, when he fell out of bed and broke his arm at the elbow.

The doctors told Nannie and Marvin that Si's arm would be stiff for life, so they decided to take their son to a faith healer. In the middle of a copse of pine trees, a faith healer and his followers had built a temporary church—a "bush arbor" Si called it—where pine boughs were stacked high in a square formation, surrounding a bunch of felled logs for sitting. That was their church. Amidst singing and preaching and chanting, baby Si was delivered up to the healer who rubbed ointment on the arm and prayed over it. Two days later, the arm had not improved, so Nannie returned to the church in the woods for a second visit. There, a member of the little congregation put a cookie in Si's hand, on his bad side. He lifted the cookie to his mouth with the bad arm and began to eat, something he had not been able to do since the accident. The arm was healed. "Now that's a true story, so help me God," Redd said. "That's a true, true story . . . I'd just have to be a terrible hypocrite [if] I didn't believe . . ."[22]

Although Marvin Redd may have been the primary religious tutor in the family, Nannie Redd passed on her own form of wisdom to her children. She was a strong advocate of positive thinking, and she passed her message on to her children at every opportunity. His parents' religious and philosophical lessons, Redd claimed years later, helped shape his life and his business philosophy.

Early in his life Si Redd made a decision—consciously or not we cannot know—that he would not be a product of his environment or of his time. He would be more. How, where, or by what means, he had no idea, but he had no doubt it would happen. His greatest ally in this quest was his mother Nannie.

Nannie Eatman Redd was the practical one in the family. She was born and raised in nearby Meridian, and it seemed to be her life's goal to improve her family's lot. "If we say 'better living' . . . and desire . . . to get ahead, what formed our character was really my mother," Si Redd said. "Her burning desire [was] always [that] we do better or get an education."[23]

Perhaps it was the influence of living in Meridian that had inspired the young Nannie Eatman. Between 1890 and 1930 Meridian was the largest city in Mississippi and a leading center for manufacturing in the South. It was also the regional rail center. Nannie was surrounded by culture: the huge, ornate Grand Opera House that still serves the city today, and two wonderful Carnegie Libraries, one for whites and one for blacks.[24] It is not known if Nannie came from a middle class family, but the proximity of culture and education certainly rubbed off on her regardless.

Life on the farm outside Union was a constant whir of activity for Si, Paul, and Marie. In addition to the farming and the cattle, they also kept hogs and chickens; but the real workers were their mules. "I'll bet we were ten or twelve or fifteen years old . . . before we ever had the occasion to ride on a horse," Si laughed.[25]

From the Redd farm, it was five or six miles to the nearest grocery story, and the family would make the shopping trip in an old buckboard pulled by one of their mules. The closest shopping, other than for basic items, was the tiny town of Neshoba. The town had a post office, a railroad depot, a bank, a drug store, a doctor's office, a hardware store, a wagon and buggy store, a two-story hotel, and a small mercantile. About three miles south of Neshoba, down the old dirt road in Union, stood the area's most stately structure. Boler's Inn is a two-story, pre–Civil War stagecoach inn that stands as proudly today as it did almost 150 years ago when General William Tecumseh Sherman was quartered there on his march through the South. Sherman may have been impressed with his quarters, but it did not stop him from burning most of the town as he rode out.[26]

Si Redd recalled as a small boy helping his mother with chores around the farm. Doing the family wash was one of his most vivid memories. They would boil the clothes in homemade lye soap, "[made] from the fat of hogs, I would suppose," Si said;[27] then they would beat them and hang them out to dry. Si's chores also included lugging water to the fields, mucking the hogs, feeding the chickens, milking the cows, and chopping firewood.

Despite all the hard work to be done around the farm and Marvin's frequent absences due to his street corner preaching, there was never any doubt that the children would attend school. Nannie Redd simply wouldn't have it any other way. Si recalled his first school was a little one-room log schoolhouse at a rural log camp crossroads—now vanished—named Tigville. After one or two years, the Redd children transferred to another school in Beech Springs in Neshoba County.[28]

The family moved a number of times over the next few years as Nannie Redd constantly sought to improve their position. Si recalled a small town named Shady Grove, then finally a move to the "big city" of Union itself. "I'll never forget, we moved in[to] a very poor old dilapidated house. The only way you could clean this house . . . it was so black and so much dirt that all we could do was get lime. You know, if you take lime and put it in water, you can use it for paint.

"I remember the first night we were there, it was very cold and we had to take newspapers . . . and stuff them in the holes of the floor to keep the cold air from coming up."[29]

During this period, World War I was raging in faraway places the Redds and their neighbors had never heard of, places such as Lorraine, the Ardennes, Tannenberg, and Isonzo. In school the teacher would point to these spots on the big round globe that sat in the corner, and each child would include the name of a Neshoba or Newton County soldier in their daily prayers.

Every able-bodied male between eighteen and forty-five was required to register for the draft in 1918, and thirty-nine year old Marvin Redd did his duty, according to World War I Draft Registration records. Marvin listed his occupation as "Minister," and he was described as being of "medium height, medium build with blue eyes and dark hair."[30] The Redds were fortunate, however, as the war ended soon afterwards and Marvin did not have to serve. Many Neshoba County young men did serve, however, and fourteen made the ultimate sacrifice for their country.[31]

The Redds had an uncle, a dentist, who also lived in Union, and the children loved having cousins close by. The doctor's name was Dr. Sim Red—with only one "d," Si explained. "He never did fool around putting that extra D [in]," he laughed. Actually, Marvin had originally had only one "d" in his name too, but Nannie had changed it sometime after they married, believing it made them sound more educated.[32]

It also appears that she changed her given name at some point. Second- and third-generation Redd family members who are still living remember her as Nancy. However, every official record, including one in Marvin's own hand, lists her as Nannie.

For fun, once the chores were completed, Si, Paul, and their cousins would probably sneak down to take a cooling swim or dip a fishing line in the Chunkey River, a small river that gathered its headwaters right outside of town.

Soon, however, Nannie Redd would move the family again, to the Neshoba County seat of Philadelphia, a town of 1200 people by that time. Though they continued to farm, working a twelve-acre plot right in the city, this would mark a turning point for young Si Redd, who had never known anything but abject poverty.[33]

— CHAPTER 2 —

A GOOFY BEGINNING

The town of Philadelphia the Redds moved to in the late 1920s was a very different place from what it had been only two decades earlier. At that earlier time, it had been a sleepy village of less than one hundred people, virtually isolated from the rest of the nation. But when the railroad and the telegraph finally arrived in 1905, everything changed: its population grew, and the county seat finally began to gain some respect, becoming the entertainment hub for the area. Church festivals, minstrel shows, the Neshoba County Fair, an annual circus, traveling medicine man shows, and the Great Swain Show with its lively melodramas drew people from as far away as Carthage and Decatur.[1]

"By the 1920s of my childhood," wrote Neshoba County author Florence Mars, "some of the streets of Philadelphia were paved, and the square was filled with one- and two-story brick buildings with flat wood awnings that covered the sidewalk in front."[2]

Mars went on to paint a vivid picture of everyday life in the small but bustling town when the Redds arrived:

On Saturday people came to town to shop for everything from plowstock to the latest in ladies' millinery. Crowds of Philadelphians—white farmers, Negroes, Choctaw Indians—filled the lawn of the old red brick courthouse and the sidewalks around the square. Most of the country people dressed differently than we did in town—the men in overalls, khakis, and flannel, the women in homemade cotton dresses. The Negroes dressed more colorfully, the women often wearing aprons and bandanas. . . . The Choctaw men wore white shirts, black pants, and hats; the women wore colorful, ankle-length dresses with ruffles on the bottom. Almost all adults, except the Choctaw women, wore large-brimmed soft straw hats to protect themselves from the sun; some women wore their Sunday hats.[3]

Although it was still a far cry from the "metropolis" of Meridian, where she had grown up, Nannie Redd must have been delirious with joy to be surrounded by all the trappings of civilization again. Needless to say, the crowded streets of downtown Philadelphia were a boon to Marvin too. Here he was able to join other jackleg preachers and evangelicals—men and women such as Miss Nannie Ogletree, Railroad Spinks, and the Billy Sunday–trained Howard Williams—on the steps of the courthouse, or on the lawn under the sweeping magnolia tree, as they took their turns trying to save souls.

Young Si also fit right in. He could see there were opportunities aplenty for an ambitious young fellow looking to make a few dollars. His first foray into the business world had come even before he entered his teen years; later in life he said he was seven years old when he started earning some cash.[4]

Somewhere, as a young boy, he had discovered a "miracle" product named White Cloverine Brand Salve, a petroleum jelly product sold in a round tin box. According to the label, the patented medicine was highly recommended for "sores, burns, cuts, ulcers, chaffed hands, face and lips, common sore throats, chafes, galls, nasal catarrh, itching piles, sun burn, and tired, sore and aching feet." Because these were all common afflictions in rural Mississippi, the perceptive young boy saw an opportunity.

He also became aware of another product, a monthly magazine designed for rural folks called *Grit* that had been around since the early 1880s. So with a case of his White Cloverine Brand Salve and a stack of *Grit* magazines, bought at wholesale prices, Si Redd hit the road, walking to every farmhouse within a ten-mile radius.

"We were so far out in the country, you had to scare the hoot owls off the drinking dipper," Redd said years later in the folksy, homespun style of speaking that became his stock-in-trade.[5]

Si explained about the distributors for the two products he sold: "They would charge a nickel; well, you got a dime. If they charged a dime, then you got twenty cents, and that was the profit."[6]

Though never a whiz at math, young Redd understood at an early age that buying low and selling high was a very good thing. He followed that up by learning another basic business principle probably not taught at the Harvard Business School: the concept of contract labor.

Entering their teen years, Si and his brother Paul were expected to pick a certain amount of cotton each week to help the family survive. Cotton picking was hard, painful stoop labor. "You got up at daybreak. You stopped for . . . dinner, thirty minutes, at twelve. Then you go back again, and you stopped when it was dark," Si remembered.[7]

Redd could pick about 250 pounds of cotton a day. However, the bending and stooping; the strain of the heavy, scratchy burlap sack you dragged behind you; the raw, cut fingers from plucking the hard, sharp cotton bole from its plant; the blistering sun; the gnats buzzing into your eyes and ears; and the stinging no-see-ums feasting on the salt trail left on your face and neck from sweat, made it a very, very long, arduous day.

The inventive Redd discovered he could hire three or four young neighborhood boys—black or white, it didn't matter to the budding entrepreneur—to do the picking for him. Then he could go downtown and get a better-paying job working as a helper on a lumber truck at the local mill. To the best of his recollection years later, Redd believed he was paying the young boys a nickel each a day, fifteen or twenty cents total, while he was making forty or fifty cents a day at the mill. The work was much easier to boot. Again, this was a math the young man could understand.

At some point in his midteens, Redd entered Philadelphia High School, and he found a job at a local dry cleaning plant. "I'd get up in the morning at, oh, six o'clock and solicit—pick up dry cleaning," he said. "Then I'd go on to school, and then in the afternoon I'd come back and work in that dry cleaning plant . . . and on Saturday and Sunday."[8]

About the dry cleaning job, he told *Forbes* magazine with a grin in 1982, "I'd go out and walk the streets and talk men into giving us the hats off their heads so we could block them."[9] Having discovered the pride and value of having some money jingling in his overalls, Redd also worked at a bakery on Saturday night. Between the two jobs, he was making about three dollars a week, a princely sum in the late 1920s in rural Mississippi. Then came October 29, 1929— Black Tuesday—and the beginning of the Great Depression.

The Depression affected different people, and different areas of the country, in different ways. To go from being rich, or even financially comfortable, to being poor was a stark, life-shattering change. To go from being poor to being dirt-poor was not nearly so traumatic. Perhaps a poor Mississippi farm family such as the Redds would eat potatoes with greens or turnips five times a week, rather than the customary three times; or maybe a small sack of butter beans, rather than a nickel, would be dropped into the collection plate at church on Sunday morning for the preacher's wife, or to be shared with the congregation's less fortunate. Or perhaps the annual family outing to the Neshoba County Fair would have to be cancelled, and the year-long dream of cotton candy and exciting midway rides and two-headed cows would exist only in the memories of the young ones.

The Great Depression was all a matter of one's perspective and one's position in life. Eudora Welty, Mississippi's marvelous writer and photographer, toured the state during the Depression for the Works Progress Administration, recording her thoughts in words and snapshots as she traveled the rural roads of the state's eighty-two counties.

"The Depression, in fact, was not a noticeable phenomenon in the poorest state in the union," she wrote in the foreword to her first photo collection book, *One Time, One Place.* "In New York [where she did graduate work at Columbia University] there had been the faceless breadlines; on Farish Street in my home town of Jackson, the proprietor of the My Blue Heaven Café had written on the glass of the front door with his own finger dipped in window polish: . . . 'The cook will be glad to serve U with a 5 and 10c stew.'"[10]

It was all a matter of one's perspective.

By his senior year at Philadelphia High, Redd was still working at a number of jobs. Despite his work, he still found time for fun. Redd had a girlfriend, probably his first one, a pretty girl named Ivy Oliphant who was also attending Philadelphia High. Si and Ivy had been sweethearts since the eighth grade. In fact, he admitted, it was Ivy's help that had gotten him through most of his math tests.

The Oliphants were a reasonably prosperous Philadelphia family. They owned and operated Spivey & Ross Furniture store. Like most of the town's middle-class white families, the Oliphants were very traditional and conservative.[11]

"Small towns are cliquish," Ivy's younger sister Jonnie said. "My folks didn't really approve of Ivy going with Silas. I think they probably saw each other on the sly a lot."[12]

Perhaps reflecting her parents' attitude toward the sharecropper's son, Jonnie admitted she did not particularly like Si when they first became acquainted. "Silas was a very flamboyant boy," she said. "I always compared Silas and Ivy to Professor [Harold] Hill and Marian the librarian from *The Music Man*. People respected Si but many thought he was too big for his britches."

Because of his hard work, Redd usually had money in high school, another fact that set him apart from most other young people. Jonnie believed many classmates were jealous of him because of that, but it didn't seem to bother him one way or the other.

As for Ivy, the comparison to Meredith Willson's Marian the librarian was a good one. Although she had a spunky side, she was

Si Redd's 1929 high school graduation photo. At about the same time he made a speech at the Neshoba County Fair. *Redd family photo.*

normally prim, proper, and quiet. She was, her sister Jonnie said, very picky about who she associated with, making her interest in the outspoken, pushy Si a classic case of opposites attracting.

In high school, Redd's grades were not stellar. He would often admit that he wasn't the smartest kid in school, but he made up for it by working harder than any of his classmates. Along the way, he had also discovered that he possessed a valuable aptitude. Through all his years of selling Cloverine salve and *Grit* magazine, in addition to a natural gift of gab, Redd had developed a real talent for oration. Perhaps he had even inherited some of his splashy, theatrical Harold Hill personality from his street preacher father.

He was smooth and persuasive, and the more he talked and the more self-confidence he gained, the better he got at it. It was during this period that the Mississippi sharecropper's son first began to dream about becoming a lawyer. To advance his dream, he had joined a competitive debating club at school called the Adam Byrd Literary Society, named for a turn-of-the-century U.S. congressman who had lived in Neshoba County. A Philadelphia High graduate and successful Mississippi real estate entrepreneur, Mark Bounds, who was a member of the society many years after Si, aptly described the experience: "It was like our version of the *Dead Poets Society* and it was great inspiration for all the members."[13]

Redd was also in the drama club. He loved to participate in the annual graduation plays the club performed. It allowed the true "ham" in the comedic young man to emerge and helped him gain self-confidence in all sorts of situations. Years later, Redd recalled that the drama teacher, Mr. L. O. Todd, said of the plays, "All of those graduating plays at Philadelphia High School were nothing more than three-act comedies featuring Si Redd."[14]

It was in his junior or senior year that Redd won the right to speak at the annual Neshoba County Fair, one of the highlights of his teen years. It was also during this period, in the summers of his high school years, that Redd and a few of his cousins and friends followed the hobo life. "We'd get on a freight train from Mississippi and ride up to Memphis and then get on another freight train, ride out to Kansas and work in the wheat fields," he related. "We belonged to what you called the Four H Club . . . only then it wasn't agriculture; it was Herbert Hoover's Hungry Hoboes."[15]

He recalled that during one summer's vagabonding, the group made it all the way to Reno, Nevada, where years later Si would strike gold in gaming machines. "We . . . saw that 'Biggest Little City in the World' [sign] . . . when I was probably fifteen," he said. They continued on to the central valley in California, where they picked pears for a season, before making their way home from their *Grapes of Wrath* journey.

Si returned and finished high school, then took a year or two off from his schooling; but there can be little doubt that his mother Nannie kept nagging him about continuing his education.

In 1933 or thereabouts, Redd enrolled in East Central Junior College (ECJC), today East Central Community College, in Decatur, in Newton County. Ivy had also enrolled there. The school had accepted its first students only five years earlier, meeting in buildings that had once been part of the Newton County Agricultural High School.[16]

By this time the Redd family's fortunes had taken a slight uptick, probably through Nannie's prodding and pushing. By some means, Si's parents now owned their own small farm; and Marvin had started a second business, buying and selling used pianos and organs.

"We'd keep the barn full of those old organs," Redd related. "He [Marvin] would . . . sell an organ to the school, and also bring corn and do other things to help me pay my tuition at junior college . . ."[17] This was the barter system that Redd's father used to help pay his son's junior college fees, a common practice during the Depression.

One of Redd's professors at ECJC was William D. McCain, a young man only five years older than Si himself, who was in his first teaching job following college. McCain would go on to earn his master's and doctorate degrees, and eventually serve as president of Mississippi Southern College, now the University of Southern Mississippi.

McCain would teach Redd another valuable lesson that he carried with him throughout his life, one that helped him achieve such great heights in the business world.

Redd was very weak in math. "I never did learn the multiplication tables," he laughed years later. When McCain gave him a complex geometry problem to solve, Redd threw up his hands in frustration and defeat. McCain said to him, "Silas, it's not too important whether you work this geometry class . . . it's how you live, and how you approach things."[18]

Redd grasped something valuable from that remark. "It doesn't matter whether you know the multiplication tables or not, if you just work that much harder, you can go on anyway," he said, another lesson he learned to live by.

* * * *

Gambling had always been part of Si Redd's life, even as a young boy. "We learned how to shoot dice as kids at eight, ten years [old.] I don't think there was anybody in Union, Mississippi, or Philadelphia, Mississippi, that didn't know how to shoot craps," he laughed. Remembering a typical game, he said, "We'd be shooting dice, two or three little black boys and six, seven of us white boys." Everybody was equal in the crap game. "That little black boy—it was his money—and he had just about as much authority as anybody."[19]

It was while he was attending East Central Junior College that Redd had his first serious brush with coin-operated amusement machines, slick devices that had interested him from the first time he saw one. When the concept of the two things—gambling and coin-operated machines—finally coalesced in his fertile imagination, Si Redd would never be stopped. He vividly remembered his first commercial venture with the coin-ops.

"There was a boy named Lamar Trapp in Philadelphia, [who] purchased a little amusement penny pinball machine," Redd said. "It was right in the middle of the Depression. Trapp saw an ad in *Billboard* magazine [and] he . . . purchased an amusement machine for sixteen dollars."

Trapp's only problem was that he didn't have the sixteen dollars, so he turned to his buddy Si for help. Redd was still working in the dry cleaning and pressing shop, and he shined shoes at a small pool parlor, so he had a little money saved. He loaned Trapp the sixteen dollars.[20]

Trapp bought the machine he had seen advertised in *Billboard,* a brand new 1932 Bally Goofy penny pinball machine, and waited nervously for his prized possession to be delivered. When it arrived, he installed it in a restaurant in Philadelphia and began collecting his pennies. The pennies added up quickly, and before too long Trapp had the money to pay Redd back. But just as he was prepared to do that, he saw another ad that would forever change the life of his benefactor.

The second ad said that a Cleveland, Ohio, distributor had a used Goofy machine for sale for only six dollars, and Trapp quickly put in his order.[21] When the machine arrived he offered Redd the used machine as repayment on the loan for his new machine. Although it was probably one of the few times in his life that Si Redd would be taken advantage of, he accepted the offer.

* * * *

Pinball machines, in one form or another, have been around for centuries. The modern era of pinball machines came along in 1931, when Automatic Industries introduced the Whiffle. These early pinball machines were horizontal wooden-framed boxes, slightly inclined from top to bottom, with simple but colorful layouts, or playfields, under a sheet of glass. Most of the early ones were countertop machines. A player would drop a penny into the slot—one usually got seven balls for a penny—and a metal ball would emerge from the top of the box and roll and ricochet its way down the playfield toward the bottom. There were a number of holes in the playfield, each partially protected by a fence of small metal pins around it, thus the name "pinball." Each ball would score a certain number of points if it fell into one of the holes; if it rolled all the way to the bottom, it scored no points. These early machines did not have the lighted rubber bumpers or noisy bells and whistles of later models, or the flippers at the bottom that allow the player to keep a ball in play. The flippers came about in the mid 1940s.

The Great Depression was the mother's milk for pinball machines and other coin-operated amusement devices. During the Depression men were looking for an inexpensive way to spend their leisure time, and an affordable escape from the bleak landscape of hard times. Arcades and pool halls with coin-operated machines were favored gathering places. Then when Prohibition ended in March 1933 and taverns and bars reopened, the pinball machine found a new home. Some pinball operators awarded small prizes— or illegally, cash—for a player who scored a certain number of points. But most often, the men bet among themselves to see who could score the highest point total. Mississippians have always loved to gamble.

Of course, these post-Prohibition good times didn't last too long in the Magnolia State. It had had its own prohibition laws as early as 1907, and when the Twenty-first Amendment legalized the manufacture and sale of 3.2 beer and light wine, the state legislature was quick to take advantage of the Amendment's language allowing state or local control of alcohol sales. Legislators banned it again, and

A 1933 Bally Goofy pinball machine was Si Redd's first coin-operated amusement machine, and it launched him on a sixty-five-year career in the industry. Redd paid $16 for the used Goofy. *Courtesy of Wayne Namerow Collections, www.pinballhistory.com.*

Mississippi did not repeal its own prohibition until 1966. To this day, about half of Mississippi's counties are still dry.

None of this had much effect on the burgeoning pinball revolution, however. There were still restaurants and pool halls and drug and sundry stores and many other places where the machines could find a home, and an eager audience.

A new company was founded in 1931 that would have a lifetime influence on Si Redd: Bally Manufacturing Company. Raymond Moloney, another young entrepreneur, founded it as the sales and distribution arm of his parent company, Lion Manufacturing Corporation of Chicago. Moloney's first product, offered in 1932, was a pinball machine called Ballyhoo. He coined a catchy advertising slogan to promote his entry in the burgeoning pinball market: "What'll they do through '32 . . . play Ballyhoo!"

And indeed they did.

But competition was intense, and each manufacturer had to constantly improve his machines. Ray Moloney turned to a New York industrial designer, Jack Firestone, to get a leg up on the competition. Firestone designed a playfield that used one of Bally's most popular features, the Bally Hole, which gave the player a free ball. And he added exciting new features such as a difficult side alley that awarded additional points if reached. Moloney named the colorful new machine Goofy, and came up with another catchy slogan: "Thru '32 'twas Ballyhoo—Goofy'll smash all records too!"

Si Redd must have been excited, but perhaps also somewhat skeptical, when he took possession of his sixteen-dollar, secondhand Goofy pinball machine. He took it back to Decatur, where he was still attending classes at the junior college, and he built a wooden frame on which to stand it. He found a local hamburger joint, Joe's Café, and offered the owner a share of the profits if he could install his Goofy on a trial basis. The owner agreed. "I'd take half the money [and] give the storekeeper half of it. That's the way that business is done," Redd explained.[22]

Joe's Café had bare dirt floors. "We just had a heck of a time getting that machine to sit level—we finally used pieces of wood under the legs, and that seemed to work alright," Redd laughed years later.[23]

In about a week, Redd went back to the hamburger joint to check on his investment. His expectations were modest as he opened the machine, but he was absolutely stunned when he counted all the coins. There were thirty-two dollars in pennies in the Goofy coin-box! Redd's half of the take was sixteen dollars, exactly what he had invested in the business.

Si Redd saw his future clearly at that moment, and he would never be the same man again.

—— CHAPTER 3 ——

MUSIC TO HIS EARS

Si Redd was earning about eight dollars a week at the dry cleaner. That money, plus his share of all the pennies he took out of the pinball machine, was immediately invested back into the business: "Every quarter or dime I could get my hands on, I'd continue to . . . buy another amusement machine," he said.[1]

It is probable, although not verified, that Redd didn't limit himself to just pinball machines. Coin-operated pool tables and cigarette and food vending machines were possibly part of his inventory as well. One type of machine that Redd didn't own was slot machines. These were the old-fashioned three-reelers, or one-armed bandits, with oranges, bells, cherries, and the much maligned lemon symbols. For a penny or a nickel, or even a quarter if you were really flush, a man could get one pull of the handle, and if he was lucky that day a few coins might clank into the return tray at the bottom of the machine.

Although slot machines, like moonshine whiskey, were illegal in Mississippi, they could be found by those who knew where to look. "You could . . . go to the sheriff and buy a license. You'd give him three hundred dollars for a twenty-five-cent slot machine . . . a hundred dollars for a dime model, and fifty dollars for a five-cent model, [and] he would issue a license to put on that machine," Redd said.[2] Although the license didn't make the machines legal, it sufficed.

Redd was probably tempted—there was a fellow who had some slot machines in Philadelphia—but he eschewed the illegal machines.

Si Redd, just barely twenty-one years old, set up a company he named Mississippi Vending Company, and began calling on stores, restaurants, pool halls, barber shops, and anywhere else he could place a machine as he could afford to purchase it.[3] It was not unusual during the Depression to step into a barber shop for a haircut and shave and smell the strong, haunting aroma of Bay Rum, rose water, and talcum mingling with the acrid scent of cigarette smoke from the men hanging over a pinball machine in the back of the shop, behind the shoeshine stand. The Depression was a great enabler, and few merchants were unwilling to chance anything that might bring in a few extra coins.

After about a year in the coin-op business, Mississippi Vending Company encountered its first stumbling block. The Mississippi legislature, searching for a new revenue stream, enacted a new law requiring that a license be purchased for every coin-operated machine in the state. Redd recalled the license was twenty dollars per machine, a significant investment considering all the machines he had in operation.

Each separate license documented the machine's owner, its make and model, and the date the license was granted. The law also stipulated that each license must be clearly displayed on the appropriate machine. Redd came up with a clever scheme. He'd cut a license into four parts, and paste one part under the glass of each of four machines, folding the edges under to make it appear that it was a full, folded copy. Thus, he saved 75 percent on the licensing fees.[4] Redd's uncle on his mother's side was the man responsible for collecting the licensing fee, but it's uncertain if that benefited Redd in any way.

Speaking of quartering his license fees, Redd said, "Not having the money—and whether that's [right] or I should be ashamed of it or not, [I won't judge]." Years later, with a twinkle in his eye, Si Redd said, "If they'll tell me the proper [amount], I'll be glad to pay it now, as long as they don't compound the interest."[5]

Although Si Redd had completely broken away from his nuclear family after high school and was earning his own livelihood, his mother and her steadfast teachings were still an ingrained part of who he was. Shortly after he had hired one of his first employees, he discovered that the young man was stealing from him, and he fired him. A few days later he heard from his mother.

Nannie Redd told her son that the young man's mother was quite active with her in the church, and that they were a good family. "In her opinion," Redd said, "I just wasn't paying him enough. My mother said, 'Silas, you hire that young man back.'"[6]

Always the obedient son, Redd did as he was told.

There can be little doubt that Nannie Redd also continued to hound her son to finish his education following his first two years at junior college. Probably his girlfriend Ivy did too, as she wanted more for Si than a pinball machine route. So sometime in the mid-1930s Redd enrolled as a prelaw student at the University of Mississippi—Ole Miss—in Oxford.

"I hitchhiked up there . . . and [met] my roommate, a guy named Earl Beall," he said. "There was a . . . craps game down on the floor; shooting dice, eight or ten or twelve . . . college boys . . . I mean, they're loaded; those guys had all kinds of money."[7]

Redd made a lot of money that day, and throughout his short Ole Miss career, shooting craps, a game he had been weaned on since he was a small boy. He pledged the Alpha Tau Omega fraternity, and lived in the dorm. Redd was surrounded by young men who came from better-off families than his, members of Mississippi's genteel old money circle. Ole Miss was a haven for such young men, especially during the Depression, when few men of meager means were able to attend college.

Redd readily admitted that he was not a good student. He attended what he described as "some classes," but he was more interested in making money than in gaining an education. He discovered he could visit the nearby Depression-era Civilian Conversation Corps camps and buy Ole Miss football tickets at a discount, then return to Oxford and scalp them at a nice profit. He also delivered hamburgers at night, and spent a lot of time successfully shooting craps with "the freshmen from the Delta."[8]

Redd would often stop in Noxapater, a small crossroads outside Philadelphia, on his way back up to school in Oxford. He knew the location of an old moonshine still hidden in a stand of timber where he could buy a gallon of white lightning for about $1.50. He did not drink, but he'd sell the ugly brew to his fraternity brothers.[9]

As if trying to live up to his sister-in-law's comparison of him to Professor Harold Hill, the Music Man, Si said, "I didn't go to school very much. I was just out there . . . hustling all the time."[10]

But Redd's main priority was to extend the reach of his profitable pinball route. He went to the Delta, in the western part of the state, and set up machines in Greenville, Clarksdale, Itta Bena, and other small towns. But it was a chance trip to Memphis, Tennessee, that introduced Redd to another opportunity that would play a significant role in the next phase of his business career. He discovered jukeboxes.

* * * *

Like pinball machines—which Si Redd had discovered in the early 1930s, just as they entered their heyday—jukeboxes too had been around for a long time, and like its coin-op cousin, the jukebox would enjoy a rebirth of popularity. The machine's prime began in the late 1930s and early 1940s, and again Si Redd was fortunate— or visionary—enough to sense and seize the opportunity at its onset.

Thomas Edison is generally credited as being the progenitor of the jukebox, but he was a reluctant father.[11] He had invented sound recording in 1877 while trying to invent the telegraph machine; and he was working on perfecting the Dictaphone a few years later when he invented the phonograph by chance. He sold the rights to the machine, and for the next twenty years, the device—like a disowned child—tried to find a place for itself on the entertainment scene. It met with little success.

In 1889 the first coin-operated jukebox model was developed and installed in a San Francisco saloon; but it still failed to gain any popularity. Perhaps it was because the only way you could listen to the music was by putting one of the machine's four listening tubes to your ear. It was clumsy and cumbersome, and certainly didn't encourage dancing. The player piano was king, and as the twentieth century dawned, it was that machine that garnered the nickels and dimes for the popular ragtime music of the day, or the stirring John Philip Sousa or George M. Cohen marches.

For the next quarter-century the jukebox languished, forgotten by almost everybody, including its famous inventor.

Rudolph Wurlitzer, a German immigrant, was one of the pioneers in mechanical music, and his extensive line of player pianos commanded a high share of the market in the early 1900s. But in 1920, Prohibition dealt the entire mechanical music industry a severe blow. With the closure of saloons, bars, and taverns—by far the most popular haunt for player pianos—business plummeted. The advent of radio in the 1920s only exacerbated the problem for Wurlitzer and his competitors. But ironically, it was a major technological advance that first appeared in radio that also gave new life to the jukebox: sound amplification.

By the end of Prohibition the jukebox finally came into its own. With the reopening of taverns and bars, the machine found a home, and by the end of the 1930s there were approximately 300,000 of them attracting listeners and dancers across the country. Leading the pack was Wurlitzer.

One of the customers Redd had on his pinball route was a small café located on the Ole Miss campus. During one of his service calls, the owner told Redd he would give him sixty dollars if Redd would get him a jukebox for the restaurant. They had become all the rage, and the café's student clientele was demanding that the owner install one. Redd promised he'd look into it.

He did some research, probably in *Billboard* magazine, which covered the industry, and found a machine for sale for forty dollars in Memphis. It was an older Mills "ferris wheel" model, in which the records were rotated into place on a mechanism resembling the famous circus ride.

"I didn't know anything about jukeboxes—I didn't even know how to put the records on it," Redd said. But the promise of a twenty-dollar profit was too great to pass up.[12] On his next swing north, Redd drove up to Memphis, bought the jukebox, and brought it back to Oxford. But when he delivered it to the café, the owner had had second thoughts and backed out of the deal. Panicked, Redd talked the owner into putting the machine in on a fifty-fifty revenue split. So, with Eddie Duchin, Fats Waller, Tommy Dorsey, and Guy Lombardo serenading the Ole Miss Rebels and their co-ed dates, Si Redd raked in the nickels and dimes. The sound of each coin dropping into the old Mills jukebox was indeed music to Si Redd's ears.

Although Redd had completed the two years at ECJC before entering Ole Miss, his girlfriend Ivy had been forced to drop out after the first year because of the financial crunch of the Depression. In order to distance Ivy from Si, her parents had urged her to travel to Freeport, Illinois, to spend some time with her older sister Hettye and her husband "Doc" Howington, also from Neshoba, who worked on the Illinois Central Railroad.

Redd was heartbroken without his sweetheart close at hand. After spending the winter in Freeport, she too couldn't stand being apart any longer. When she took the Illinois Central's Panama Limited down to Batesville, near Oxford, to visit Redd, they decided to get married on the spot. That was March 4, 1936.

The Redds moved into an apartment in Oxford, but a short time later he had had his fill of the academic life. He dropped out of Ole

Miss. They continued to live in their downtown apartment in Oxford, and Redd worked harder than ever extending his amusement machine routes.

As time passed, the routes grew, and the travel time required to service all the machines grew as well. The Redds probably had a hundred or so machines by this time, and Ivy became Si's partner in business as well as in life. Maintaining all their machines became quite a challenge.

Redd bought an old International pickup truck and he serviced the machines out of the back of the noisy old clunker. "Tuesdays we would head all the way back up to Oxford [from Philadelphia], stopping in Louisville, Ackerman, Durant, Eupora, and Grenada," he related. "We would get back on Thursday, and then Friday and Saturday we would hit Newton, Union, Decatur, and Philadelphia. We would come back with $1,300 or maybe $1,900 in pennies, dimes, and nickels."[13]

Rolling all those coins became Ivy's job. "She would swear to God, 'I will never go with you [again] as long as I live,'" Redd said. "Then the next week she would get in the truck again."[14]

Redd fondly recalled that Ivy did get one extra reward for her labor. The couple no longer had many penny machines, and they agreed that Ivy could keep all the pennies she rolled. When she had saved about one hundred dollars, she bought a fur coat.

"It was a muskrat coat," Redd said. "That was rather a high point."[15]

Si Redds' rural Mississippi coin-op "empire" would eventually grow to nearly 1000 machines spread out over northern and central parts of the state. Business was booming, and although the Redds would not have considered themselves wealthy people, they were living quite comfortably, particularly by Depression-era standards. Redd was also the main support for his parents by this time.

By the mid- to late 1930s he estimated his share of the income from the business to be about ten dollars per machine per week, or about $150,000 a year. "I would suspect," he told one of his oral history interviewers, "that [after] the overhead of the labor and the depreciation . . . well . . . I'll bet we were earning a net profit of probably fifty thousand dollars a year."[16] Never too absorbed by the concept of money, Redd did not seem to appreciate the fact that they were earning a princely sum in Depression-era Mississippi.

He roughly estimated the value of Mississippi Vending Company at that time to be about $150,000 to $200,000. They had a small office in Grenada, and a warehouse in Jackson with a number of machines awaiting repair, and a large inventory of parts. There was a second warehouse in Philadelphia, in the back of Ivy's father's furniture store. He had also added routes that included Jackson, Carthage, and Canton.

Redd admitted that Mississippi Vending Company was pretty much "a one-man operation."[17] One of his sisters-in-law had moved in with Si and Ivy, and she was paid six dollars a week to keep the books. Redd would also occasionally hire some young men to help him service the routes. But otherwise, it was all Si and Ivy.

One day when Redd was out servicing one of his routes, he received an unpleasant surprise. "[I] found the big operators from Birmingham—about 200 miles away had put their big fancy amusement machines in my locations," he said.[18] Locations—the stores, parlors, pool halls, and restaurants where a businessman installed his machines—were his bread-and-butter, his most valuable asset after the machines themselves. Redd was frantic with worry.

The Birmingham operators had been illegally giving cash prizes as payouts on their pinball machines, and they had been forced to leave town. A 1931 Alabama law had outlawed gambling devices in the state, and by issuing payoffs in merchandise or cash, pinball operators had exposed themselves to that law. Also, the Alabama attorney general had just begun to put teeth in the law's enforcement because of the rise of organized crime, prostitution, and gambling in Alabama's notorious Phenix City. It amounted to a "perfect storm" for the Birmingham operators, so they had hightailed it to Mississippi and into Si Redd's life.[19]

Redd insinuated but never directly accused these operators of being unsavory characters, perhaps even mobsters. His language in a magazine interview in which he discussed this situation, and the deference he showed to these men in the years to come, give the impression that he believed they were mobsters. Moreover, Alabama historians admit that Birmingham, like Phenix City, was a hotbed of lawlessness, and perhaps even mob activity, during the 1920s and 1930s.

Bob Jones, Redd's good friend and employee in Illinois and Massachusetts, was doubtful that the Birmingham men had mob connections. "I never heard anything like that," Jones said. "These fellows from the Birmingham Vending Company were friends . . . they had a very friendly relationship."[20]

Redd saw the handwriting on the wall and decided the best thing he could do was coexist with this new competition. So he traveled to

Birmingham and had a meeting with them. "To make a long story short," Redd said, avoiding mention of any details, "I went into partnership with them on a fifty-fifty system—the store kept 50 percent and then we split 50 percent."[21]

Redd indicated that he considered it a great opportunity to be affiliated with a large, financially stable organization. Whether that was true, or that he was just trying to put the best possible face on the situation, is uncertain. He and Ivy continued to service the routes. "When my wife and I used to take off the money, we would actually give my partners more than their share just so they'd be pleased with how I was running things.

"We were doing so good," he said, "I was afraid that they might want to take away my share if they thought they were being cheated."[22]

His Birmingham partners also had a large number of jukeboxes in their inventory, so Redd also placed and serviced those machines in Mississippi. His experience with his sole jukebox on the Ole Miss campus had been positive, and he was excited about the prospects for this new revenue stream, especially because it did not cost him a cent in cold, hard cash to purchase the machines.[23]

In 1937 Si and Ivy traveled to Freeport, Illinois, to visit Ivy's sister and brother-in-law, Hettye and Doc Howington.[24] When Doc learned that Redd was in the coin-operated amusement business, he suggested they visit Sterling, a small community about thirty miles downstate, which he believed would be ripe for some jukebox machines. Si and Ivy took a drive, and entering the Sauk Valley they soon arrived in the small town of Sterling, snuggled up to the banks of the Rock River.

Sterling had originally been a farming community, but just a year earlier the Northwestern Steel and Wire Company had opened a large steel mill in the town. It joined the Wahl Clipper Corporation, manufacturer of barbering equipment, and Lawrence Brothers Hardware, manufacturers of farm equipment, forming a healthy industrial base for the small town. Si and Ivy did a little shoe-leather research, and soon discovered there wasn't a single jukebox in town, despite a significant population of men who stopped off for a few drinks after work at one of the local taverns.

Redd had seen how well jukeboxes could do—in fact he probably thought about that each time he emptied the cash box in his old Mills jukebox on the Ole Miss campus—so when he returned to Oxford he began planning.

He called the Rudolph Wurlitzer Company—likely the plant in DeKalb, Illinois—and inquired about buying some used machines. They told him they had 150 obsolete M/412 jukeboxes manufactured in their North Tonawanda, New York, plant. Redd arranged to buy the machines on credit, with no down payment. The company also told him he could have a route that included parts of northern Illinois, excluding Chicago, southern Wisconsin, and eastern Iowa for his machines.

A beautiful, wooden-cased 1936 Wurlitzer M/412 jukebox launched Redd on a new career path when he purchased 150 of the obsolete machines. *Courtesy of* Always Jukin' *magazine.*

The M/412 was a twelve-record machine. Wurlitzer had manufactured 17,700 of the M/412s in 1936, before moving on to sixteen-record models.[25] Like most jukeboxes of the day—which were called phonographs or automatic phonographs until the late 1940s—the mechanics were housed inside a beautiful but heavy walnut console. A large window at the top front of the cabinet exposed the inner workings, called the Wurlitzer Simplex Multi-Selector, showing the twelve records sitting atop one another and the mechanical arm that would lift the selected record from the stack and position it on the turntable for playback. Beneath the large window was a small glass-covered listing of the twelve records available for play. In 1937, songs such as "Sweet Leilani" by Bing Crosby, "One O'Clock Jump" by Count Basie, and "It's a Sin to Tell a Lie," by Fats Waller, would all be included.

Below the selection list was the coin slot and a colorful round selector knob for indicating the records to be played. The bottom half of the cabinet was the cloth-covered speaker with beautiful wooden scrollwork fronting it. The M/412 accepted nickels, dimes, or quarters, up to a total of one dollar at a time, with each play costing five cents.

That same year, 1937, a few months after Wurlitzer came up with a sixteen-record machine, the company also perfected a twenty-four record machine. Called the Model 24, it would revolutionize the jukebox industry. It was the first machine to eschew the wooden console and incorporate illuminated plastics into its design. This transition from the old heavy wooden consoles to colorful, back-lit, modern deco plastic machines propelled Wurlitzer even further ahead of its chief competitors, Seeburg, Rock-Ola, and Mills.

But to Si and Ivy Redd, the bulky wooden boxes of the earlier generation that they purchased were works of art, and they were about to propel the young couple on the first grand adventure of their new life together. Leaving his family behind in Mississippi was likely difficult for Redd, but throughout his entire life he would be a man who always looked forward, never backward.

— CHAPTER 4 —

THE MUSIC GOES ROUND
AND ROUND

Si and Ivy Redd arrived in Sterling, Illinois, in 1938 with all their worldly possessions. It's likely they had had the Wurlitzer jukeboxes trucked or shipped by rail to Sterling. The nation's first coast-to-coast highway—US 30, the fabled Lincoln Highway—passed just outside of Sterling, and as a matter of fact, one of the earliest paved seedling miles of the historic roadway was only fifty miles east, in the town of Malta.

Although Washington Irving had called most of the land traversed by US 30 the Grand Prairie, this northern part of Illinois in the late 1930s was more rolling than flat. Forested moraines, left over from the last Ice Age, shared the landscape with peaceful, prosperous farms of corn, hay, wheat, oats, and often cattle, sheep, and hogs. Even an occasional herd of goats could be glimpsed from the highway, feeding in a barnyard or in a woodland pasture.

Si and Ivy quickly settled in. Redd had invited Ivy's brother-in-law Doc Howington to join him in the new enterprise, and together they began to call on bars, taverns, bowling alleys, restaurants, and other likely spots to place the jukeboxes. They immediately ran into an unexpected problem that could have scuttled the entire business on day one.[1]

"Everyone was very enthusiastic," Redd said. "But on the second or third place we went to the owner [and] said, 'Fine, put 'em in, but they're against the law, you know.'"[2]

Redd was incredulous. Nearby Dixon and Freeport had jukeboxes; Pecatoma, across the river, had jukeboxes. Gambling was even legal—or at least tolerated—in Sterling; and many of the same stores where he hoped to place his jukeboxes already had slot machines. Why not a harmless jukebox in Sterling? he wondered.

"It's amusement," he was told. "It's a violation of [an] ordinance."[3]

Redd went to see the police chief who told him he'd have to see the mayor, the man who ran Sterling. So Redd promptly went to visit the mayor. "Si was a helluva persuasive individual," Bob Jones, who later joined his team, related. "He cried and moaned and groaned, and finally the mayor said, 'I don't really see anything wrong with a jukebox, so you go ahead and put 'em in.'"[4]

The ambitious young Mississippi country boy with his strange accent and funny Southern dialect had fascinated the mayor. He asked Si to repeat his story just so he could hear him talk some more, complete with all the "y'alls," "sho nufs," and "over yonders." Redd also recalled that it was cold, and he wore a Union suit under his clothes with the cuffs of the arms and legs sticking out.

"He could tell I was a hillbilly," Redd laughed. "If I'd been a horse, my fetlocks would have been dragging on the ground."[5]

The mayor explained that the local ordinance had been passed at the behest of a popular local orchestra leader who didn't want any musical competition in the town. He gave Redd written authority to place his jukeboxes, and opined that the ordinance would eventually be changed. But in the meantime, Redd was the only person with the authority to install jukeboxes in Sterling. Northwestern Music Company's business was off and running.

The business expanded rapidly. Routes were established westward all the way into eastern Iowa, northward into southern Wisconsin, and eastward to the suburbs of Chicago. They put machines on the campuses of the universities of Wisconsin and Iowa, and on as many small college campuses as they could cover.

Ivy was pregnant by now, and she couldn't help any longer, so Redd hired a number of people to service the routes and assist him with the business. One noteworthy hire was a young man named Robert Marshall Jones.

Bob Jones hailed from Chicago. About six years younger than Redd, he had graduated from high school and took the only job he could find during the Depression as a soda jerk in the city. But friends told him about a company named Sloane-Birch that had the exclusive Wurlitzer route franchise for Chicago. Route managers were always looking for assistants to train in the business, Jones's friends told him. Route assistants received no pay, and they were expected to learn how to change records, make minor repairs, and clean the machines in hopes of eventually earning their own route.

Jones found a route manager who was willing to take him on, even offering him seven cents a day for bus fare. He accepted the job, and after some time he had earned his own route.[6] But Sloane-Birch fell on hard times, and eventually found itself on the cusp of bankruptcy. Northwestern Music Company was doing much better in the small cities and towns, and Redd made an overture to buy some of Sloan-Birch's jukeboxes and outlying routes. Bob Jones became aware that his employer was going to scam Redd by selling him the machines, but not include the routes in the transaction, something the naive young bumpkin never suspected.

Jones warned Redd about the scheme, and saved him from disaster. Redd liked the honest young man, and he hired Jones, who ended up running Northwestern Music Company's routes out of Moline, on Illinois's western flank. Bob Jones would work for Si Redd on and off for the next half-century, and the two men became fast friends, "almost like brothers," Bob Jones likened it.

This penchant of Si Redd for "shootin' from the hip," as he called it, without doing all the necessary due diligence, would haunt his business career from start to finish. Redd was only of average intelligence—he often told people he wasn't very smart—and he was particularly weak in accounting and legal matters, and in leadership qualities. However, his indefatigable drive, innate sales ability, crafty nature, and keen instinct for knowing what people wanted, always managed to keep him one step ahead of his competitors. It was only in his later years, when he had worked his way up to the lofty heights of international commerce, that his sly, folksy ways were no longer enough to ensure his success.

****

In late 1938, Si and Ivy had their first child, a daughter they named Vinnie. Less than two years later, a second daughter, Sherry, would join the family. When the doctor told Si he had another daughter, he didn't believe him. "No, no, Ivy put you up to this," a perplexed Si said to the doctor. But when he studied the new baby for himself, Si discovered it wasn't a practical joke. Years later, Sherry said, "I was supposed to be a boy."[7]

Si and Ivy were very much in love, and he adored both his babies. He often gave Ivy credit for whatever success he achieved. "Ivy Oliphant, my wife, was absolutely the greatest [person] I ever met in my life," he swore on more than one occasion.[8]

Ivy was one of those rare individuals who never had a bad word to say about anybody. She rarely complained, and was a constant source of love, support, and optimism for her entire family. She and Si—she always called him Silas—bought a small house in Sterling, and they fit right into the community. Redd often described Sterling as being a lot like a Mississippi small town, peopled by outgoing, friendly, neighborly folks.

It was a beautiful place to live, too. Sterling nestled on the north side of the Rock River, whereas its twin city, Rock Falls, sat just across the water on the south side. Lawrence Park sat on an island in the middle of the river, and was equally enjoyed by residents of both towns.

Sterling's early nineteenth-century days were centered along the river, which supported a number of gristmills and lumber mills. But a long stretch of rough rapids running through the town greatly hampered navigation, so the river never achieved its hoped-for promise. However, the beautiful limestone cliffs that line the river make it one of the most scenic waterways in the state. When the city was originally laid out in those early days of great promise, nine broad, sweeping avenues one-hundred-feet wide ran from the river into the town to handle the heavy traffic that was anticipated. Those broad tree-lined thoroughfares, plus the river's scenic beauty, gave the city a grandeur that was enjoyed by few other municipalities of its size.

The Redds loved living in Sterling. Redd still owned his route business in Mississippi too. He had a man named Lester Griffin overseeing the operation down there, and he was required to make only periodic trips to check on things. Between the two widely separated concerns, the Redds were doing very well financially. Not yet thirty years old, they were very successful by any yardstick in the late 1930s and early 1940s.

In 1939, after a number of visits to Sterling, Ivy's younger sister Jonnie also moved up to the town from Mississippi. During one of her earlier visits she had met one of Si's customers, a café owner named Dick McClanathan, and the two had fallen in love. They

Ivy and Si Redd, circa 1940, when they lived in Sterling, Illinois. *Redd family photo.*

eventually got married, and McClanathan gave up the café and went to work for Redd as a route manager.[9] The job entailed convincing restaurants, taverns, and retailers to accept a jukebox on a revenue-shared basis, then following up with service work. Each box was serviced weekly. The most important part was emptying the cash box and carefully recording the results so everyone would get his fair share. The machines were also dusted and cleaned, worn needles replaced, records changed, mechanisms greased and oiled, and burned-out bulbs replaced. It was a good job, and Redd's friends and family members were often promoted to more responsible positions as they learned the business.

This pattern of providing for his extended family would be prevalent throughout Si Redd's life. He always believed in sharing whatever good fortune he had with those closest to him. His sister-in-law Jonnie McClanathan said that wealth didn't seem to mean much to Redd in and of itself; it was important only for what it could do for his family and close friends. That theme would be repeated again and again throughout Si Redd's life, and each new generation of family that followed enjoyed his generosity.

* * * *

Redd expanded his Northwestern Music Company's reach in the Midwest by buying up other small route operators when they fell on hard times. In neighboring Lee County, in a small town named Dixon, he placed a few jukeboxes. Shortly afterward, he received an anonymous letter threatening him if he didn't pull his machines out of Dixon. Amusement machines manufacturers did not grant exclusive territory rights except in very large cities, so Redd knew he had a right to place his machines wherever he wanted. Also, he didn't like being threatened. Redd assumed the letter had come from a small Dixon operator who had about 500 jukeboxes and illegal slot machines in Lee County. He called on his competitor, and with a small threat of his own—saying that he could go to his senator or to the attorney general over the illegal slot machines his competitor had—the man backed down. Redd left his boxes where he had put them.

Wurlitzer jukeboxes—although they were called automatic phonographs in the trade, the term *jukebox* was used in popular culture as early as the late 1930s—were sold by the factory to distributors, who then re-sold them to route operators. They were never sold directly to stores, restaurants, and taverns. So if a diner or a pool hall wanted to install a jukebox, he had to deal directly with a route operator such as Si Redd.

By the late 1930s, the coin-operated music business was booming. A typical Wurlitzer ad of the period promised operators a great future:

Never before has business been so good for Operators of Automatic Music. . . . Operators are lining up locations that they were never able to "crack" before.

Today, as never before, the Wurlitzer-Simplex is the acknowledged leader—the automatic phonograph that the biggest and best locations demand.

To be sure of getting your phonographs when you want them, place your orders now. If you aren't operating in music, cash in on this big opportunity—find out if there is room for another Wurlitzer-Simplex in your locality . . . the wise Wurlitzer operators will put the newest records on his phonographs and change them often! It pays![10]

Wurlitzer was easily the coin-operated music industry's leader through the 1930s and 1940s, with Seeburg and Rock-Ola contending for the number two spot. The growth and prosperity of the industry went hand-in-hand with the growth of another booming industry, the record business. Jukebox operators were the record industry's largest customers.

Operators such as Si Redd bought their records wholesale. Records that retailed for thirty-five cents wholesaled for nineteen cents, fifty-cent records for about twenty-eight cents, and seventy-five-cent records for forty-seven cents. A record was good for only about 125 to 150 plays on the jukebox, and then it could be resold to outlet stores for two or three cents. Jukebox operators rarely gambled on which records would be big hits. They waited until a particular song had been thoroughly popularized on the radio before placing it on their machines.[11]

Working with Wurlitzer, the industry leader, provided Si Redd and his fellow operators with a number of advantages. First there was the fact that their turf was protected because the distributors sold machines only to the operators. This was the structure the industry had used since the beginning, and there was no appetite to change it. Another advantage was that Wurlitzer took old machines back on trade-in for newer models at liberal allowances, and destroyed the old machines so they wouldn't water down the market. Finally, as the leader, Wurlitzer machines were the best on the market and the machines most often demanded by restaurants, taverns, and other locations.

However, there were also a few serious problems in the industry that made life difficult for operators such as Si Redd. Except in large cities, operators were not given exclusive distribution rights in their territories. So Redd competed not only with operators of Seeburg and Rock-Ola machines, but also with other Wurlitzer operators who might be serving the same territory.

Perhaps the biggest problem Redd had to contend with was the tendency of Wurlitzer and other manufacturers to pressure their distributors and operators into buying machines that they did not need. New models were introduced far too often, generally more than once a year. Often the "improvements" in the new machines were cosmetic only, but the manufacturers pressured operators to upgrade their inventory with every new model. They would even send promotional literature on the new models directly to the bars, tavern, and cafés where the machines were located, urging the owners to badger their operators for the newer, "better" machines. The fact was that the life of an average jukebox was four years, but operators were forced to turn over their inventory much more frequently so the manufacturer could earn bigger profits.

Operators were also pressured to buy more units than they needed. If Redd tried to place an order for a half-carload of jukeboxes, he would be relentlessly badgered to buy a full carload with threats and recriminations if he didn't relent. Because the machines were always purchased on credit, that meant additional financing charges as well.[12]

"Well, he [the Wurlitzer sales manager] would load us up with inventory," Redd said years later. "I went to the factory . . . and we would sign the contract in blank and . . . they would just fill it out."

"Today, I wouldn't do [that] in a thousand years," he laughed. "I wouldn't do it—sign it blank—for anybody."[13]

Being forced to overbuy was troublesome for Redd while he was a route operator in Illinois, but when he became a Wurlitzer distributor in New England the practice would almost bankrupt him on a number of occasions.

Despite the problems, Northwestern Music Company prospered. Redd would probably have been content to spend the rest of his days in rural Illinois if another, larger opportunity hadn't eventually surfaced. It came about as a result of the excellent reputation Si Redd had earned in the coin-operated amusement industry—but it would not turn out to be the blessing he initially believed.

—— CHAPTER 5 ——

THE LUCKIEST MAN ALIVE

In the early 1940s, the United States shook off the last vestiges of the Great Depression. However, the war that raged in Europe and the Far East was a matter of great concern to all Americans. When the United States was forced into the war on December 7, 1941, with the bombing of Pearl Harbor, everything changed.

In early January 1942, while the nation was still reeling from its entry into World War II, Si Redd received a phone call from Homer Capehart at Wurlitzer in North Tonawanda, New York. Capehart, often called "the father of the jukebox industry," was Wurlitzer's vice president of sales. A company he had founded in 1932 had developed the Simplex technology for automatic record changing, and when Capehart sold his company to Wurlitzer, he went along as part of the deal. Capehart would eventually leave the music business and go on to a career in politics as a three-term U.S. senator from Indiana.

Capehart told Redd that the outstanding job he had done building his route business in Illinois and adjoining states had not gone unnoticed in North Tonawanda. The man who held Wurlitzer's distributorship for the six New England states, Capehart said, had decided to tackle a distributorship in northern California, and the company wanted to know if Redd would be interested in moving to Boston to buy that enterprise.[1]

The hillbilly from Mississippi was dumbfounded. "I didn't even know where in the hell Boston was," he said. "I thought it was close to Baltimore."[2]

Despite his ignorance of geography, Redd was overwhelmed. "I was very happy," he said. "I would have gone anywhere to be a Wurlitzer distributor."[3]

There was a significant difference in being a distributor and a route operator, as Redd had been in Mississippi and Illinois. A distributor bought machines directly from the factory and resold them to the route operators. Distributors could and often did run their own routes as well, and they had a big edge over other route operators because they were able to buy the machines at a lower cost. Also, distributors often handled competitive products from different manufacturers, whereas route operators were restricted to only one manufacturer per product.

Redd traveled to Boston to check out the deal. He was told Wurlitzer would help him arrange whatever financing was necessary to purchase the company and get started, and that he would have the complete backing of the company in every way. Redd was sold, and the deal was consummated. He put his affairs in order in Illinois, packed up the family, and headed for Boston.

The Redds arrived at their new home on November 28, 1942. A man named McIlhenny had been a district manager with Redd's predecessor, and the two had become friends even before Redd's purchase. McIlhenny would stay on and become Redd Distributing Company's marketing director.

McIlhenny had arranged for Si and Ivy to accompany him to the famous Cocoanut Grove nightclub for dinner that very evening of their arrival.[4] Boston College and the College of Holy Cross from nearby Worcester were huge football rivals, and their annual game was being played that afternoon. Boston College was undefeated and ranked number one in the nation. After the game, and the inevitable Boston College victory, McIlhenny told them, the nightclub would be jammed with rabid Boston College fans. Redd was a huge football fan, and his friend knew this would be a great chance to introduce Si and Ivy to many of the city's civic and business leaders.

To McIlhenny's embarrassment, and Redd's chagrin, when they arrived at the Cocoanut Grove, they discovered their reservations had been lost. Try as he might, McIlhenny could not get the problem resolved. To save face, he finally suggested they have dinner at a famous Boston lobster restaurant instead.

It was Si and Ivy's first Maine lobster dinner, and they enjoyed it thoroughly. They probably listened to at least part of the game over the radio in the car on the way to dinner. The McIllhennys and the Redds, like thousands of other Bostonians, were stunned at the 55-12 trouncing their Boston College Eagles took at the hands of their cross-state rivals in one of the greatest upsets in college football history. But this news would pale in comparison to the news screamed in the headlines of the next morning's *Boston Globe.*

The prior night, the Cocoanut Grove had been jammed with Bostonians reliving the pain of their Eagles loss to Holy Cross. Over 1000 people were crowded into the restaurant, bars, and lounges of the two-story building, which had a capacity of only 460 people. At about 10:15 p.m., a small fire started in one of the downstairs lounges when a match was carelessly dropped in one of the decorative paper palm trees. A massive inferno developed quickly, and when it was over 492 people were dead and hundreds more injured. It is still the deadliest nightclub fire, and the second deadliest single building fire, in U.S. history.

Although he was undeniably loud and flamboyant, Si Redd also had a humble, self-effacing side. Throughout his life, when questioned about his success in business and in life, he often claimed he had been the luckiest man in the world. Never was that more true than on November 28, 1942.

****

The fire provided an unholy welcome for the Redds, but they comfortably settled into their new Boston life. This was the first time either Si or Ivy had lived in a large metropolitan area, and they instantly took to the vibrancy and excitement of city life.

One of President Franklin Roosevelt's WPA programs was the Federal Writer's Project. It was designed to put unemployed writers back into the workplace during the Depression. One of its most lasting projects was the American Guide Series, a library of forty-eight guidebooks, one for each state in the Union. These books provide a broad and colorful look at each U.S. state and its leading cities in the late 1930s and early 1940s, just as the Redds arrived in Boston. Of this city and its many divergent faces, the authors wrote:

It is the Boston of wide streets, overarched by spreading elms, of crooked, narrow streets called "quaint," of magnificent parks, fine public buildings, handsome residences, and a general air of well-scrubbed propriety and gracious leisure. It is the Boston where acres of ugly wooden tenement houses line the drab streets; where ten dollars a month rents a three-room flat in a wooden firetrap without heat, lighting, or any sanitary facilities; where, despite a magnificent park system, thousands of children must still play on sidewalks. It is the Boston of music-lovers . . . the Boston of art-lovers . . . the Boston of well-to-do churches and prosperous universities . . . [and] the Boston of manufacturing establishments.[5]

As the family absorbed their new surroundings, Redd quickly realized how large his new business opportunity would be. He knew he wouldn't be able to juggle the new six-state New England distributorship and still hold on to his Illinois and Mississippi route operations. He set about making arrangements for his employees in both states to buy the routes and inventories. In Illinois he sold the business to Ivy's brother-in-law Doc Howington, who then sold part of it to Ivy's other brother-in-law Dick McClanathan, keeping the enterprise in the family.[6]

When he left Mississippi, Redd had tried to keep the business he developed in the family too. His older brother Paul was the manager of a small general merchandise store in Louisville, Mississippi, barely eking out a living for himself and his family. Redd offered to sell the business to his brother for a very generous price, even offering to allow him to pay the note off in a number of easy installments out of his profits. After thinking about it, Paul declined the offer, telling his brother, "Well, I guess you just can't put a square peg in a round hole."[7]

Redd would eventually sell the business to Lester Griffin, who had been running it for him. "I really gave it to them," he said, explaining that the business was worth at least a quarter-million dollars, but that he sold it to Griffin for "eighty, ninety, or a hundred thousand dollars, and let him pay for it out of the income."[8]

"I didn't know the real, true value," he shrugged. Despite the "aw, shucks" country boy demeanor that Si Redd often hid behind, he was a shrewd businessman. He likely knew exactly what he was doing when he sold the business to his employees. Throughout his career, Redd's generosity to family and friends never wavered. He had the knack for making money, and liked to share it with those closest to him.

Making money never seemed to motivate Redd, nor did spending it, perhaps because he was able to do both with such ease. What was important to him was what the money stood for: winning. Si Redd loved to win. Whether it was a craps game in the dorm at Ole Miss, a c-note bet on a college football game, or a multimillion gamble in the boardroom of one of the country's largest corporations, he wanted—perhaps even needed—to come out on top. As kind and generous as he was to family and friends, he could be brutal and ruthless to competitors or those who sought to thwart his goals.

Dale Rodesch, who worked for Redd when his company first began popularizing video poker in the 1970s, said of his boss, "Si was a great guy, and a terrible guy. There's never been anyone like him." Rodesch said Redd had an open mind and would listen to anyone who came to him with an idea. "But he was always conniving too. You always had to watch him," Rodesch added.[9]

So the innocent-old-country-boy mask that Si Redd hid behind was very honest in one respect, but it could also be deceiving if taken too seriously.

* * * *

With war raging in both the Pacific and European theaters, it was inevitable that Uncle Sam would come looking for Si Redd, who was able-bodied and in his early thirties. Shortly after the family arrived in Boston, the draft letter arrived in their mailbox. Redd was willing—although, by his own admission, not anxious—to serve his country. He recognized what a great country it was, a place where a young man with no particular skills, born on the very bottom rung of society's economic ladder, could accomplish great things if he was willing to put forth the effort. But Si Redd turned out to be one of the lucky ones. A very severe case of hay fever and allergies had first struck him while he was in Illinois, and the move to Boston had exacerbated it. Redd reported for his physical, but he was classified 4F—physically unqualified to serve—and sent back home.

With the threat of military service out of the way, and his other businesses handed off to others, Redd was ready to go to work. But for once in his life, his timing was terrible. Wurlitzer, like other major manufacturers of nonessential products on the market, found that shortages of raw materials put a screeching halt to its production. The same happened to all other amusement machine manufacturers that Redd had anticipated representing. In fact, in early 1942 the coin-operated amusement machine industry was the first to be ordered to severely reduce or even completely cease production for the war effort. Thus the only goods Redd had to sell were whatever had been stored in the warehouses when he bought the company, and that inventory was quickly depleted.

Never one to whine about things out of his control, Redd made the best of the situation. Because he had no goods to sell through his distributorship, he began buying other route operators who found themselves in the same predicament. "I feel like I bought more jukebox routes than anyone else in the world," he would explain later. "I owned routes all over the New England area including New York State. It was very successful from a financial point of view."[10]

In this process, Redd also made excellent connections with finance companies, and he quickly learned the subtle techniques of using someone else's money to his advantage. Over the years, as he became more and more prosperous, he became a significant moneylender himself, especially after moving to Nevada. He would finance some of the men who became the biggest names in the Las Vegas and Reno gambling industry.

Toward the end of World War II, the government allowed Wurlitzer to begin building some of its older model cabinets again, though it still couldn't build the interior mechanisms because that required metal parts. So Redd and other distributors would jury-rig used mechanisms to fit into the "new" old-style cabinets, which provided them with what appeared to be new products to go into the field with. Redd made the most of the opportunity. Because of all the routes he had purchased—which always included the jukeboxes as well—he had huge inventories of old machines, which allowed him to put together thousands of the renovated old mechanisms into their "new" old-style cabinets.

The production of records had also been severely restricted because of the shortage of shellac. But Si Redd again saw and seized an opportunity. He discovered that if he changed the records more frequently than his competitors on all the jukes on his routes, he could keep his clientele happy. Because of the shellac shortage, he'd put whatever brand new records he could buy with the most popular songs *only* on the jukes of his largest customers; then the records he had replaced would be installed on the machines of his next largest customers; and so it went all the way down the line to the smallest cafés and taverns. Everybody was happy, and few customers asked Redd to take out the jukes, or threatened to do business with another route operator.[11]

Si Redd was a genius at customer service long before it became the mantra of modern-day business. Later, after the war ended, Redd even bought a small record manufacturer so he could produce his own records.

The Redds made their home in Newton Highlands, a suburb southwest of the city proper, and they thrived there.[12] It was an upper-middle-class neighborhood, not pretentious in the least according to Redd's friend Bob Jones, who lived with the family for a while after his service in World War II. Their neighborhood was one of fourteen individual Newton villages, according to the Federal Writers' Project, and "consist[ed] of more and yet more fine residences clustered around a small business center."[13] The neighborhood's most celebrated dwelling was the 1681 Woodward Farmhouse, a brown clapboard house with a massive central chimney and small-paned windows, which was still occupied by a descendant of the original owner.

In the Redds' neighborhood, all the families became close, as neighbors did all across the country during the war. Redd gave each neighbor a jukebox for their basement or rathskeller, and block parties became all the rage.

Redd was also a huge sports fan. He bought season tickets to Boston College, Holy Cross, and Harvard football games, and rarely missed a game. He always bought enough tickets so he could share them with his best customers too. He was also a regular attendee at Boston Red Sox and Boston Braves (now the Atlanta Braves) home games, where he maintained box seats behind the first base dugout. He became friendly with many of the players from the 1940s and 1950s. Bobby Doerr and Johnny Pesky, among others, often appeared at his office to sign baseballs and promote his jukeboxes.

Redd not only loved watching the games, he also bet heavily on them, particularly football, a habit that accelerated right along with his disposable income. Bob Cashell, a good friend and customer of Redd's from years later in Reno, said, "Si was a big-time gambler; he was no one-hundred dollar bettor. He had people all over the country who handicapped for him. He'd get on the phone and call some city whose university was playing a game and he'd chat them up, then he'd ask, 'What's the weather like there, or who's injured?'"[14]

Because of his contacts, expertise, and ability to remain unflappable under pressure, Redd was generally a successful gambler, a fact that could be traced all the way back to his Mississippi boyhood days. As he got older, however, and became more reckless, he would not be as successful with his sports wagering.

Si Redd loved being among friends. He was the consummate people person, and he was happiest in any social setting where conviviality and good conversation reigned. He was a great raconteur, and could tell stories with the best of them. His "aw, shucks" self-effacing demeanor, ribald sense of humor, and Southern country boy charm and wit made Redd a favorite at every party. Another country boy, Nevada's powerful U.S. senator Harry Reid from rural Searchlight, Nevada, said, "I could never get enough of [Si's] stories."[15]

In the 1950s, the Redds bought a summer home on Lake Wequaquet, near the town of Centerville on Cape Cod. They joined the Craigville Beach Association, and teenagers Vinnie and Sherry Redd spent a lot of time on the beach with their Cape Cod friends. One young man particularly caught Sherry's eye: Alan Green. Alan's family had summered on Cape Cod for years, and he was the head lifeguard at the beach. Sherry would eventually become Mrs. Alan Green.

Si Redd loved his summers on Cape Cod, but he did miss the "action" of the city. Bob Jones said he often complained about being out of the main business orbit of Boston. It did allow him to spend more time with his family, though, which he enjoyed very much.

Si Redd at his Cape Cod cottage, circa 1952. Throughout his life, fishing was a favorite hobby. *Redd family photo.*

Alan Green recalled that Si became a hero to many of the young people on the Cape. He took them to ball games, ferried them around the Cape, bought them ice cream, and just sat and visited with them. Redd had a childlike streak in his personality that never abandoned him. He always loved being with young people, especially his grandchildren and great-grandchildren later in his life.[16]

Bob Jones had gone to work for Redd again. He described his position with Redd Distributing Company as "a jack-of-all-trades," a sort of right-hand man who did anything that was asked of him. "We were such good friends," he laughed, "that I even babysat with his kids when he and Ivy had to be out of town."[17]

****

In early 1943, a brief and seemingly innocuous news item had run on page 59 of *Billboard* magazine. It announced that two men had been granted a Wurlitzer distributorship for parts of New York, New Jersey, and Connecticut. It is impossible to determine if this new distributorship overlapped with that of Redd Distributing Company's "exclusive" territory, or if it just butted up to his territorial limits.[18] But in either case, anyone reading between the lines could have sensed eventual trouble for Si Redd. The names of the men who had purchased the distributorship were Ed Smith and Meyer Lansky.

Gangsters had been attracted to the coin-operated amusement business from its inception, both because of the large amount of cash that could be generated and because the proceeds could easily be shielded from prying government eyes. Redd's career had been surprisingly free of such intrusions. He did have suspicions about the Birmingham men who had horned in on his Mississippi operation, but that fact was never confirmed. And in Illinois he knew the Chicago jukebox distributors were gangsters, but their territories never overlapped with his. But Meyer Lansky was different.

Already one of the Mafia's top leaders, despite his Jewish heritage, Lansky was organized crime's chief banker, and head of its feared assassination unit, Murder, Inc. During World War II he had aided the war effort by arranging for the Mafia to provide security against German saboteurs in the Navy's waterfront shipbuilding operation. Perhaps this service was being rewarded by the Wurlitzer distributorship, but that is only speculation.

In any case, this new development must have been closely watched by Si Redd in the years to come. Eventually he would brush much closer to this feared organization than he ever imagined.

* * * *

The postwar period brought with it renewed prosperity for most Americans, and certainly for those involved in the coin-operated amusement business. But there was trouble brewing in the jukebox industry, and few realized it had already reached its zenith before the war.

Redd Distributing Company began handling a wide assortment of coin-op machines in addition to jukeboxes, which remained its primary product. These included pinball machines, vending machines, arcade games, shooting galleries, shuffleboard games, and kiddie rides. In the late 1940s and early 1950s Si Redd began to represent some of Bally Manufacturing Company's products, such as its horse racing games, bingo machines, and coffee vending machines. That was a particularly nostalgic reunion for Redd, who had begun his coin-operated career with a single Bally Goofy pinball machine two decades earlier.

Bally had also made its first foray into the slot machine business. Before the war, they had come up with an innovative slot machine they named Bally Baby. It was a tiny replica of the three-reel one-armed bandit, a little tyke that measured just 2 × 7.5 inches and weighted only 8 pounds. The unexpected success of the machine convinced Ray Moloney, who still ran the company, to extend his line and produce slot machines. However, the war would put Bally Baby and all of the company's other products into cold storage for the next five years.

The postwar period found Redd Distributing Company's bread-and-butter product, jukeboxes, in trouble. A decade-long internal struggle to move the industry from its traditional nickel-a-play standard pricing to a dime-a-play split the industry in two. Jukes had also reached what many considered a saturation point in American society, and the advent of television further threatened to weaken the industry.[19]

Kerry Segrave's chronicle of the industry, *Jukeboxes: An American Social History,* aptly describes the beginning of this fall from prominence:

For distributors as well, 1948 was a bad year. Prices for jukes were too high, inventories were too large, and there was a lack of credit. Most manufacturers canceled a large number of distributing contracts to appoint new sales representatives. Distributors changed lines; some simply closed their doors or went into other lines.

Many operators who were solely juke owners had added pinball games along with cigarette machines in response to increased operating costs.[20]

Although the decade of the 1950s was anticipated to be a rebirth for the jukebox industry, it never materialized. It was, in Segrave's words, "a stagnant decade," and he described the 1960s as the industry's "slow fade to obscurity."

Si Redd's problems were typical of the industry. He told his University of Southern Mississippi oral history interviewer that he came close to bankruptcy two times during the 1950s and 1960s, barely escaping each time. The only thing that kept him solvent was his route operations. "It [took] six months to a year period [each time] to straighten out my whole life," Redd said.[21] Once during this period he even tried to sell his entire operation to his friend and employee Bob Jones. But Jones was unable to handle the large outstanding debt that the business carried.[22]

One of his biggest successes during the period, although short lived, began in the mid-1950s, according to one of his Boston employees, Dick Olsen. Although cash payouts on pinball machines was illegal throughout the region, many men's clubs, fraternal halls, and other types of venues that were not open to the public began making monetary payoffs for winnings. Even some of the bolder bars and taverns began doing it too, on the sly of course. "These were really quasi slot machines," Olsen said, "and they were enormously profitable."[23]

Because the machines on his routes were generating so much cash, and were so profitable, Redd didn't want to waste a lot of time counting the exact proceeds of each machine when he went in to empty them. So he would dump all the coins—thousands of them— from an establishment's machines onto a large table and quickly separate them into two approximately equal piles. Then he would tell the hall or tavern owner to select whichever pile he wanted. "This saved a lot of time, and time was money," Olsen said. "Si was a real efficiency expert."[24]

Unfortunately, this profitable gig ended in the early 1960s, when law enforcement cracked down and put an end to the cash payouts.

Of the three major jukebox manufacturers, only Wurlitzer depended primarily on music machines—jukeboxes and electric organs—for its sales. Seeburg and Rock-Ola, numbers two and three in the business, respectively, were heavily involved with other types of coin-operated amusement games as well, and these allowed the companies to continue to prosper. In late 1948 Seeburg introduced its 100 series, which held fifty records, or one hundred songs. They followed that with the introduction of a machine that played only the newly developed 45-rpm records. These and other Seeburg advancements left Wurlitzer in the dust, and Seeburg replaced its longtime rival at the top of the jukebox mountain.

"All we had was the 24-record systems," Redd remarked. "The Wurlitzer jukebox business rather went to hell from a competitive marketing standpoint when the Seeburgs hit the market."[25]

Redd jumped ship. He knew Seeburg owner Dale Coleman, and he arranged to drop Wurlitzer and become a Seeburg distributor. This honeymoon lasted about ten years, but when Seeburg began shipping Redd more units than he had ordered—the same scheme Wurlitzer had used—he offered to sell the distributorship back to them in the early 1960s. They accepted.

"But I made a serious financial business mistake," Redd said. "I sold them the assets, but not the corporation." In essence, Redd had sold Seeburg the company's physical assets only, not the $3 or $4 million in conditional sales contracts he carried for the bars, taverns, and restaurants that still owed him for the jukeboxes he had installed. "Believe it or not," he said, "the Seeburg people came in and told the people [who owed me money], 'Hey, don't pay those conditional sales contracts. Si won't bother you. Those machines aren't any good anyway. Buy our *new* machines.'"[26]

That's exactly what many of them did. However, Redd had offset those debts to leading Boston banks, and he was still responsible for repaying them whether or not his borrowers paid him. It was a brutally expensive lesson for Si Redd. He lost millions on the deal.

By his own admission, Si Redd had an itchy trigger finger when it came to buying and selling his business ventures. "Other than talking it over with [Ivy]," he said, "I'd make a shoot-from-the-hip decision to do it without thinking it out." Of the Seeburg decision, he added, "You look back again and [there] was no question from a business point of view it was damn wrong. In other words we were successful in spite of ourselves."[27]

Redd was a business genius, but primarily in sales, marketing, and customer service matters. He never completely understood the complex financial aspects of big business, and as a result he made many of the same mistakes over and over throughout his career. But he always forced himself to look forward, not backward, as his mother Nannie Redd had taught him.

"My jukebox business in New England was on the skids, and I had to start over somewhere," Si Redd said.[28] He still had his route operations, so in 1960 he again began to search for new opportunities in that field. For the remainder of his time in New England, however, Redd's business was hit-and-miss, and he would have as many failures as successes.

One scheme Redd pondered during this period was food vending. Although he had hundreds of cigarette and coffee vending machines on his routes, he had never branched out into other areas of food vending. He decided to try to become a distributor of food vending machines and products.

Dick Olsen, a lifelong Bostonian, was a good friend of Vinnie's husband, John Copeland. Redd had met the young man and was

Ivy and Si Redd in Boston, circa 1958. They spent a quarter century in New England. *Redd family photo.*

impressed with him. In fact, Olsen had even brokered a midtown apartment for Si and Ivy when they decided to move from their Newton Highlands house. Both daughters were now married and into their own lives, and Si and Ivy wanted to move to town where they could enjoy the restaurants, theaters, and other amenities Boston had to offer.

Redd decided that Dick Olsen, who was just finishing his master's degree in business entrepreneurship from Babson College, would be the ideal fellow to set up his food vending business. "He was at my commencement," Olsen said, "and he grabbed me out of line and said, 'I want you to come work for me.'"[29] Olsen accepted the challenge.

He spent about three months analyzing the food vending opportunity, and decided it would not be a good fit for Si Redd. "It wasn't the kind of margins Si was used to," Olsen said, pointing out that the business generated profits of only about 3 percent.

The business also required carrying a huge amount of perishable inventory, and needed a lot of warehouse space. Olsen gave Redd his report, and Redd took the advice and dropped the food vending idea.

Another of Si Redd's "golden opportunities" came close to costing him his life.

Tennessee U.S. senator Estes Kefauver was chairman and chief flag waver for the Senate Crime Investigating Committee, a now famous group that studied the influence of organized crime in U.S. business at the beginning of the 1950s. During their proceedings, the committee released a list of seventy separate types of businesses into which "hoodlums had infiltrated."[30] Among the items on the list were the amusement industry and jukeboxes, giving Redd double exposure to potential trouble, which wasn't long in coming.

United Manufacturing Company of Chicago had introduced a coin-operated arcade game called Shuffle-Alley, a bowling game, which was beginning to capture the public's fancy in a big way. It was a miniature 9-foot-long bowling alley built into a wooden cabinet that stood on four legs. Ten small bowling pins sat at one end of the machine, topped by a scoreboard-like device with blinking lights that kept a running score of the game.[31]

One or two players would stand at the other end of the machine, drop their coins into the slot, and slide a heavy metal-encased puck down the alley to knock down the pins. The puck actually hit mechanical switches in the alley just in front of the pins that caused a relay to retract the toppling pins upward in a realistic pattern. Then the puck was returned to the player for his second shot.

An early ad for Shuffle-Alley, targeting those in the industry, promised what the new machine could do: "[It] puts operators 'in the chips' almost overnight . . . the first shuffle type bowler ever manufactured . . . making money for the operator every day."[32]

By the time Redd got interested in the game, it was already a hit. He sensed the same optimistic future for this game that he had seen for pinball machines in Mississippi and jukeboxes in Illinois, so he arranged with United to become the distributor for Shuffle-Alley in Massachusetts. He got the machines licensed in the state—a formality that had to be followed with each new type of coin-operated amusement machine—and began selling Shuffle-Alley to area route operators and putting them out on his own routes.

At the beginning of every year Redd would arrange for a line of credit to cover his inventory-purchasing expenses for the coming year. It was a practice he had followed for years, and he always paid his notes off promptly, so he never had a credit problem.[33] One day, as Redd was sitting in his office, two tough-looking characters came in to see him. "We're your new partners," they told him insolently.[34]

"I don't have any partners. I run this business myself," Redd said, puzzled.

The men informed Redd that their associates had purchased one of his notes, and that $20,000 was due and payable. Redd knew the note was not due for another year, and that even then it was only a $10,000-note. He told them so.

The two thugs smiled malevolently and told Redd that the difference was the vig, or interest, on the note, and that it was due and payable immediately . . . or else. Then they left.

Si Redd knew he had come face to face with the Mob. The *capo* of the New England Mafia was Raymond Loreto Salvatore Patriarca, a Massachusetts-born thug who ran New England for the Profaci-Colombo family from New York. Patriarca's underboss, Jerry Angiulo, ran the rackets in Boston, and raked a cut off of every illegal gambling game in the city.[35] The Mob was always trying to muscle in on legitimate businesses that caught their fancy, and Shuffle Alley had become their latest focus of attention.

Redd considered his circumstance for a few days and decided to take it to the top. Patriarca was headquartered in the heavily Italian city of Providence, Rhode Island, and it was there that Redd headed.

Atwells Avenue sits atop Federal Hill in downtown Providence, the center of what was once the most densely populated Italian neighborhood in the nation. It served as "Little Italy" for the entire state. The strong smell of garlic lingered in the air from dozens of Italian restaurants and delis that crowded the neighborhood; and salamis, plump sausages, and prosciutto legs hung from hooks in the windows of small grocery stores and meat markets. Other vendors sold their goods from pushcarts in the streets, and the sounds of live chickens and rabbits clucking and chattering in their wooden cages created a cacophony of sound.

This was "the hood" if you were Italian in the 1950s and 1960s in Providence, and Si Redd elbowed his way down the crowded sidewalk to the office of Raymond Patriarca. What actually happened during his confrontation with the *capo* was known only to the two men themselves, and perhaps to a few thugs who hung around to see that no harm came to Raymond Patriarca. According to Redd's version, "I showed a lot of fight."[36] And as he told and retold the story in years to come, the raconteur in him took over and he even adopted a heavy Italian brogue to go with his story.

His son-in-law Alan Green heard the story innumerable times, and he still smiles at the recollection. Redd said he had written a long letter to his friend Mississippi U.S. senator John Stennis, and to major Mississippi newspapers, outlining the threats Patriarca had made against him. When he confronted Patriarca, he told him about the letters, and boldly said that if anything ever happened to him or his family the letters would be made public and Patriarca would go down. Whether it happened that way or not is open to speculation, but it's a great Si Redd story.[37]

Redd may have been brazen, but he was not foolish. However the meeting with Patriarca had gone, Redd began to think about it afterwards, and the full impact of what could happen to him and his family finally sunk in. He decided to sell the Mob the Shuffle-Alley distributorship, "for a very small amount,"[38] he said, and move on with his life.

Somewhere in the mid-1960s Redd sold his route operations too. He was weary of New England, and he began yearning for a fresh start. In the meantime, he retired from business.

Summing up the up-and-down business cycles of the quarter century Si Redd spent in New England, Bob Jones said, "Si felt a drag on him because he couldn't find the key to make it all work. Si was basically a gambler, and he made a lot of mistakes which were the result of taking a lot of bad gambles."[39]

But retirement soon grew boring, and in the absence of anything better, Redd took another look at the food vending business. United Servomation had been incorporated in 1960 as an amalgamation of eleven independent food vending companies, some of which Redd had likely done prior business with. The new company wanted to begin establishing its own vending routes, not only in food but also jukeboxes, cigarettes, and other products in order to supplement the low margin of profits in the food business. Redd proposed the idea of going around the country and buying routes for them.

"They would furnish the money and I'd go out and buy the routes all over the United States and keep them long enough to make a little profit," he said. "I could buy them cheaper than they could because I knew the business."[40]

But the idea had its disadvantages, too. Redd would be working all alone, which would have been unpleasant for the gregarious promoter. And he'd be away from Ivy for weeks at a time, living out of a suitcase. It wasn't a very exciting prospect for the man who loved to make deals and break new ground, but it beat sitting around his lake house chatting idly with the neighbors. So he put his toe in the water.

"I . . . placed ads in the trade magazines," he said. "'We'll pay cash dollars. Sell your whole route.' I started traveling all over the United States . . . answering these ads."[41]

Redd's first call was in Gary, Indiana. Because he was nearby, he decided to stop in Chicago and see his friend Bill O'Donnell at Bally. He wanted to let O'Donnell know what he was up to, and see if perhaps he could bring Bally into the venture with its coffee vending machines.

Little did Si Redd know that at fifty-five years old, and after four decades in the coin-operated vending business, he was about to come face to face with the biggest opportunity of his lifetime.

— CHAPTER 6 —

THE BIGGEST LITTLE CITY

It was spring of 1967 in Chicago. At 2640 Belmont Avenue, on the North Side, Bally Manufacturing Company's Chicago headquarters hunched down next to the west bank of the Chicago River. In nearby Brands Park, in the remnants of Chicago's Old Settlers' picnic grove, the delicate white blossoms on the flowering dogwoods were just beginning to emerge, in stark contrast to the crumbling old red brick field house that stood nearby. Along the river bank, the gray branches of the birch trees were just beginning to sprout the emerald green leaves that would soon envelope them.

Lounging comfortably in Bill O'Donnell's office, Si Redd described the Servomation opportunity to his friend. O'Donnell listened respectfully. Redd had sought Bill O'Donnell's advice because the men had become friends over the years, and Redd admired and respected the Bally executive. A dozen years younger than Redd, O'Donnell, a handsome man with thick, wavy brown hair and a ready smile, had joined Bally in 1946 as a brash young amusement machine salesman, and had risen to the position of vice president of sales. But with the death of Bally founder Ray Moloney in 1958, the company began a period of slow descent into fiscal insolvency, and O'Donnell became uncertain of his future.[1]

Moloney's two sons tried desperately to convince debt holders and court trustees to allow them to develop a new generation of electro-mechanical slot machines, but their pleas fell on deaf ears. In 1963

O'Donnell and a few other investors stepped in and purchased the company's assets for $2.85 million, saving it from bankruptcy.

O'Donnell, as the new president, quickly led a turnabout for the company using a combination of personal charisma, business acumen, and an iron will. Within five years he would turn the company from a manufacturer of pinball and amusement games into the world's largest maker of slot machines as well.

As an ex-salesman, O'Donnell appreciated Si Redd for the natural promoter and salesman the man was. Redd's New England distribution business and slot route operation had included a number of Bally's amusement machines, and he'd always done an outstanding job selling them. O'Donnell may have also felt a nostalgic connection to the man who had begun his career with a single Bally pinball machine nearly four decades earlier. Knowing Redd as he did, O'Donnell instinctively realized the Servomation deal would not be a good fit: it would be, he knew, like harnessing a racehorse to a plow. However, the Bally executive also had a selfish motive for deterring Redd from accepting the Servomation opportunity.

"Si, you don't want to do that . . . you want to go out to Reno, Nevada. Heck, you'll make a million dollars," O'Donnell told him.[2] He then shared some key information with Redd about his company and its plans.

Early in its history, Bally had competed in slot machine manufacturing against the industry's leading companies: Mills, Pace, Watling, Jennings, and Caille. But in 1951 a new federal law had been passed banning the sale of slot machines in all states except Nevada. Concurrently, Illinois passed a state statute outlawing slot machine manufacturing within its borders. So Bally was forced out of the slot machine business.

But in 1963 Illinois repealed its ban on the manufacture of slot machines, and Bally, under its managing partner Bill O'Donnell, was ready to reenter the market with the design of the industry's first electromechanical slot machine, Money Honey. Ironically, these were the same machines Ray Moloney's sons had tried to develop to save their father's company. O'Donnell had been wise enough to appreciate the value of this advanced technology, and had quietly continued its development once he was in charge of Bally.

It is important to understand that in the mid-1960s, the term *slot machine* referred almost exclusively to spinning reel machines with three or four reels, machines often referred to as one-armed bandits.

The almost unlimited variety of slot machines that a casino visitor can play today simply did not exist in the 1960s.

So, with its brand new, technologically advanced Money Honey slot machine ready to be introduced in the nation's only gambling market, Nevada, O'Donnell traveled to the state to obtain the necessary license for Bally to sell its new slot machines. However, from information gleaned from a 1981 lawsuit against Bally by one of its shareholders, it is revealed that certain "questionable business practices and associations" of some of the company's directors—notably president O'Donnell and vice president Sam Klein—prevented Bally from being granted a license.[3] This was an unexpected turn of events, but Bill O'Donnell was up to the challenge.

Because Bally couldn't distribute its own machines, O'Donnell convinced two experienced Nevada gaming executives to become independent distributors for Bally's products in the state. Mickey Wichinsky, who had been involved in the Nevada gaming scene since the mid-1950s, set up Bally Sales Company in southern Nevada, whereas Dick Graves set up Currency Gaming Devices in northern Nevada.[4]

Graves, like Si Redd, was a natural-born promoter and salesman.[5] In the 1940s, after the war, Nevada's northern neighbor Idaho had found itself surrounded by states in which slot machines were operating either legally or illegally, draining much-needed cash away from the small logging, mining, and farming communities in the state. So in 1947 Idaho legislators legalized slot machines. Although the new law did slow the cash drain, it wasn't a perfect solution. Slots, it was charged, were "like a virus in the body politic, dividing Idaho citizens against each other, changing the shape of towns, [and] altering social life," *Time* magazine reported in 1953.[6] So, at the end of that year, legislators acted again and banned the machines.

Graves had been running a very successful slot machine route in Idaho, and when the machines were banned he simply moved his business lock, stock, and barrel to northern Nevada. He also opened a small casino in Yerington that he named the Nugget, then built Nugget casinos in Carson City, Reno, and Sparks, Reno's next-door neighbor.

When Bill O'Donnell convinced Graves to set up a Bally distributorship in northern Nevada, the old gambler was already contemplating retirement. He was in the process of selling his last remaining Nugget casino in Sparks to his general manager, John Ascuaga. But he agreed to help O'Donnell out. O'Donnell, meanwhile, had managed to get a personal gaming distributor license in his own name. And in late 1965 he invested $63,600 for a 30 percent stake in Graves's distributorship. A year later, as a temporary measure only, O'Donnell purchased the remaining 70 percent of Currency Gaming for resale, with the condition that Graves manage the venture until he could find a suitable partner.[7]

All of this O'Donnell related to Si Redd as they sat in his Chicago office. Graves was itching to retire, so Si Redd's visit was a serendipitous occasion for O'Donnell. He explained that if Redd liked the opportunity, O'Donnell would install him as manager of Currency Gaming until he acquired his gaming license—which he did in late 1967—and would then sell him the 70 percent stake in the business.

Redd would later say that O'Donnell was also completely open and honest with him about future plans for the distributorship. He told Redd that he planned to take Bally Manufacturing Company public, and that at that time he would want to repurchase the northern Nevada distributorship in Bally's name. But he assured Redd he'd get a fair price for the business when it happened, and that he could make a lot of money in the meantime.

Redd had no problem with the condition; in fact, he was intrigued with the whole proposition. He had been involved with almost every type of coin-operated machine there was, but except for a casual

The 1964 Bally Money Honey, the first electromechanical slot machine, revolutionized the casino industry, with Si Redd's help. *Courtesy of Marshall Fey.*

brush with slot machines on a few occasions, he had always steered clear of the illegal devices for fear of being caught. He agreed to travel to Reno and take a look.

By the mid-1967, Bally was manufacturing the new Money Honey slots, but in a very limited quantity, as the demand in Nevada had been light. Marshall Fey, whose grandfather Charles Fey is credited with inventing the three-reel one-armed bandit slot machine, wrote the book that is the definitive source on slot machines through the 1990s. His book is quoted often in this story. Of Money Honey, he wrote:

Using an updated mechanism from their floor consoles cased in a front-opening cabinet, this new machine vaulted them [Bally] into the casino slot market. A hopper payout unit was added . . . with a capacity of 2,500 dimes. It had the capability of accurately paying out numerous variable sized jackpots as well as multiple coin and line pays, creating a major improvement over the 20-coin maximum of the slide pay. Bally's electro-mechanical machine utilized multi-contact boards which could sense more than 50 different payout combinations. These features led the way to multi-coin, three and five-line machines, as well as left-to-right and right-to-left payouts.[8]

With a purely mechanical slot machine, the maximum automatic payoff possible was twenty coins, the number that would fit into the coin tube inside the machine. If a player won more than twenty, he had to wait until a slot attendant verified his win and paid him the remainder by hand. According to longtime Reno casino owner Warren Nelson, "This didn't just slow up play, it kind of suggested closure, an end to the game. . . . [I]t tempted the customer to cease play and walk out the door with his winnings."[9] All that ended with Bally's electromechanicals, which featured a large "hopper," or coin-collecting and coin-disbursing mechanism, controlled by an electrical circuit.

Once more, like so many times during his coin-op career, Si Redd was in the right place at the right time. It's difficult to believe that blind luck or serendipity smiled on the man so often. Instead, it's obvious that an innate, finely honed sense of the marketplace led Redd to the pinball machine, the jukebox, and the new and improved slot machine at just the right moments in history. The normally self-effacing Redd called it luck; other industry watchers called it genius. Perhaps it was a little of each. In any case, once these opportunities presented themselves, nobody was ever quicker or surer to take advantage of them than the sage old Mississippi country boy.

Redd left immediately for Reno to check on the opportunity O'Donnell had outlined. The idea must have sparked a big interest in him, because on his way West he didn't follow up on any of the other leads he had developed for the Servomation routes. He made a beeline for Reno.

When he arrived at the Reno airport, Redd rented a car and drove the short distance to downtown. He passed through a couple of residential neighborhoods with sturdy little 1920s and 1930s brick houses and welcoming tree-shaded streets; crossed the clear,

The casino corridor in downtown Reno, Nevada, is shown at night in this late 1960s photo, when Si Redd first arrived in town. *Courtesy of the Nevada Historical Society.*

sparkling Truckee River; and parked on Virginia Street, in the middle of the casino corridor.

"It was a beautiful late summer evening on the Truckee Meadows when the air has that soft, mellow quality that you only find on mountain meadows at the end of a warm summer day," Redd recollected poetically some years later. He instantly began to fall in love with the town. "Reno, Nevada, was in a way more just like Mississippi. . . . Everybody was friendly. . . . [I]t was just a charming place," he said.[10]

He wandered up Virginia Street with its blinking neon lights and net-stockinged young ladies shilling in front of every open door, over the railroad tracks, and across Commercial Row, where most of the small sawdust joints huddled side by side, and back down Sierra Street, passing casinos, bars, and cheap souvenir shops with big fuzzy dice and gaudy Indian artifacts in the windows. Redd was struck by the excitement and the carnival atmosphere of the place. "I've never seen slot machines like that in all my life! People were playing them and—cling, clang, clang—the noise that they were making!"[11]

He was especially impressed with one particular machine. "I saw the Big Berthas," he said, "[and] I saw the opportunity. It wasn't because I was smart; I should have moved to Nevada in the first place," he laughed.[12]

Big Bertha impressed everybody who saw it. It certainly wasn't technology that made Big Bertha such a hit, for it was just another mechanical slot machine. It was the size. Big Bertha was B-I-G! A giant-sized replica of a regular slot machine, the Big Bertha was nearly 8 feet tall and 5 feet wide, with three huge reels and a handle on the side that was so big that many players required two hands to pull it down. Big Bertha accepted only silver dollars, and when a player won, the sound of a handful of coins tumbling into the tray was ear shattering. Most Reno casinos of the day opened onto the sidewalk with large triple or quadruple doors, creating a gaping maw into the noisy, brightly lit interiors. Big Bertha would sit right in the middle of the open doorway, enticing everybody who walked by to drop a dollar into the slot. Often, scantily clad young ladies would stand beside the giant machines, purring sexily to passersby about what a great chance they had to win a stack of silver dollars.

Redd related his initial experience with the machine. "At the Horseshoe Club—right across the street from Harrah's, where I was standing—they had one of those Big Bertha machines. . . . There was a big, heavy woman playing it, and darned if she didn't hit the jackpot! She started screaming, bells started ringing, cars started stopping in the streets, and a crowd started to form. I ran across the street just in time to see her being paid off."[13]

Big Bertha was great fun, especially when somebody won. It's a sure bet that Redd dropped a few coins into the big machine as he stood in front of the Horseshoe. Nevada was the zenith of the coin-op business, and Si Redd couldn't wait to join the party.

"I'd had all those years of experience in the coin-machine business, and here was an opportunity that I never dreamed existed," he said.[14]

No question Big Bertha was an anomaly, but like a very large, heavy child born to normal-sized parents, it still bore the same DNA as its progenitor, which could be traced all the way back to 1899.

The Industrial Revolution in America, often called the Second Industrial Revolution, had ended, but the great advances that had been fomented continued, as American inventors sought new ways to make life easier and more enjoyable for their fellow citizens. Charles Fey was such a man.[15]

Born August Fey in 1862 in Bavaria, Germany, Fey began work as a teenager in a Munich farm tool factory, then perfected his trade as an apprentice in a marine nautical instrument workshop in London. Fey later emigrated to New York, and in 1885 left it for the warmer climes of San Francisco, eventually finding work to support his growing family as an instrument maker at California Electric Works.

While working, Fey met two other like-minded men of Germanic origin, Gustav Schultze and Theodore Holtz. By 1895 all three men had moved their families across the bay to Berkeley. They shared stories, swapped yarns, and discussed their future as they traveled daily by ferry to their jobs in the city. Schultze had been manufacturing and operating slot machines—nickel-in-the-slots, they were called at the time—and with his encouragement Fey and Holtz quit their jobs and formed a partnership to compete with California Electric Works. Fey's grandson, Marshall Fey, has said that the two men also made parts for Schultze's slot machines.

In his spare time Fey began tinkering with nickel-in-the-slot machines in his basement, and eventually sold out to his partner Holtz to devote full-time to this new passion. When nickel-in-the-slot machines were declared legal in San Francisco in 1897, Fey came

Charles August Fey invented the Liberty Bell in 1899 in San Francisco, the forerunner of all reel slot machines that would follow over the next 110 years. *Courtesy of Marshall Fey.*

up with the first machine with an automatic payoff feature, a poker game he named Card Bell. (There is more on the history of poker slot machines in Chapter 10.)

In 1899 Fey revamped his Card Bell machine into a spinning reel slot machine that he named Liberty Bell, and the modern-day slot machine was born. As other manufacturers began copying Fey's work, the name Liberty Bell became the generic name for any spinning reel slot machine, which later were more popularly called one-armed bandits.

Charles Fey's 1899 mechanical Liberty Bell slot machine, the first "one-armed bandit," would remain virtually unchanged for more than a half century before the advent of electromechanical slot machines in 1964. *Courtesy of Marshall Fey.*

Nearly seven decades later, in Reno, an excited Si Redd returned to his car thinking about the magic spell Big Bertha had cast on everybody. He headed east toward Sparks and the newly renamed John Ascuaga's Nugget. Ascuaga was a second-generation Basque-American. His father, Josè, had left his home in the Pyrenees in

1914 and found his way to Caldwell, Idaho, where he began tending sheep, the predominant occupation for native Basques. John Ascuaga had just finalized his purchase of the Nugget from Dick Graves.

"I checked in at the Nugget's little motel, had a nice meal, and right away got into a crap game," Redd laughed. "I started shooting craps like they was goin' to close up the place. I must have shot dice until two or three in the morning, and lost all the money I had on me. But what the hell, it was a lot fun," he said.[16]

The next morning, with happy visions of the crap game and Big Bertha still dancing in his head, he called Ivy back in Cape Cod and told her they were moving to Reno.

* * * *

The 1967 Nevada that Si and Ivy Redd would soon call home was basically a bifurcated state. It had two principal markets, Las Vegas (Clark County) in the south and Reno (Washoe County) in the north, and two principal time periods, prelegalized gambling and postlegalized gambling.

The Reno–Sparks, Nevada Metropolitan Statistical Area is today an area of nearly 350,000 people. Originating from Lake Tahoe and cutting right through Reno and Sparks is the sparklingly clear, tree-shaded Truckee River, which makes the area a year-round outdoor sportsman's paradise. Biking, hiking, swimming, fishing, kayaking, skiing, and snowboarding are favorite activities. Reno's downtown core, home to most of the old-time gambling parlors and "burley-cue" (burlesque) joints, is today home to many of the area's high-rise casino resorts, too. But there are also a few grand spots in the eastern part of the city, along South Virginia Street, and in neighboring Sparks.

Reno was founded in 1868 as a stopover on the Central Pacific Railroad.[17] Throughout its early history its fortunes were tied to the discovery of silver in Nevada's mining camps, most notably nearby Virginia City. Its population rose and fell along with the intermittent discoveries of silver ore deposits.

Quickie divorces were Reno's earliest claim to fame, as the state lowered the residency requirement for divorce to six months, then to three, and finally to six weeks. "The City of Broken Vows," one writer called the place that helped separate Mary Pickford, Cornelius Vanderbilt Jr., Sinclair Lewis, and Jack Dempsey, among others, from their spouses. To entertain all the folks who stopped over to establish residency before untying the knot, illegal gambling speakeasies flourished in downtown Reno. Gambling had been legal in the state from 1869 until 1910, when it was outlawed, but the new law certainly hadn't stopped the practice.

In 1931, state legislators reduced the divorce residency requirement to six weeks, a law that would be a bonanza for Reno. At the southern end of the state, the dusty little town of Las Vegas was looking forward to its own miniboom: contracts were about to be let for the construction of Hoover Dam. But town leaders were looking further down the road, and had been agitating for an open gambling law, as we can see in this January 24, 1931, excerpt from the *Reno Evening Gazette:*

While no gambling bill is in sight in the legislature, it is expected that one will be introduced with excellent chances of favorable action. No one can be found, as yet, who will admit having been approached to offer such a bill, but all the legislators profess a lively interest in one. None of the Clark County [Las Vegas] delegation has an idea in mind of introducing a gambling bill, although the latest agitation for such legislation started in that county.

It took a twenty-nine-year-old cowboy from Humboldt County, freshman assemblyman Phil Tobin, to get up the nerve to introduce a gambling bill. Similar bills had failed in 1925 and 1927, so Tobin showed a lot of courage in tackling the moralists who opposed it. His bill passed the Assembly (24 to 11) and the Senate (13 to 3), and Governor Fred Balzar quickly signed the bill into law.

In an ironic twist, it would be two years before the U.S. government repealed Prohibition, thus for a spell making it legal to gamble and visit a prostitute in Nevada, but not to enjoy a cocktail.

One magazine writer noted that the impact of the new gambling law wasn't felt overnight. It took two nights, he penned. "Saturday, March 21 [two days after Governor Balzar signed the new law] was a big evening in Reno as crowds of locals, Californians, and out-of-state reporters jammed the Bank Club, which had done a hasty remodeling, and other establishments."[18]

With the legalization of gambling, Reno's back alley speakeasies became the nation's first legal casinos, and the town became its first gaming center. (The term *gaming* has been used in Nevada since the 1920s. It is synonymous with the word *gambling*.) The Owl Club on East Commercial Row was the first location in the state to be granted a gaming license after the new law was passed. Owner Dan Shoemaker was licensed to install a number of table games and four slot machines (two nickel, one dime, and one quarter machine). Other games were available nearby at the Sage Brush, Louvre, Palace, and Wine House, where men played faro, poker, craps, pan, three-card monte, and chuck-a-luck.[19]

Slot machines were also popular gaming options from the earliest days of legalized gambling. As today, they weren't limited to just casinos. They could also be found in bars, nightclubs, restaurants, hotel lobbies, bowling alleys, bus stations, cigar stores, dance halls, pool halls, and drugstores. They were also a prominent form of entertainment at dude ranches, swimming pools, newsstands, gas stations, and grocery stores. They could even be found in some of the most unlikely places, such as root beer stands, bakeries, candy stores, and even in local brothels.[20]

Did legalized gambling fulfill its early promise to help Nevada through the worst years of the Great Depression? "You bet it did," said Silvio Petricciani, whose pioneer gaming family owned Reno's Palace Club. In his University of Nevada oral history interview, Petricciani said, "All the clubs made money during the Depression."[21] The tourists the casinos brought to town also provided the trickle-down effect the law's proponents had anticipated, bringing in just enough additional revenue to allow most businessmen to keep their heads above water until the Depression ended.

A historian describing Reno in the late1930s and early 1940s wrote,

From a distance we can picture this Reno as a Babylon of miners, dudes, sheepmen, prospectors, lawyers, cowboys, bewildered women, bartenders, roulette wheels, dressed-for-Sunday Indians[,] . . . the University, the minis-ters, the priests, the hot springs baths [and] the regulated Stockade with its regulated whores—put them all together and run the bubbling Truckee River down the midst of them and . . . we have this Reno.[22]

But it was the advent of such downtown Virginia Street places as Harolds Club, built by San Francisco carnival games operator Harold Smith, Harrah's Club, founded by California bingo operator Bill Harrah, and the Art Deco–style Mapes Hotel-Casino, built by the grandson of a Reno cattleman, that put Reno on the map and eventually made it world famous. The city earned the moniker "The Biggest Little City in the World" and gave its visitors the opportunity to rub shoulders with hard-core gamblers such as Harry the Horse, Hard Luck Johnny, the Iceman, Looking Glass Harry, and Joe the Grinder.

Today, Reno takes a back seat to Las Vegas, its southern counter-part, whenever the conversation turns to gambling and billion-dollar destination resort casinos. That was not so in the beginning. One historian described Las Vegas in the pre–Boulder (today Hoover) Dam era of the 1920s, before gambling was legalized:

Las Vegas . . . was a raw western settlement of approximately five thousand souls, the last frontier town in America, but really dying in its boots. It was a place where prospectors, cowboys and tourists gathered to get blind drunk in the saloons that flourished in open defiance of Prohibition; to sing, shout, and gamble in the dingy clubs that lined Fremont Street; to stagger to the houses and cribs on Block 16 of North First Street, the sorry red-light district where gaudily-dressed women sat on porches or on tipped-back chairs under cottonwood trees.

   . . . Rip-roaring, no-holds-barred pursuit of pleasure was Las Vegas' stock-in-trade, and all that separated it from the frontier towns of the nineteenth century were the automobiles parked in front of the battered hitching posts and the flicker of neon tubes where wooden sideboards had once creaked in the wind.[23]

The early 1930s construction of Hoover Dam just south of town and the legalization of gambling spurred growth in Las Vegas, and the city gradually began to shake off its frontier image. The Boulder Club had received Las Vegas' first gaming license, followed quickly by the Las Vegas Club, the Exchange Club, and the Northern Club, all located downtown on Fremont Street. But gaining national respect would take longer.[24] *Time* magazine had referred to the city in 1940 as "a scraggly tank town with a tumbleweed economy."[25]

Time magazine's demeaning description of the small desert city began to change later that same year. The small town's leading businessman—car dealer James "Big Jim" Cashman, who had been around town since 1904—had a cup of coffee with Tom Hull at a sidewalk table in front of the downtown Apache Hotel. Hull was a one-time wildcat oil driller, a World War I Army flight instructor, a movie theater operator, and finally, by the time he reached Las Vegas, a successful hotelier. Cashman was trying to talk Hull into building a *real* hotel in Las Vegas, the type Hull ran in Hollywood, Beverly Hills, and Sacramento—with bellhops, chambermaids, a swimming pool, and all the other amenities that turned a sawdust joint with rooms into a real first-class operation. It would spur tourism in the city, Cashman believed.[26]

Hull was intrigued, although his motivation was quite different from Cashman's. Las Vegas was only a place to gas up and perhaps get a quick meal on the drive between Los Angeles and Salt Lake City, he believed, and nothing would change that. "This was a good stopping off place," Hull is quoted to have said. "I'll build a hotel here for people to stay on their way through on Highway 91."[27]

The next day he and Cashman toured the town looking for a suitable site. Cashman drove him to the east side of town and pointed out some nice acreage on Maryland Parkway. "I don't want to build there," Hull told him. "I want to build on the road going into town."[28]

He found just the parcel he was looking for, sixty-six acres at the corner of San Francisco (today Sahara Boulevard) and the Los Angeles Highway, Highway 91. Hull was a cagey businessman. The parcel he selected was just a few feet south of the city's boundary, qualifying him for the much lower county tax rate. However, one local legend has a much simpler explanation for his choice of the site. Hull, it is said, once had a flat tire at that very corner. While he waited for a tow truck to rescue him, he began counting the number of cars passing the intersection, quickly becoming convinced that the traffic would support a roadside resort.

On April 3, 1941, the El Rancho Hotel opened, the very first resort hotel in Las Vegas, on the north end of what is today the most spectacular collection of resort hotels in the entire world—the Las Vegas Strip.

The hotel was a sprawling ranch-like complex, built in Spanish mission style and surrounded by large expanses of lush green grass sprouting from the desert sand. It had all the amenities Cashman had envisioned: sixty-three well-appointed bungalow or cottage rooms with full room service; the Round Up Room Restaurant and the Chuck Wagon Buffet, the forerunner of Las Vegas' famous all-you-can-eat buffets; premier entertainment in two venues, the dinner theater and Nugget Nell's cocktail lounge; a health club; and the city's first on-site retail shops.[29]

Like the rest of the resort, the casino, too—which was not part of the original hotel—may seem small by today's standards, but it was groundbreaking in the 1940s. There were four table games—two blackjack tables, a roulette wheel, and a craps table—and seventy slot machines. All in all, the El Rancho Hotel would set the standard for Las Vegas for years to come.

While World War II may have put a damper on Reno, it was a bonanza for Las Vegas. The U.S. government desperately needed military bases in the West. Because the government owned more than 90 percent of Nevada land, it was a cheap place to build, and far enough inland from the coast to ensure safety from enemy attack. A massive magnesium plant, Basic Magnesium, was built southeast of town, creating a payroll of 10,000 jobs overnight. After the war that area became the city of Henderson, today Nevada's second-largest city.

North of Las Vegas, a gunnery school was built. After the war, it became Nellis Air Force Base, a giant facility used for training fighter pilots, adding thousands of jobs to the community. And finally, in 1950, the government moved testing of its new atomic arsenal from the South Pacific to the Nevada Test Site just 65 miles north of town, creating thousands more jobs until testing ended in the early 1990s.

After the war, the Las Vegas' casino scene was perfectly positioned for growth. Benjamin "Bugsy" Siegel, a Mafia hood and ex–hit man, was sent west by the Mob to open the Flamingo Hotel on the Las Vegas Highway (later the Las Vegas Strip), about 2 miles south of the El Rancho Hotel, now renamed the El Rancho Vegas. When the Flamingo finally opened for good on March 27, 1947, it was another turning point for the "scraggly tank town." The city's fortunes would never again be described as a "tumbleweed economy."

The Flamingo Hotel was a mixed blessing. On the positive side, it launched an entirely new era in tourism for the city. But on the other side of the ledger, it spawned a tide of gangsters and ne'er-do-wells who would milk the city's tax roles, tourists, and casinos for the next quarter century.

Meantime, the Golden Nugget, Fremont, El Cortez, Horseshoe, El Dorado, California Club, and a number of other hotel casinos opened north of the Strip, huddling together downtown and earning that area the nickname Glitter Gulch. Downtown's icon was Vegas Vic, a huge 75-foot neon cowboy who stood atop the Pioneer Club and waved his arm in greeting visitors. Every fifteen minutes, Vegas Vic shouted, "Howdy, Podner!" to anyone within earshot until 1966, when city fathers decided it was time to silence the giant greeter.

During the 1950s, resorts such as the Tropicana, the Desert Inn, the Sahara, the Sands, the Dunes, the Riviera, and the Hacienda joined Hull and Siegel's resorts along the Las Vegas Strip. As a result of all these efforts, by the mid-1950s Las Vegas had eclipsed Reno in both population and gaming revenue.

In the 1960s, Las Vegas continued building on its dominance, taking another giant leap forward, thanks to another extraordinary entrepreneur. Jay Sarno, like Si Redd a poor southern boy who came of age during the Great Depression, began his working career as a house builder in Atlanta. A chance meeting with Teamsters union leader Jimmy Hoffa led to a loan that allowed Sarno and partner Stanley Mallin to launch a small motel chain in 1958. In the early 1960s Sarno visited Las Vegas, and like Tom Hull a quarter century earlier, he thought it would be an ideal place in which to expand his business. This time he wanted to build a grand European-style hotel that offered more—of everything, including gambling—than any hotel in Las Vegas ever did.

"He was a man who loathed plain vanilla," one of his daughters said. "Las Vegas hotels at that time just oozed mediocrity."[30] Sarno wanted more, much more.

He and Mallin broke ground for Caesars Palace on the Las Vegas Strip, and in 1966 they opened their grand hotel casino. It was the city's first themed property, and it set the stage for the future of Las Vegas. Only three years later the two men who had built Caesars Palace for $24 million sold the resort for $60 million, and built Circus Circus, a huge casino that featured circus acts under the big top to entertain the wives and children of the gamblers. The original Circus Circus, though it was built to appeal to families, had no rooms. It would fall on hard times when a gas crisis hit the nation, so Sarno and Mallin leased the property to two other Nevada legends, Bill Bennett and Bill Pennington.

"Both [of Sarno and Mallin's] properties were funded by loans from the then mob-connected Central States Teamsters Pension Fund," according to the Las Vegas Sun newspaper, a fact that would leave a permanent stain on the two men. But the genius of their impact on Las Vegas was never in question.[31] Like Tom Hull and Bugsy Siegel before them, they set a new standard that would be followed until the 1989 introduction of the megaresort era by Golden Nugget owner Steve Wynn and his Mirage Hotel-Casino.

Over the years Reno's city fathers watched all this unchecked growth occurring down south, and decided it wasn't for them. So with the prodding and encouragement of downtown casino owners, they "redlined" their casino corridor, restricting new casino growth to the downtown area only. This law would remain in effect until the early 1970s. Although it accomplished its purpose, it doomed Reno forever to being a handmaiden to Las Vegas as far as gaming and tourism were concerned.

* * * *

By the time Si and Ivy Redd arrived in Reno in the summer of 1967, casino gaming was a well-established industry throughout the state. Redd had made the deal with Bill O'Donnell, paying him $60,000 for 70 percent of his Bally distributorship. That was all the money Redd had after folding up his New England enterprises. His quarter century in the East had taught him a lot of valuable lessons, but it had not made him a wealthy man. O'Donnell also promised Redd that he could buy the remaining 30 percent in the future, when he had the money, but Redd would claim years later that O'Donnell reneged on that promise when he attempted to purchase it in the early 1970s.[32]

Redd renamed the company Bally Distributing Company, rented a building at 44 West Liberty Street, and set up shop. His early headquarters was small and basic: a door set on crates served as a desk, and empty cardboard cartons filled in as file storage cabinets. But it was sufficient, as Graves had not left much inventory when he sold the distributorship to O'Donnell.[33]

Even before Redd had closed the deal with O'Donnell, he had made a fact-finding visit to Warren Nelson, managing partner of the Club Cal-Neva and a legendary Reno gaming pioneer. Nelson had arrived in Reno in 1936 from his native Montana to run a keno game at the old Palace Club, and for the next quarter century the big-hearted cowboy would work at almost every job in almost every major casino in town. A World War II combat marine, Nelson was ready for his own place by the early 1960s. He and five partners bought the downtown Club Cal-Neva, a hotel casino with a checkered past that went back to the late 1940s.[34] When Nelson and his partners purchased the Cal-Neva, Bally had just come out with the new electromechanical slots, and Nelson had ordered forty of them for this casino with a 4 percent hold, or casino winning percentage.

"They had a few glitches in them, which we worked out," Nelson said. "Then they just took off, making twelve or fourteen hundred [dollars] a month, which was unheard of for nickel machines." Nelson's casino was still one of the few in town that had any of the new Bally electromechanical slot machines on its floor. Si Redd wanted to find out why. "Yeah, I've got 40. I think they're a hell of a machine," Nelson told him. "The Bally is twice as good as the others. I'd like more of them, but I can't get anymore."[35] That told Redd all he needed to know about the new Bally slot machines.

Nelson related another story that indicates how broadly Lady Luck had smiled on Si Redd. "Dick Graves . . . and I were friends," Nelson said. "When he decided to retire he offered the Cal-Neva his Big Berthas and his interest in the Bally franchise for $40,000 [prior to O'Donnell purchasing it.] True to form, my partners vetoed the idea," he laughed. "I was interested in taking over the Bally distributorship myself, but I was discouraged by partners who felt it would take up too much time that I should be giving to the Cal-Neva," he said.[36]

What Nelson failed to mention was that another Nevada gaming pioneer also had a shot at buying Bally Distributing. Dick Raven, one of the earliest innovators of electronic slots, had a slot route installing a few of his advanced technology keno games. The Cal-Neva was a customer, and Warren Nelson told Raven about the opportunity. Raven had the money because his keno games had been selling well, so he considered the purchase. He even visited Bill O'Donnell in Chicago, but eventually decided against the venture.

Instead, Raven said, "We bought property across from the Reno airport as a little sideline." A decade later in a magazine interview, he admitted in blazing understatement that the result of his decision was "something where we missed out."[37]

Warren Nelson and Si Redd would go on to be good friends, and in years to come Redd would often refer hesitant Bally slot buyers to Nelson, who always opened his books to show how well the machines performed.

After his initial visit with Nelson, Redd had signed the contract with O'Donnell. But as soon as the ink was dry on the paper, he turned his attention in a different direction. The Big Bertha machine that had so excited him on his first visit had been manufactured by Graves and a partner, Bob Weiss, and had been on location for only a short time. There were only two of them, and they were out on a revenue-shared basis to the Horseshoe and another casino. Redd wanted more of the lucrative machines. He went to a local banker—Redd swore the man's name was Jesse James, but he referred to most money lenders by that name—and borrowed enough money to have more Big Berthas manufactured. The Big Bertha deal would be an aside to his business with Bally, but O'Donnell, as a part owner of the business, was also in on the big machines. However, they were not being manufactured by Bally.

When the machines were ready, Redd put a few in Reno and Sparks, and he also put them on location in a few smaller northern Nevada towns such as Elko, Winnemucca, and Wendover. He knew

the popular and productive machines would make good money for
the casinos and ingratiate him with the owners.

"The machines were each making us about $15,000 a year. That
was . . . our part," Redd said. "They only cost $3,000 or $4,000 to
make, so they were paying for themselves four or five times a year. It
was fabulous."[38]

Turning his attention now to the Bally business, Redd made
rounds of all the casinos in his territory, both large and small. His
distribution area included Reno, Sparks, Carson City (the state capital), the eastern shore of Lake Tahoe, and a welter of small towns
such as Elko, Winnemucca, and Wendover. He quickly discovered
three truths about the slot machine business in northern Nevada.
First, there was competition. Only a few of the casinos were operating with Bally machines. Others had mechanical machines made by
Mills, Jennings, or Pace.

The second truth was that almost all the machines were old, some
very old. "The fact is that when I did go to Nevada," Redd said, "I
noticed that all of the machines were fifty to seventy-five years
old."[39]

The market for slot machines and other gaming devices was limited. The 1951 Transportation of Gambling Devices Act, better
known as the Johnson Act, restricted the transportation of slot
machines into any state where gambling was not legal. At the time,
Nevada was the *only* state with legalized gambling. It would be more
than twenty-five years before Atlantic City joined the fray, and even
longer until Indian tribal gaming became a major force. Thus this
law essentially drove most manufacturers of slot machines out of the
business. And for years, Nevada's legal casinos hoarded their existing machines as if they were gold. If really interested, a person could
even find a few old Caille slot machine models from late 1930s still
taking in coins.

Before the passage of the Johnson Act, there had been a lot of slot
machines made and sold for amusement purposes. These machines did
not have a hopper, or coin paying unit, in them (this was often referred
to as "the gray-area market"), and it certainly was not enough to keep
a half-dozen manufacturers humming. In 1965, for example, there
were only 22,890 slot machines operating in the entire country. So
most makers, like Bally, devoted the majority of their manufacturing
to other, more profitable amusement games and devices.[40]

The third truth Redd discovered was that there had been very few
changes to slot machines for decades, for many of the same reasons.

The Bally electromechanicals were the exception, but given their cool reception among casino owners, no other manufacturer was eager to begin making them. All the mechanical slot machines were pretty much the same as they had been in the 1930s and 1940s. A good example were the machines at play at Harolds Club, the first casino to emphasize slot machines, and the first to do coast-to-coast advertising with their now-famous "Harolds Club or Bust" billboard ad campaign.

Harolds Club was an anomaly for its time. General manager Harold "Pappy" Smith, and his son Harold Jr., who owned the place, used Pace "Comets," bright red, cast-iron machines, many of which had been in service for decades. Whereas most casinos considered one armed bandits a necessary nuisance, the Smiths embraced them. Harolds had modified their Pace machines so they provided larger and more frequent payouts, and a bigger coin tray to hold the winnings, something nobody else was willing to do. But the machines themselves had the same old mechanism everyone used, with only paint, decoration, and signage delineating one brand from the next.[41]

With the exception of the Big Berthas that Bally Distributing had built and installed on its own, Redd's first Bally slot machine sale was to Karl Berge at the Silver Club in Sparks. He sold only three Bally machines in his first month of operation, and it's likely all three were to Berge. In the second month, he sold twelve. "Then," Redd told a reporter from *Loose Change* gaming magazine, "I met Clyde Keeting [Keeling] up at the Riverside."[42]

Redd tried a new approach with the Riverside, selling them new Bally slot machines with the understanding that they only had to pay him out of the *increase* in revenues from each machine. He thus installed one hundred machines in the Riverside on that basis. That was a win-win situation for both the casino and Redd. It was also an idea that helped launch his business in a big way.

Unfortunately, the Riverside would not remain a Bally customer for long. The Nevada Gaming Commission shut down gambling at the Riverside on September 16, 1967, for using crooked dice at the craps table, then completely closed it on December 29, 1967. It would not reopen for gambling until April 1971. Because the machines had been installed on the usual credit basis, Redd had to take them right back out.

"Again, I got lucky," Redd said. "[I] moved them over across the street to the Holiday [Hotel] and got the same [deal]; it didn't cost us anything."[43]

With four decades in the coin-operated machine industry behind him, Redd had an innate sense for what would work and what would not, what would appeal to his machines' end users and what would not. Of course he wasn't correct 100 percent of the time, but he was right a lot more often than he was wrong.

In every spare moment, Redd strolled northern Nevada's casino floors, watching men and women plug their nickels, dimes, and quarters into the slot machines, looking and listening for inspiration. Walking among the gamblers, chatting with them, being surrounded by the action, gave Redd an almost primal high. The excitement on a slot floor was palpable for one attuned to it like Si Redd.

A crowded slot floor in the days before quiet electronic slot machines, and wide, well-spaced aisles was a banquet for the senses. The machines themselves played a loud, clamorous symphony: the scratchy metal-to-metal swoosh of a nickel as it slid down the coin slot, ending in a satisfying thud as it engaged the gears; another tinny swoosh as the one-armed bandit's handle was pulled down, then a sharp crack when it was released and banged back into place; the whir of the three reels as they took motion, spun around their axes, then stopped one by one displaying their symbols inside small windows; then the satisfying clang-clang-clang of the coins as they bounced into the metal tray if Lady Luck had smiled on the slot player. Joining this chorus were the bells and whistles the machines played with each winning hand. And all these magical sounds mixed with the laughter, the snorts, the cheers, and the curses of the people lined up at the machines or those serving as cheering sections for each player.

The slot floor also provided a visual treat. All the slot machines were painted bright, garish colors. Some were custom built into the center of colorful, life-sized wooden figures: a stoic Texas Ranger, an angry Indian warrior, a one-armed bandit, or a smiling, jewel-bedecked chorus girl, each with a shiny metal handle topped by a bright red knob protruding from their sides, just begging for a pull. Some casinos were brightly lit, whereas others, particularly the old-fashioned sawdust joints, kept the lights down low to mask their shortcomings.

And there were the smells too. The acrid odor of cigarette smoke and the thick, heavy smell of grease from the casino's restaurant mingled in the air with the scent of perfume, toilet water, pomade, hair tonic, aftershave lotion, and sweat of hundreds of slot players, all creating a virtual stew of aromas.

Even on weekends, Redd would spend his time wandering through casinos. But he often took his wife Ivy along. They liked to drive the few miles southwest to Lake Tahoe, where on the Nevada side of the lake a number of casinos clustered along the lakeshore. "We would have some fun too," he said. "My wife would play the slot machines, [and] . . . we'd see a show and have a wonderful meal. And while she'd play the slot machines, I'd call on the customers."[44] These were usually two-day minivacations for the couple, and they got a big kick out of them.

Si Redd instinctively knew the casino bosses were underestimating the potential of their slot machines. "The slots were just a convenience for the wives and girlfriends while the men played craps," Redd said.[45] "The slot machine business didn't have anything new. The machines were basically a piece of iron with a lemon in front." The lemon was like a bad luck sign, a symbol that stood for losing. "If a lemon came up on the first reel," Redd explained, "the customer said, 'Aw, shit!'"[46]

Every time a lemon appeared in one of the three side-by-side windows on a standard three-reel one-armed bandit, the player automatically lost his money. Redd thought it was a stupid design. He immediately recommended to Bally that they stop using the lemon symbol. They took his advice.

Then he studied the different coin denominations the slot machines accepted, and discovered another startling fact: smaller denomination slots—penny, nickel, and dime machines—paid off better than the quarter and dollar machines. "The whole industry made a mistake," Redd said grinning and shaking his head in disbelief. "The dollar machine was tighter than the nickel machines[,] where it should have been just the opposite. I stumbled on that and had a field day. It was like shooting fish in a barrel."[47]

Next Redd chided Bill O'Donnell to alter a machine so the bettor could double up, inserting two coins at a time instead of just one. When that was done, he asked why not three coins, why not even five coins—and O'Donnell's engineers went to work again.

If you can play multiple coins, why can't you play multiple lines, he wondered. And he started on O'Donnell once more. So Bally went to three lines. Why not make it five lines, Redd asked, and crisscross it with the option to play five coins? So they did.

Bally had three engineers, and Redd had them constantly hopping to meet his demands. "They thought I was a son of a bitch," Redd said. "Just when they had things set, I'd be looking to change this or that."[48]

He then went to work on stagnant slot machine designs. "[T]he gambling people treated a slot machine the same way they do a blackjack table or a dice game. As long as you can put a new cover on it, it won't ever wear out," he said. "[But] you must have something new."[49]

Redd recalled his years working with coin-operated amusement games, pinball machines, and jukeboxes. Companies such as Williams, Gottlieb, Mills, Chicago Coin, Wurlitzer, and even Bally constantly added new models with new designs, new features, new color schemes, and new win tables. He couldn't understand how slot machine manufacturing executives were so far behind their coin-op brethren in their thinking.

Redd also argued for more liberal machines. "The whole secret to gaming is to make the games liberal," he said. "Let you use two hours instead of one hour to lose your money. Enjoy it, make it entertainment."[50]

All of these things he related to Bill O'Donnell, and chaffed him for allowing Bally's slot machine division to slip into such shoddy practices. The fact was, most of the innovations Redd had championed were made possible only because Bally had introduced the electromechanical machines. For the improvements Redd extolled, the machines simply had to be modified somewhat. With the old style mechanicals, none of these new enhancements would have been possible. Despite that, there's little doubt that the two men probably exchanged angry words on more than one occasion. But every change Redd recommended increased sales and market share for Bally machines.

Redd's good friend Bob Jones related a ploy Redd would often use in those early days to get his machines in the door at a reluctant casino. He'd ask for a tour of the slot floor, and during the inspection he'd key in on a little group of twenty or thirty slot machines off in a corner somewhere, or next to the restrooms, machines that he knew from experience would be low-grossing machines.

"How does this little group of machines do for you?" he'd ask innocently. Generally he'd be told that the machines in question were not very important, that they took in very little revenue. "I'll tell you what I'll do for you," Redd would respond. "Let me put my machines in there. I'll buy these old machines at a fair price, and charge you nothing for these new Bally electro-mechanical wizards.

We'll split the take fifty-fifty, and I'll even guarantee you more than you're making now."[51] It was an offer few casino managers could turn down, and in every case the Ballys outperformed the older mechanical machines.

Tony Mills, who competed against Redd in Reno in the late 1960s, talked about another scheme Redd would often employ. Mills was the scion of the multigenerational family that founded the Mills Novelty Company in Chicago in 1889. A manufacturer of amusement arcade games and slot machines, Mills was one of the largest and most respected of the early game manufacturers. In 1953, however, the company was forced into liquidation. The surviving Mills Bell-O-Matic Corporation had a large assembly plant in Reno, turning out Mills mechanical slot machines for Nevada's casino industry when Redd bought Bally Distributing Company.

"When a new casino would open, or when we'd try to get into an established casino," Mills said, "we'd offer to put a Mills slot machine in at no charge for them to try. But when Si came along, he'd go in and offer to put in twenty new machines on a trial. He was grandiose; he was out-doing everybody. We couldn't afford to put twenty machines in," Mills lamented. "He just flooded the market."[52]

Offering to install new Bally slot machines in a casino with no upfront money required was a very successful gambit for the shrewd promoter. Bob Cashell, who arrived in Reno at about the same time as Redd, bought a small slot joint called Bill & Effie's. Eventually he and his partners parlayed the place into Boomtown, a large hotel casino complex on the highway leading to California. Cashell would go on to form a very successful casino management and consulting business, and would serve as mayor of Reno for many years.

Cashell related that Bally Distributing Company often put machines in his places, or in those he managed, on a trial basis. "He put free machines in for a lot of people, but it worked," Cashell recalled. He developed a real fondness for Redd, even calling him "Uncle Si" from time to time. "I was young at the time, and very impressed with him—I really liked him," Cashell admitted. "But I also found out that he was . . . full of it; and you needed to really be on your toes with him 'cause he'd out-talk you in a heartbeat."[53]

In 1972 Redd also began selling Bally slot machines in the southern Nevada market. Michael "Mickey" Wichinsky, who had been part of the gaming industry in Las Vegas since 1957, still owned the Bally distributorship in southern Nevada. His company, Bally Sales

Corporation of Nevada, was not having as much success selling Bally's new generation of slot machines in southern Nevada as Redd was having in northern Nevada. From stories related by two of Redd's employees, it appears that Redd—undoubtedly with Bill O'Donnell's tacit approval—simply muscled in on Wichinsky's territory. Wichinsky complained to O'Donnell, but it did little good. Bally had seen what having the right man in place could accomplish in the sale of its products, and they wanted the same result in the growing Las Vegas market.

Mickey Wichinsky, who is still in the gaming business in Las Vegas, commented without elaborating that Bally bought him out. Si Redd, in his University of Southern Mississippi oral history interview, said that he purchased the Las Vegas distributorship, but provided no details. Wichinsky wouldn't discuss it at all. Thus, it is not known how much money Redd had to come up with in order to expand his Bally Distributing Company statewide. Nor is it known if Bill O'Donnell also owned a percentage of Wichinsky's distributorship. But Redd never skipped a beat once he entered southern Nevada. And in a matter of only a few years he had built Bally's dominance in Las Vegas to the same heady heights as in Reno.

* * * *

Chevis Swetman, chairman of a Biloxi, Mississippi, bank that did a lot of business with Si Redd when he opened gambling in that state in the late 1980s, said of Si Redd: "He loved visiting the slot people. . . . [H]e was the consummate salesman." Swetman pointed out that Redd knew everybody in the casino industry's top management, where most slot machine sales were made. "But he also knew the guys on the floor and what their problems were," he added.[54]

Not everyone in Nevada's gaming industry bought into Si Redd's ideas. Charles Mapes, who owned Reno's Mapes Hotel-Casino, thought Bally's machines were inferior. He also believed Redd was involved with the Mafia that held a stranglehold on southern Nevada's casino industry.

Redd went to see the crusty Mapes. Born in Reno, educated at the University of Nevada–Reno, and a fierce debater like Redd himself, Mapes wielded a certain amount of power among Nevada's casino elite. When he built his hotel in 1945, it was the first high-rise hotel built in the U.S. postwar period. Charlie Mapes took no lip from anybody, especially a newbie such as Redd.

Unfazed by Mapes's reputation, Redd told him, "I'll make you a deal. Let me install fifty of my machines in your casino at no charge to you. I'll reinstall your [old] machines at no cost if you're not happy."[55]

Mapes, hard as nails but no fool, agreed. His income jumped from $20 a day on each old machine to $80 a day with Redd's machines, and he became a regular customer.

Another legendary gaming executive, Lincoln Fitzgerald, owner of Fitzgerald's Hotel-Casinos in Reno and Las Vegas, used only Jennings slot machines, and he wasn't about to change. "Don't talk to me; get out of here," he told Redd. "We don't want your machines. . . . [W]e do so much play that your metal is too soft, and it will wear out. . . . A Bally machine, it won't take that wear."[56]

A temporary holdout was "Pete" Cladianos Jr. When Pete Sr. had first come to America from the isle of Zante, off the coast of Greece, he peddled fruits and vegetables from a pushcart in Sacramento. In the early 1920s he and his brother came to Reno to open a store, and in 1932, after gaming was legalized, he opened a small sawdust joint with five slot machines he had bought for twelve bucks each. In 1965 Pete Jr. and his sister Katherene entered the business when they purchased the Sands Motel, a seventy-nine-room motel just west of downtown with three slot machines. By 1970 their Sands Regency had 103 rooms, qualifying them to install 415 slots.[57]

"We bought the machines from Bally Distributing Company, at that time being run by Si Redd," Pete Cladianos Jr. said. "We also put in a Big Bertha machine." All the new machines were the Bally electro-mechanical slots, which were the only type the company manufactured. "When Bally came out with that electro-mechanical, it pretty much knocked everybody else out of the market," Cladianos said. "Harolds and Harrah's were still running Paces, and Fitzgerald's was running the old mechanical Jennings, but everybody else went to Ballys, because they were a far superior machine in terms of the drop [profit]."[58]

A number of the smaller sawdust joints also held out. The holdouts had varying reasons for not wanting to replace their old slots with the new electromechanicals. One reason was money—it was an expensive proposition to change over a casino's entire slot floor. Another reason was that some operators didn't like or trust Bally Manufacturing Company, and by extension, Bally Distributing Company. The company had a shady reputation that bothered some operators. Others just didn't like Si Redd. Redd was a "love him or hate him" kind of guy, and there were many men on both sides of that argument. Some thought he was Mob-connected, which he was not, whereas others just couldn't stomach his pushy, assertive style.

Finally, a few casinos eschewed Bally slots simply because they preferred the old-fashioned, clunky mechanicals, even though they may have realized the drop, or profit, on the Bally machines was greater. Harrah's Club was one of those.

Bill Harrah was a maverick, a one-of-a-kind casino guy who always marched to his own drummer. As early as the 1950s he had built a top secret, off-site research lab to study slot machine design and production. Harrah did not want to be beholden to Bally, Jennings, Mills, or any of the other slot machine manufacturers. He wanted to build his own machines, using his own design and his own personnel. He wanted something so unique that nobody else had even thought of it before.[59]

In 1975 Bill Harrah believed his innovative slot machine was ready. He dubbed it the "Experimental." It was a different type of three-reel machine in many ways, but it had taken Harrah so long to design and build it that some of its basic technology was already being used by other manufacturers. Still, there were enough novel features to make the Experimental different from anything else out there. Unfortunately, Bill Harrah died only a few years later, and his successors decided it was not worth the money to continue developing their own machines.

Mead Dixon, a gaming attorney, had been given a strong hand in overseeing Harrah's operations after Bill Harrah passed away. It was Dixon who was primarily responsible for arranging the merger between Harrah's and Holiday Inns the following year. As he dug into the company's records he discovered that every phase of Harrah's business was dictated by ironclad rules and procedures that Bill Harrah had set down over the years. One of the primary purposes of these rules was to keep all but the highest executive level personnel from knowing what was going on in the company. So Harrah's slot managers had no idea, for instance, what their slot drop was, why their machines were located where they were, or which machines paid off well and which did not. They were expected to run their division with blinders on, which is exactly the way Bill Harrah and his top lieutenants wanted it.[60]

Rome Andreotti was Harrah's operations manager, and a true-blue company man to the bone. Bill Harrah had loved the old Pace machines and his own Experimentals, and had believed the Ballys were too noisy. So when Mead Dixon suggested to Andreotti that they put in some of the new Bally dollar slot carousels, and perhaps replace their aging Paces with more productive Bally machines in a new casino they were building, Andreotti said, "Bill would never allow it, and it's going to be over my dead body."[61]

"As you elect," Dixon said, and pulling rank, he put in the Bally machines anyway. Harrah's, the last major casino to embrace Bally's electromechanicals, became another satisfied Bally customer. Dixon was particularly impressed with the more productive machines, and with Si Redd. " [H]e was one of the greatest salesmen in the world— really a great salesman," Dixon once remarked.[62] A few years later, after Redd's split from Bally, Dixon would even contemplate buying Redd's entire operation.

It had finally become apparent to Pace and Mills-Jennings—these two companies had been absorbed by the much larger American Machine and Science Company of Chicago—that they had to change. Both tried unsuccessfully to launch electromechanical models of their own, but both failed to gain acceptance in the only market that counted, Nevada. It was a case of too little, too late.

Of Harrah's and Harolds eventual capitulation, Cladianos said, "They had to give in because . . . the new [Bally] machines did four or five times what the old mechanical machines would do. If you wanted a good machine that would make you money, you didn't have anywhere else to go."[63]

So, although the Bally machines were far superior to the old mechanicals, it was Si Redd, not Bally's technology, that built their business in Nevada. Dick Graves had been the distributor for the new electromechanical machines in northern Nevada for a few years before Redd arrived, but Graves had never penetrated the casinos to any significant degree. Tony Mills of Reno-based Mills Bell-O-Matic slot machines said he had not even been aware there was a Bally distributorship in Reno until Redd arrived. But, Mills said in deference to his new competition, "Redd was a forceful salesman."[64]

John Ascuaga, owner of John Ascuaga's Nugget in Sparks and a northern Nevada gaming legend, defended his good friend and benefactor, Dick Graves. "Si Redd always operated on high energy," he said, "and everybody liked Si." But Ascuaga pointed out that Graves was an exceptional salesman and promoter himself, and he thought that perhaps Graves was a little too early with the new machines. "People just couldn't adjust to change," Ascuaga said, referring to the casinos' slow adaptation to the Bally electromechanical slots. "It's just like everything else; change takes time."[65]

Like Graves, Mickey Wichinsky in southern Nevada had made few waves with the electromechanical machines before Si Redd strong-armed his way into that market. In both ends of the state, it took the old Mississippi sharecropper's son, with his thirty-five years of experience and his occasionally obnoxious style, to make a difference.

By the early 1970s Si Redd and Bill O'Donnell had everything going their way. Bally's competition in Nevada was virtually nonexistent: a whopping 95 percent of all slot machines being sold in the state were Bally machines.

Likewise, Si Redd had no competition. He was now the majority owner of the statewide Bally distribution company that serviced every gaming establishment in Nevada. He was also making more money than he ever dreamed possible. In 1968, its first full year of operations, Redd's company grossed about $1 million. By 1970 that amount had increased two-and-a-half-fold. "Then our hard work began to pay off rapidly," Redd said. And by 1975 sales were an astounding $10 million.[66] As it would turn out, however, Si Redd had barely scratched the surface.

CHAPTER 7

NEW BEGINNINGS

Despite the brisk, often hectic pace of Redd's business activities from the early to mid-1970s, and despite all its successes, a dark, ominous cloud hung over Si and his wife Ivy during the period. His soul mate, moral compass, chief advisor, and best friend for nearly a half century, Ivy, was suffering from cancer. She had had her first bout with breast cancer just after they moved to Reno, but surgery, chemotherapy, and radiation could not halt the spread of the disease.

Si Redd had lived his entire life believing in the mantra that hard work could overcome adversity. "Keep on keepin' on," he was fond of saying. It was something his mother Nannie had drilled into her son's head from his earliest days. Si now grabbed at this straw, and took Ivy from one promising cancer facility to another—in San Diego, San Francisco, Boston, and Texas. Ivy dutifully followed her man from place to place with the same calm and dignity that had always been her hallmark. She seemed to recognize the futility of it, but she also realized it was something Si needed to do, so she went along without complaint.

In February 1972 Si and Ivy traveled back to Cape Cod for the marriage of their daughter Sherry to Alan Green. The wedding day was one of those wild, stormy Cape Cod days with high winds accompanied by snow and rain. The reception was to take place at the venerable Barnstable Inn, in Barnstable. The wind whipped through the cracks in the boards and the roof leaked, but everyone had a grand time despite—perhaps even because of—the wicked weather. Ivy, despite her illness, was a picture of calm, and reassured the wedding couple that everything would work out well, which of course it did.[1]

Back in Reno, the Redds had initially made their home on Flagg Drive, in the southern part of the city, behind the Park Lane Mall. However, the year after they arrived they moved into the penthouse apartment at the Arlington Towers, a twenty-two-story high-rise residential apartment building that had just opened. Just across First Street from their building, the sparkling clear Truckee River tumbled by, carrying muscular young men downriver in their sturdy, colorful

Ivy and Si Redd at home in Reno, Nevada, in the early 1970s. He began his career in gaming in Nevada in 1967. *Redd family photo.*

little kayaks. Directly across North Arlington Avenue stood the ornate 1908 stone-and-brick St. Thomas Aquinas Cathedral, with twin Baroque towers and huge copper-covered doors fronting the street.

Arlington Towers was at the edge of downtown Reno, with all its activities and exciting vibes, and the Redds loved living there. They entertained friends and enjoyed frequent visits from their two daughters, their husbands, and all their grandchildren from Massachusetts. They maintained their home on Cape Cod, too, and Ivy spent summers back East with family while Si worked. They also kept an apartment in Las Vegas, where they traveled regularly for Si's growing statewide business interests.

On September 24, 1974, Ivy passed away in Reno, surrounded by her large family. Son-in-law Alan Green related a poignant story about Ivy's lasting influence on her lifelong love, Si. Toward the end, while the two were alone together in the hospital, Ivy playfully poked Si in the stomach. "Silas, you're too fat," she said. "I want you to promise me that you will lose that weight and get in shape."[2] He faithfully promised.

After Ivy's death, Si began to take his health very seriously. He ate better and began a regimen of exercise. He became a regular guest at the exclusive Golden Door Spa in San Diego County, and even hosted family members at the ultraexpensive spa. He began to run, despite being in his mid-sixties. He worked his way up from short runs to competitive 5K, then 10K races. Up until his late seventies, before leaving Reno to live in Las Vegas, Redd was still a familiar sight at the local YMCA, where he swam six laps in the pool on a regular basis, and along the walking path beside the Truckee River, where he walked or jogged almost daily.

Alan Green recalled one 10K race in San Francisco, when both Si and his company IGT were beginning to make big news in the nation's press. His employees had slipped a T-shirt on him just before the race, and all along the course he heard fans and supporters screaming, "Go, Si, Go!"

Redd was delighted. He thought all the positive public relations he had paid so dearly for was perhaps beginning to make him famous. At the end of the race, covered with sweat, he stripped off the T-shirt and noticed some lettering on the back. "I'm Si Redd," it proclaimed, explaining to his chagrin his instant celebrity.

Following Ivy's death, Redd plunged even deeper into his work. It was his balm, his way of dealing with life without his partner. But Si Redd was not cut out to be a solitary person. Upbeat, jovial, and fun loving, he couldn't bear to be alone at those times when he wasn't buried in his work. In the summer of 1975, only nine months after Ivy's death, sixty-four-year-old Si showed up on Cape Cod to visit his daughters. To their astonishment, he introduced them to his new thirty-nine-year-old bride.[3]

Marilyn Shaw was a successful Las Vegas commercial real estate broker, twice married and divorced, with a valuable portfolio of properties she had acquired over the years. Tall, stately, and attractive, Marilyn stood out in any crowd because of her beautiful curly red hair that was always carefully coiffed atop her head. There were a number of amazing similarities between Si and Marilyn. Both had achieved success through hard work and determination; both had outgoing, voluble personalities; and neither had a shy bone in their body. One of Si's good friends described his new wife as "a tough broad."[4] Redd's secretary, Barbara Rich, said, "She was a very intelligent lady; you couldn't pull the wool over her eyes."[5]

Perhaps they were too much alike to maintain marital bliss for the long haul. But in the beginning, for all appearances, Si and Marilyn Redd were a dynamic pairing.

* * * *

By 1970 Redd had moved Bally Distributing Company to a larger facility on 6th Street. The building had previously been a large appliance store, and the entire front was a display window overlooking the street. The company had about forty-five employees by this time, including his personal secretary, Barbara Rich, whom Redd had hired the previous year. Ms. Rich had come to Reno from Sacramento following the aerospace industry cutbacks. She would remain Redd's secretary until 1989, and stay on at International Game Technology (IGT) for another seven years thereafter.

The 1970s, particularly toward its end, brought growth and change to the casino business in Reno. The Eldorado, Fitzgerald's, Colonial, Onslow, Sahara-Reno, Circus Circus, and Comstock all opened downtown, crowding out many of the older, smaller places. Many others expanded. East of downtown, MGM opened a hotel-casino-entertainment complex with over 1000 rooms and the world's largest casino at the time. Harolds Club was sold to Howard Hughes's Summa Corporation, and Harrah's to Holiday Inn.[6]

Meanwhile, growth in Las Vegas had temporarily slowed. The International Hotel opened in 1969 and became the Las Vegas

Hilton in 1971. The MGM Grand, now Bally's Las Vegas, opened in 1973. But most of the other activity was in expansions and renovations. More important was the appearance of legitimate moneymen in Las Vegas, replacing the Mob influence. Real estate developer Del Webb was the first to enter Nevada gaming in 1961. Billionaire Kirk Kerkorian had also initially begun investing in Las Vegas in the early 1960s, followed later in the decade by Howard Hughes. In 1967 and 1969 Nevada gaming laws changed to allow corporate ownership of casinos, a development that changed everything for the state and led to the almost unbelievable growth in Las Vegas in the 1980s, 1990s, and the first decade of the twenty-first century.

As these changes were occurring in Nevada's gambling markets, Si Redd continued to push for new and exciting innovations in slot machines. He never let up on the Bally engineers in his quest for products that were bigger, better, smarter, flashier, and more profitable. In the mid-1970s he turned his attention to dollar slots. He had already led the charge to make them more liberal than slots of lower-denomination coins; but now he wanted to find ways to maximize their potential with gamblers. The Riverside Hotel in Reno was a perfect example of the low esteem in which the dollar slots were held.

"At the Riverside we had only one dollar machine," part owner Jack Douglass said. "That was because of a very wealthy lady who was there as a permanent guest and she loved to play it. It was her machine! The other customers avoided it."[7] Such was the dismal acceptability of dollar slots by both players and casinos.

The problem with dollar slots up to Redd's time was twofold. First, they were set too tight, many times paying back as little as 75 percent. Odds were much better on a quarter machine, and the serious slot players all knew it; so they avoided the dollar slots.

Second, the interior coin collection and payout mechanism, or hopper, on Bally dollar machines was too small. They used the same hopper that was used for smaller coins, causing the machines to jam and the payout to be slow and laborious. Because of these flaws, when a casino ordered one hundred Bally slot machines, they might include only one or two dollar machines in the order. Si Redd believed that could be fixed.

"The biggest thing of all? It's the dollar machine," he told a magazine writer in 1990. "The making of the dollar play is the thing that really made Nevada what it is today, the foundation for gambling's growth in the last ten years."[8]

To fix the problems, Redd traveled back to Bally Manufacturing in Chicago and told the engineers, "We've got to fix our hopper to where it works faster. . . . We've got to make [it] bigger and make it handle the big [silver] dollars."[9]

While the Bally people went to work on the problem, Redd had a couple of his own in-house engineers jury-rig three machines to his new specifications, and ratchet up the win percentage until the machines were paying out 90 to 92 percent. He installed his three prototype machines at the Silver Club in Sparks on a sixty-forty revenue split. The three machines were arranged in a round carousel with flashing lights and ringing bells—another Redd-inspired innovation—and the dollars began to pour in. Soon John Ascuaga's Nugget in Sparks added a few, and before long the demand was far greater than what Redd could meet.

"We were . . . bringing silver dollars into Reno by train—boxcar loads of silver dollars," Redd said.[10] Soon Bally's dollar slot carousels with the reconfigured hoppers were ready, and the growth accelerated.

Dwayne Kling, the general manager of the downtown Reno Silver Spur, recalled the new loose-dollar slots affectionately. "We started out just putting in two of the dollar machines," he said. "They were about 97 or 98 percent machines—and the money was just pouring out of the hopper . . . and I thought, boy these are going to be some real losers for us, they're paying off so much. But when we dumped the buckets [emptied the hoppers] the profits were really good. I couldn't believe it."[11] The Silver Spur immediately placed an order for a lot more of the dollar slots.

Redd's friend and good customer Warren Nelson at the Cal-Neva was another success story. Nelson put in the loose-dollar carousel in May 1976. "It was an instant success," Nelson said, "increasing our drop [the amount lost by a gambler] by 40 percent over the next year and a half."[12]

To improve his profits even more, Nelson also installed louder drop bowls (the metal trays that catch the coins when the machine pays off). "We were searching for just the right sound: silver dollars from frequent jackpots clanging into the big metal trays; winners yelling in triumph, creating more commotion and more play . . . there is nothing quite like it," he smiled.[13]

Taking a cue from Nelson, Redd also began tinkering with the drop bowls on the Bally machines in his warehouse. His son-in-law Alan Green recalled one visit he made to the warehouse in Reno:

"[H]e had people dropping coins into [variously shaped bowls] and tweaking the shape and size to get the . . . type of sound he wanted. It was a unique sound, like that of a Harley Davidson motor, that he was looking for," Green said.[14]

A casino in Las Vegas had thirty of the new dollar machines grouped together in a giant carousel. A third of the machines were set at a very loose 99 percent. Casino shills played at those machines, screaming and laughing and pointing to the silver dollars cascading into their drop bowls. The other twenty machines were set at a more normal 88 percent, and people were lined up to take their turns at those machines.

Jeanne Hood, president of the Four Queens Hotel-Casino in Las Vegas, said, "We were the first ones to have a [dollar] carousel on Fremont Street. We had it right up near the door, and all the numbers were just out of sight. . . . I could see they made an entire difference in the numbers in our slot department."[15]

There were detractors too, of course—not of the fantastic new dollar slots, but of the man who promoted and sold them, Si Redd. One such man was James "Reggie" Parker, general manager of the Silver Spur Casino in downtown Reno. Dwayne Kling, who followed Parker as general manager, told this story.

"We had some Bally slot machines in there, but he [Parker] didn't want to get in bed completely with Si Redd," Kling related. "He thought Si Redd was too flamboyant, that he was too full of baloney[;] . . . he always felt that if you gave Si Redd an inch, he would take a mile from you." When Parker retired back to Arkansas, Kling found his casino was way behind on dollar slots. "We kept going along with those old 'doggy' dollar slot machines. We had very little dollar slot play," he said.[16] Personalities aside, Kling was quick to bring Redd's dollar slots into his casino, and Redd was only too happy to sell them to him.

Redd was fond of repeating one less-than-flattering story about how he sold some dollar slots to the Hyatt Regency Hotel and Casino on Lake Tahoe. Despite his personal success, he admitted he could still be mightily impressed when he met some of the legendary captains of industry. Any good salesman—and Si Redd was one of the best ever—knew that when the prospect said yes, it was time to stop selling. "When a guy says yes, you shut up and give him the pad to sign," Redd grinned.[17] But on one occasion, he just couldn't shut up.

Si and his second wife, Marilyn, were in California when he had a chance to make a sales call on Hugh "Skip" Friend, the president of the Hyatt Corporation, which had a hotel casino on Lake Tahoe. When the Redds arrived for the appointment, Si was amazed to see that the legendary founder and owner of the luxury hotel chain, eighty-year-old Abram Pritzker, was also there.

"I had my speech ready, just like a lawyer," Redd said. "I'm telling them the story . . . and I get about two-thirds through and old Abe Pritzker, he just dismisses me."

"Hell, you don't have to sell me anymore," Redd said the old man told him. "Where do we have to sign?"

But Redd was jazzed up, and he didn't want to stop. "I prepared this presentation, and you've got to listen," he told his surprised audience.

Marilyn Redd, an astute businesswoman herself, leaned over and in a voice everyone could hear whispered to her husband, "You old jackass, didn't you hear them say yes?"[18] Everyone broke out laughing then, even Redd. He had finally gotten the message and buttoned his lip.

Dollar slots were another huge victory for Si Redd, again pointing to the genius of the man at predicting what the marketplace wanted. University of Nevada–Reno professor and gaming expert William Eadington wrote in 1979, "The number of dollar slots in Washoe County casinos has increased nearly 400% in the past two years, due mainly to the introduction of so-called 'slot carousels' and the advertising of high paybacks. . . . [T]he win-per-unit with dollar slots have increased about 55% since 1971."[19] One further statistic in Eadington's study shows that whereas the dollar slots win-per-unit increased by 55 percent, nickel and quarter slots win-per-unit actually dropped by 6.7 percent and 7 percent, respectively.

Taking a broader, statewide view, Redd pointed to the increase in dollar slot play from $8 million in 1970 to $700 million in 1984, a staggering eighty-eight-fold increase. As a result of sales increases in all slots, but particularly the dollar slots, Bally's sales soared too, to $50 million in 1978, the year Redd would leave the company permanently.

Whereas most innovators would have rested on their laurels following the success of the dollar machines, that was not Si Redd's way. He had another idea: a $100 slot machine that would pay out about 99 percent. Today most large casinos have a small, secluded high-limit slot machine area where the big players can sit in comfort and not be bothered by the quarter and dollar players. They all feature Redd's $100 machines.[20]

One final innovation Redd pioneered was the bar top slot machines, though he was quick to admit there was an element of luck in it: "Sometimes we stumbled into ideas so valuable we didn't know how big they were going to be," he admitted.[21]

The slot revenue for most casinos was limited by the amount of space they could devote to slot play. It was generally a finite amount, and short of expanding the property there was no way to enlarge it. But Redd saw a way: every hotel casino had a huge expanse of bar tops that served no other purpose than as a place to set cocktails, and that space could be used for slot play.

"We spent an awful lot of money developing the bar machine, but it was worth it," Redd said.[22] Then when video poker came along a few years later—by far the most significant product Redd popularized—bar tops were ready and available to fill their most important new role.

Redd told his University of Southern Mississippi oral history interviewer a story that emphasized how valuable the bar top machines could be. "I know one very successful oil man from Texas who lived in Reno. He never gambled. He'd go to Harrah's Club with his wife nearly every night[;] . . . she probably lost a quarter-million a year in those slot machines. . . . [B]ut he'd sit there at the bar[,] . . . buy other people drinks and have fun," Redd explained. "We put one of those dollar slot machines in the bar and, as luck would have it[,] . . . he hit a four thousand dollar jackpot. And they say since then he's never stopped playing."[23]

* * * *

Bill O'Donnell had reincorporated Bally Manufacturing Corporation as a publicly traded company in 1969, and by the early 1970s he was in an acquisition mode. He had purchased Wuff-Apparate-bau, Germany's leading manufacturer of wall-mounted amusement devices, and Midway Manufacturing, an Illinois maker of coin-operated amusement games. Next he turned his attention to his top priority, Nevada-based Bally Distributing Company.

There had never been a quarrel between O'Donnell and Redd that Bally would eventually purchase both men's shares in Bally Distributing Company, although they had never discussed specifics. So a few days before they were all to appear before the Gaming Control Board for Bally to seek its gaming license, the two men began negotiating. Redd began the bargaining by asking $14 million for his 70 percent share of Bally Distributing Company. He cited the company's tremendous annual earnings, its virtual lock on Nevada's growing slot machine market, and his own important role in building it from virtually nothing. O'Donnell, on the other hand, offered $5.5 million, a figure that barely covered the company's physical assets.[24]

Very little progress was made over the next couple of days. In frustration O'Donnell said, "God damn, Si, we're running out of time. . . . We're too far apart; we've got to compromise. You know we're friends; we're going to treat you right."

Still neither man budged. Finally, at the eleventh hour, they agreed to meet somewhere near the middle of their two positions. Nine million dollars was the figure they agreed upon, Redd would later swear. When a one-and-a-half-page document cementing the deal was signed by all, Redd asked for a copy, but because they were nearly late for their appointment with the Gaming Control Board, O'Donnell promised him a copy later.

The men rushed across the street to the El Dorado Hotel for the meeting. But then an unexpected thing happened: the Gaming Control Board again denied Bally a Nevada gaming license. "It [was] all public history. They had associated with unsavory . . . people[,] . . . or gangsters were involved. Frankly, I certainly knew nothing about it," Redd said innocently.[25]

This was not surprising news, given the Mob's interest in the coin-operated machine industry. Bally's history, beginning with O'Donnell's initial purchase of the company in 1963, had been a complex web of Mob affiliations. O'Donnell had sought help from members of the New York Mafia in arranging and financing the purchase, and by the time the change of ownership had completely shaken out, a handful of mobsters owned blocks of Bally stock and sat on its board of directors. O'Donnell promised the Gaming Control Board he'd clean up his company, and he set about the task.[26]

These two licensing failures were certainly not the only brushes Bally would have with gaming regulators. In the early 1970s the company had been denied a license to put their slot machines in casinos in Great Britain because of ties to organized crime. At about the same time, the owners of the distributing company for Bally amusement machines in New Orleans, along with Bill O'Donnell, were indicted in Louisiana for making payoffs to New Orleans authorities. Finally, in 1978, after casino gaming had been legalized in Atlantic City, New Jersey regulators would also deny the company a license to open a major hotel casino in that market. That problem was finally overcome when Bill O'Donnell agreed to resign from Bally.[27]

In Nevada, the enforcement of clean, gangster-free legalized gambling is high art today. The state has set the standard that all other states that now allow legalized gambling in some form look up to. It was not always that way.

Senator Kefauver's Senate Crime Investigating Committee, discussed in Chapter 5, believed all gambling was amoral and dangerous. After studying the Mob's growing influence in Nevada in the early1950s, the committee declared, "As a case history of legalized gambling, Nevada speaks eloquently in the negative."[28] There can be no argument that was an accurate assessment in 1951. Nevada gaming had been infested with thugs, killers, and confidence men from the beginning, and until the state got serious about regulating gambling and the people who ran it, that would not change.

When the state legislature approved casino gambling in 1931, regulation was left to the individual counties where it was conducted.[29] A fee was established on each table game or slot machine, and the city, county and the state shared those taxes. What little actual regulation existed was toothless, and gangsters began drifting to Nevada to get a share of this new bounty.

In 1945 the state began to license casinos for the first time. A tax was imposed on casino winnings, on top of the per-game tax already levied. When Bugsy Siegel opened the modern resort era in Las Vegas with the opening of the Flamingo Hotel-Casino on the Las Vegas Strip, the trickle of gangsters increased to a torrent. But the Kefauver Crime Committee's work in 1950–1951 threw the public spotlight on Las Vegas and the Mob, and in 1955 Nevada, under Governor Charles Russell, decided it was time to install statewide regulation with teeth. Failing to do so, state officials realized, would likely force federal control of casino gaming, a national tax on gambling, or outright national gambling prohibition.

To prove to federal authorities that the state could regulate honest, crime-free casinos, the Nevada Gaming Control Board was created and put under the direction of the State Treasury Committee. Four years later the Nevada Gaming Commission was created, and regulation was removed from the State Treasury Commission. Henceforth the Gaming Control Board would serve as the investigative arm of the Nevada Gaming Commission, whereas the Gaming Commission would have the final say on all matters. In 1960 the state created its now famous Black Book, or List of Excluded Persons, which keeps known undesirables from even entering a casino property anywhere in the state. Finally, in 1969 the state legalized corporate ownership in casinos.

With these new regulations, and tough investigative powers to back them up, Nevada now had all it needed to keep criminals out of casino ownership and management, and off the gaming floor as players. But the bad guys didn't give up easily, and it would be more than a decade before the cleanup was complete.

For the next three years after being denied a Nevada license, Bally's Bill O'Donnell fought to cleanse his company and obtain the necessary gaming license to buy Bally Distributing Company. Meanwhile, it was business as usual for Si Redd. His business was booming. "[M]y profit [was] going up, up, up," he boasted. "Each year it's fifty thousand to a hundred thousand, two hundred to two million, two million to three million, or whatever."[30] In other words, his profits were so substantial even he couldn't keep track of them.

Redd's secretary Barbara Rich recalled those frenetic days when the company was growing at such an astounding pace. They were taking in a lot of older slot machines on trade, and Redd was selling the trade-ins to Japan, where they were put into the nation's popular Pachinko parlors. These garish, loud, smoky, over-the-top fun houses had an insatiable appetite for slot machines, so Bally Distributing had no trouble getting rid of every used machine they could take in.[31]

Despite the company's growing financial success, according to Rich, money was always tight. Probably because of O'Donnell's 30 percent stake in the firm, and because it was selling so many Bally machines in Nevada, Bally Manufacturing had a very liberal credit policy with Redd's company. "Si was an expert at juggling funds," Rich laughed. "We were always borrowing from Peter to pay Paul."[32] The accountants were constantly pulling out their hair in frustration because there was never enough money available to pay all the bills.

The ongoing financial crunch was the result of Redd's liberal credit policy to his customers. He would sell slot machines when he could, or put them in a casino on a revenue-shared basis if necessary. If pushed, he would even allow the casino customer to pay on time from the additional revenue generated by the Bally machines. Redd loved cutting a deal—any kind of deal—and it was a nightmare for the office personnel to keep everything straight.

On a personal level, Rich said Redd was a generous boss, kind and understanding, and he expected his employees to work as hard as he did. Although he had a fantastic memory for work-related things,

Redd had a terrible time with names. He called Rich "Miss Barbara," a throwback to his Southern upbringing, and he did the same with most of the women in the office, when he could remember their names. There was a slot service technician in the building named Wayne Driver, but Redd always called him Wayne Mover. Once, Rich said, she typed a letter from Redd to Larry Fox, a casino executive at Lake Tahoe. Only later did she discover the man's name was Larry Wolfe.

During these years Redd's wardrobe tended toward garish, brightly colored clothing. It wasn't that his taste in clothing was so bad—although he was never a fashion icon—but rather that he loved to draw attention to himself. It was a conversation starter, he believed. And he would laugh along with others at his plaid slacks and chartreuse jackets.

Despite his idiosyncrasies, Si Redd was very focused on business, Rich observed.

"Si had made and lost a couple of fortunes in his business life, and this was his swansong," she said. "He was determined to make it big this time[;] . . . [he] was absolutely driven to succeed. He was determined he was not going to fail again."[33]

And he didn't. Thanks to Redd's slot machine innovations, and his creative ploys to sell his machines, Bally now controlled about 90 percent of Nevada's slot machine market. Redd's Big Bertha machines continued to do very well throughout the state too.

* * * *

The 1970s witnessed a number of new beginnings for Si Redd. He became involved in a number of new ventures in addition to his Bally distributorship. In 1971, in Las Vegas, Bill Bennett and Bill Pennington had teamed up to start a slot route operation, leasing novelty electronic blackjack machines to casinos. Three years later they leased Circus Circus Casino from Jay Sarno after he could not make a go of the huge circus tent–shaped property. Bennett and Pennington would go on to become part of Nevada casino lore with their successes at Circus Circus and other properties they would build in the future. But in 1974 they needed money to lease Sarno's casino, and the banks had turned them down.

Redd said he loaned the men $3.5 million. Circus Circus was wildly successful, mostly because Bennett and Pennington added a hotel to the property and promoted it extensively. They easily repaid

Redd for his loan, including an interest rate that was rumored to be high. But a few years later the two men would wreak a small measure of revenge (see chapter 9).

During the late 1960s and early 1970s, Si Redd also branched out into casino ownership, and even began tinkering with manufacturing his own slot machines. The first happened almost by accident, and the second just fell into his lap.

Redd had planned to install some Bally machines in a small joint named Oak Room. It was basically a bar and cocktail lounge with a few slots, located in the same building as the Greyhound Bus Depot on North Center Street in Reno. In late 1971 the owner got in trouble with the Gaming Control Board and decided to sell. Redd decided to buy the place for Bally Distributing Company. However, his minority partner, Bill O'Donnell, had just been indicted in Louisiana, which precluded the two men from getting the necessary gaming license to buy the property.[34]

The Oak Room was a busy little place, and Redd believed it might be a good investment. So after okaying it with O'Donnell, he bought it himself. It did not turn out to be a good investment, but the Oak Room's corporate name, A-1 Supply Company, would become an integral part of Redd's future enterprises.

Early the next year, in 1972, Redd installed 106 Bally slot machines in the Oak Room. Until O'Donnell's Louisiana indictment was lifted ("[O'Donnell and his associates] all came out clean; they were found not guilty," Redd said[35]), A-1 Supply simply rented the machines from Bally Distributing, and licensed them under A-1's name. So, Redd was now a casino owner, and in effect a slot operator for his own distributing company to boot. That latter situation did cause a few anxious moments.

Redd hired a manager for the Oak Room, a fellow who had been in the food and beverage department at the Cal-Neva. One of the Cal-Neva's biggest draws was a huge ultracheap breakfast, and Redd's new manager decided to try the same thing at the Oak Room. He plastered the front of the building with signs declaring a full breakfast for $1.85. All of this happened while Redd had gone to Massachusetts over the Christmas holiday to visit his daughters.

When he returned, one of the Cal-Neva's partners came to see him. "Are we your best customers? . . . We always try to help you," the man said.

"Yes, sure, absolutely. You certainly do," Redd assured him.

"Well, goddamn it[!] . . . [D]o you think you'd like to take that goddamn sign down and not steal our act on the eggs?"[36]

Sheepishly, Redd agreed that A-1 Supply would stop competing with Bally Distributing Company's best customer.

In addition to the Oak Room, Redd would go on to purchase the Western Village Motel in Mesquite, a small desert community east of Las Vegas at the Utah and Arizona borders. Later he also purchased Mr. Sy's, a small slots-only casino on the Las Vegas Strip across from the Stardust Hotel-Casino, and the Tower Club, off the Las Vegas to Los Angeles Highway. Redd never operated any of the casinos himself; he hired on-site managers. Years later, when he got into slot manufacturing in a big way, he leased some of the properties to the Peppermill Company in Reno, and sold the others.

Redd's next new business venture, slot machine design and manufacturing, was totally unplanned, a serendipitous event that would eventually set him off on the most noteworthy path in his long career.

While he was still in Boston selling jukeboxes, Redd had first shown a knack for innovation with coin-operated machines. He was quick to point out that he had no expertise in engineering or technical matters. "I had no ability there," he admitted.[37] But his broad and deep familiarity with the machines and his innate sense of what the market wanted helped him see which machines might succeed. He claimed to have even modified one machine that has become a staple amusement device across the country: the coin-operated hobbyhorse.

"You put a dime [in at] Woolworths, Kreskes . . . W. T. Grants, Sears Roebuck and all those stores. I didn't originate it," Redd said, "but I think we contributed something in the design. Then, furthermore, we actually made various models of other kiddy rides, an airplane idea or a little cart. Or a ride to the moon."[38]

Redd never manufactured the machines: he sold them to Bally on a royalty basis. He also came up with a lot of improvements on anti-slug mechanisms for coin-op machines to alleviate cheating. One machine he claimed to have invented outright.

"We made another machine—I invented it completely—called the 'Pantagraph Machine,'" he said. "[Y]ou could put a quarter in and on a piece of plastic, black on the outside and white on the inside, you could [print] your name."[39]

So, given his experience with innovation, when opportunity came knocking on Si Redd's door in Reno, he was ready. It had begun some years earlier, when Warren Nelson at the Club Cal-Neva began doing some tinkering of his own. After some time, Nelson and his slot manager came up with an eight-reel keno slot machine that was unlike anything currently on the market. It had approximately the same win percentage as a regular eight-spot keno ticket, and Nelson thought he might be able to manufacture and sell the machines in Las Vegas.[40]

He traveled south with a prototype and obtained a license to become a slot operator for the machine, which he dubbed Spot Slot. He succeeded in selling one machine to his friend Bill Boyd, who was then running the Mint Hotel, and another to the Golden Nugget. He also installed a few at the Cal-Neva and at a couple of Lake Tahoe casinos.

In the late 1960s even the largest jackpot payoffs on regular slot machines were modest by today's standards. So when a customer at the Golden Nugget, against all odds, hit an eight-spot winner on Spot Slot and collected $12,500, the casino immediately yanked the machine off the floor. "[I]t's so hard for people to pay that kind of money out on the slot machines," Nelson remarked.[41]

Soon other casinos also junked the machines, and Nelson cooled on the idea of a keno slot. A couple of years later, in 1969, he and his partners purchased the Club Cal-Neva at Lake Tahoe for $1.4 million from Frank Sinatra, after Sinatra lost his gaming license. In order to afford new slot machines for that property, Nelson sold the rights to Spot Slot to Bally Distributing Company for $180,000.

So Si Redd now owned his own casinos, albeit small ones, had a successful slot route operation, and owned plans and prototypes for both blackjack and keno slot machines. The slot machine plans and prototypes he folded into Bally Distributing Company, which he co-owned with Bill O'Donnell; the casinos and slot routes he put under the A-1 Supply Company umbrella, which was solely his property.

Of all his enterprises, it was the development of new slot machines that most excited Redd. He began hatching plans for how to take the next step in this direction. And when it came time to act, his play was purely Redd.

— CHAPTER 8 —

A QUIET REVOLUTION

A very quiet revolution in slot machine technology was beginning to take shape in Nevada. Charles Fey's first slot machine, the Liberty Bell, had been introduced in 1899, and sixty-four years had passed before there were any significant changes to Fey's basic slot mechanism. Bally's 1963 introduction of the first electromechanical slot, Money Honey, set the industry off on a new path. By the early 1970s, Pace and Mills were completely out of the U.S. slot machine market, leaving only a weakened Jennings Company to offer any competition for Bally.

Replacing these venerable firms in Nevada was a plethora of small, usually underfunded companies composed of a couple of engineers or electronics professionals who were tinkering in their garages or in small rented suburban warehouses. These men, most of them refugees from California's aviation and aerospace industry, were trying to apply rapidly developing electronics and computer technology to gaming machines.

The general public, however, was far behind these early pioneers in understanding what was going on around them. Probably not a single adult in the country had failed to watch or read about the historic Apollo moon landing on July 20, 1969, so everybody knew that something special was occurring. But few were able to understand the implications of all this new technology to their everyday lives.

One of the earliest of these men who would revolutionize the gaming industry was Dick Raven. In the early 1960s Raven had been part of the advanced engineering team at Hewlett-Packard in northern California. When he learned that a friend in Reno had built a blackjack game controlled by relays, or electrically powered switches, and was looking for someone who could convert it to an all-electronic device, Raven signed on at Nevada Electronics.[1]

In its simplest form, electronics is the science of harnessing the flow of electric current to perform certain tasks such as producing motion, light, heat, or sound, among other things. In a standard three-reel slot machine that could include controlling the spinning of the reels; when and where they stopped; when a light gets illuminated to signal a winning spin; and releasing coins from the hopper into the drop bowl to reward a winning play.

For Dick Raven, converting the blackjack machine was a nightmarish project. It had 5000 wired relays, and even one bad connection would doom it. So Raven started by converting the game to a hybrid, with half old-fashioned wired relays and half electronic relays. His prototype was submitted to the Nevada Gaming Commission and was granted a conditional license.

The prototype was placed in Reno's Club Cal-Neva, where it met with lukewarm acceptance. It had reliability problems because the team had elected to use cheap Japanese transistors in the electronic relays. Worse, the machine had been accidentally gaffed—it provided the casino with too large a winning advantage—so it did not gain final approval from the Gaming Commission. Later, Raven admitted he had not known that the casino profit he built into the first prototype exceeded legal limits in the state. But within six months he was finally ready with a totally electronic version of the game, one within all legal limits, and it passed all the Gaming Commission's necessary tests. The world's first totally electronic gaming machine, dubbed Dealer 21, was now part of slot machine history.[2]

Despite the company's development of the new game, Nevada Electronics was basically a slot route operator. They placed machines, including their own Dealer 21, on a revenue-share, or participating, basis in casinos. The first year of operation for Dealer 21 saw 130 games built and installed, which generated a gross income of about $200,000 a month. It was a heady beginning for an entirely new generation of slot machines.

All of this happened just before Si Redd moved to Nevada, but he took immediate notice of it once he arrived. With his broad and deep knowledge of coin-operated machines, and the positive early results of Dealer 21 and Dick Raven's subsequent electronic keno game, Redd knew something exciting was happening. For the next few years he watched these changes very closely.

Meanwhile, Dick Raven left Nevada Electronics over a contract dispute, and subsequently developed the electronic keno game under his own company, Raven Electronics. It too was an immediate success. Early on he sold the keno machines to casinos, but then he converted the business to a slot route operation in which they were leased on a participating basis.

A series of financial reversals, however, put Raven Electronics in trouble, and in 1971 Si Redd's Bally Distributing Company bought Raven's firm. Raven had 450 games out on routes, and those locations were the real prize for Redd. Bally Distributing had begun building their own electronic games by that time and had little use for Raven's trailblazing games. The cagey Redd also insisted on a five-year noncompete clause from Raven to keep the innovative game designer out of his hair.

Redd's next coup involved another small, cutting-edge company, Dale Electronics, also located in Las Vegas. The company had three partners. Dale Rodesch, who owned 75 percent of the company, had a background working with small manufacturers providing instrumentation to the aerospace industry. Splitting the other 25 percent were Dale Frey and Bob Bonsack, who both worked at North American Aviation and were telecommuting from Southern California. Frey was an engineer with degrees in aerospace and electrical engineering, and an advanced degree in systems engineering; Bonsack was Frey's supervising project engineer at North American.[3]

Before the three men had teamed up, Frey had begun designing an electronic poker machine as part of his college master's program. Because of all the possible combinations of hands in poker, it was a much more complex game to design than either blackjack or keno. Also, Raven's earlier Dealer 21 and keno machines were built with discrete circuits, that is, circuits made up of individual transistors. Frey's machine was solid state, that is to say, it used integrated circuits, each composed of hundreds of linked transistors.

By 1968 Frey's game was completed, and he and Bonsack—both still working at North American—decided to build a prototype of the machine. They figured it would cost $1,700 to produce one. Bonsack kicked in $1,200 because Frey had done all of the work; and Frey, supporting a wife and four children, borrowed the remaining $500 from his life insurance policy.

When the prototype was finished, it was a clunky-looking machine, and it had no internal hopper, or coin-payout mechanism, but the two men were justly proud of it. Bonsack bought a ticket on a gamblers' special flight to Reno and headed off to see if he could find an interested buyer for their machine, which they had dubbed Poker-Matic. Bonsack had been directed to see Si Redd who, he was told, might be his best prospect. But to his disappointment Redd was out of town when he arrived.

Meantime, Frey and Rodesch had gotten together. Rodesch had a contact at Caesars Palace who invited all three partners to bring their prototype over and show it to Caesars's CEO, brilliant entrepreneur Jay Sarno.

"I remember one thing about that trip," Dale Frey recalled with chagrin. "Rodesch got comped at the hotel, but Bonsack and I had to pay for our rooms."

Jay Sarno showed no interest in Poker-Matic. According to Rodesch, when Sarno arrived at the door of the room where they had the machine set up, he simply looked in and snarled, "No one will ever play that damn thing. It doesn't even have a handle [to pull]." Then he departed.

The Caesars's executive who had invited them to Las Vegas told the three men they would have to get the machine licensed by the Gaming Commission and put it through a trial run in order to have any success elsewhere. Later, however, Sarno relented and allowed the Poker-Matic to be placed in his new casino, Circus Circus, for their trial. But he was still not a believer.

Rodesch, Frey, and Bonsack went back to California and adapted their clunky machine to get it ready for the big trial. They had a nicer cabinet built so it would actually look like a slot machine: they adapted and installed an old Mills hopper in it, and they converted all the interior wiring to printed circuit boards.

Rodesch took the prototype to the next Nevada Gaming Commission meeting in Carson City in late 1968. He and his partners were stunned to learn that licensing of all new electronic games had been on hold in the previous two years because of Dick Raven's accidental gaff on his Dealer 21 game. However, the state had just hired an electrical engineer from the California aerospace industry for their testing lab, and it had just reopened for business.

Poker-Matic's field test was an overwhelming success, and the three partners had no problem winning a manufacturing license for it. The first electronic poker machine—it did not have a video screen, so it was not a video poker machine—was now a fait accompli.

Rodesch began producing the machines in Las Vegas as Dale Electronics. The company had been funded by a $35,000 personal loan to Rodesch from the Bank of America in California. No Nevada bank was willing to take the risk.

Rodesch had secured a contract for sixty Poker-Matics at $3,600 each from a small route operator in southern Nevada, and Bill Pennington and Bill Bennett were named distributors for northern Nevada. Poker-Matic was an instant hit, but the partners made some business blunders, and within a year Dale Electronics was in financial trouble.

Dale Electronics's 1970 solid state Poker-Matic was the first automatic paying draw poker slot, and it kicked off the draw poker craze that has been going on for over forty years. *Courtesy of Marshall Fey.*

Bill O'Donnell, representing Bally Manufacturing Corporation in Chicago, initiated conversations with Rodesch about buying Dale Electronics and the rights to all the electronic games they were working on. At Bally Distributing Company, Redd was aware of O'Donnell's interest in Dale Electronics. Redd was mesmerized by the potential of Poker-Matic. O'Donnell, however, was less enthusiastic, and never followed up with Rodesch. Redd and O'Donnell's disagreement over the future of electronic slot machines would have huge implications for both men—one very positive, one disastrously negative—in the years to come.

While he was talking with O'Donnell, Rodesch was also talking to New Hampshire–based Centronics Corporation, inventor of the dot matrix printer, about a possible buyout. With two interested parties, things began looking up for Dale Electronics. By 1972, however, Rodesch had heard nothing more from O'Donnell. And he was infuriated when he discovered that Si Redd had gone behind his back and hired Dale Frey and Bob Bonsack to go to work for Bally Distributing Company. With its engineers gone, Dale Electronics was forced into bankruptcy the following year. Meanwhile Frey and Bonsack moved to Reno to begin their new jobs.

"What [Si Redd] wanted me to do," Dale Frey said, "was to design a poker machine for Bally Distributing. I told him I couldn't do that. . . . Dale Electronics was still in business at the time."

Si Redd was a patient man; he knew he could wait. So he put Frey and Bonsack to work in what passed for his research and development (R&D) department. It was located on Fourth Street, just a short walk to the main plant on Sixth Street, near Wells Avenue, east of downtown.

Bally Distributing was already manufacturing some machines. They had the Big Berthas, which by the early 1970s they were building themselves; they had the blackjack machines they had purchased from Bill Pennington and Bill Bennett; and they had the Spot Slot keno machines that had been purchased from Warren Nelson. They also had a dice machine they had developed internally, made of surplus parts.

"No two machines were alike," Frey laughed, speaking of the dice machines. "He [the engineer] made these things out of scrap parts from war surplus, telephone company surplus, anything. Some part—I can't recall what it was—he made out of old juice cans." Frey added, "They were popular with the players, but they didn't work too well."

The next generation of this dice machine, with input from Frey, was much improved, however. They called it Redd's Dice, and it became a staple of their offerings. The company was also producing a bingo game and a horse-racing game.

None of the games being manufactured by Bally Distributing were being produced for sale. Only Bally slot machines from the factory in Chicago were sold by Bally Distributing, although they did make cosmetic changes to some of the Bally machines before releasing them to the market.

The machines produced by Bally Distributing were all put out on the slot routes the company owned and operated on a revenue-share basis. They were rarely sold. Dale Frey did recall one instance when a very large customer of Bally slot machines in Las Vegas wanted to buy two of its blackjack machines. Each one cost about $3,000 to build, so Redd told the customers he could have two of them for $17,000 each, figuring that would discourage the man. But he agreed to the price, so Redd had to let him have them. But that was the exception rather than the rule. This lease-rather-than-sell practice was also initially used by Hughes Tool Company, and it made a multimillionaire of Howard Hughes.

One of Frey's first tasks was to work on Si Redd's favorite project, Big Bertha. All the giant machines were either three- or four-reel machines, and they were all mechanical. But Si Redd had a dream. He wanted to build a Big Bertha that would dwarf even those giants, so he had earlier ordered his engineers to put together a massive eight-reel machine. By the time Frey joined Bally Distributing, the eight-reel behemoth sat gathering dust in the warehouse because Bally engineers hadn't been able to design a reel-stopping mechanism that would work on such a large scale. Redd assigned Frey and another engineer the job of making it work.

To fix the reel-stopping problem, the men installed a Stepper motor, a versatile electromechanical motor that can divide a full rotation into a large number of precisely controlled stops. Frey designed an electronic circuit to run the motor. After these improvements, the Gaming Commission's gaming lab was called in and approved the machine, which was then installed at the Circus Circus Hotel-Casino in Las Vegas for its mandatory trial.

There were a few early problems with the Super Big Bertha. Because of all the jury-rigged internal parts, Frey described the machine as "kind of temperamental." The engineers were called in once a week or more to perform maintenance to keep it running. Also, because of the slot machine's breadth, the player couldn't see

This supersized Big Bertha slot machine that was manufactured by Si Redd's company went into the *Guinness Book of World Records* as the world's biggest slot machine in 1973. *Courtesy of Dale Rodesch.*

all eight reels at once without backing away five or six feet. Despite these shortcomings, the public absolutely loved playing it, and the machine became an instant hit at Circus Circus. After a couple of months, however, Bally Distributing had to take Super Big Bertha back into the shop for a major refitting. And Circus Circus executive Bill Pennington—angry that Si Redd was competing against him on some other slot machines—used that as an excuse to refuse Super Big Bertha reentry into his casino.

Undaunted, Si Redd arranged to have Super Big Bertha put into the Four Queens Hotel-Casino in Las Vegas after the refitting was completed. In September 1973, amid a flurry of free publicity, the machine achieved a world record. "The world's biggest slot machine (or one-armed bandit) is Super Bertha (555 cu ft) installed by Si Redd at the Four Queens Casino, Las Vegas. . . . Once in every 25 billion plays it may yield $1 million for a $10 investment," the *Guinness Book of World Records* crowed.[4] Redd now had another press clipping to add to his growing collection, and he had the last laugh on Bill Pennington and Circus Circus.

Redd's world record would not last forever, however. In 1987, after he and Bally had parted company, the slot machine maker introduced Billie Jean, a 9-foot-tall × 10-foot-wide slot that easily eclipsed Redd's previous record.

Redd achieved even a bit more celebrity thanks to Big Bertha. After he had set the Guinness record, he was invited to appear on the nationally syndicated TV show *What's My Line*, where he would be recognized as the inventor of the world's largest slot machine. In typical Si Redd style, he appeared on stage in an eye-popping light green sport coat and bolo tie, and grandly enjoyed a flirtatious on-screen repartee with panelist Dorothy Kilgallen.[5]

Redd had also installed a regular-sized Big Bertha in Jay Sarno's Caesars Palace in Las Vegas before Sarno sold the place. Redd and Sarno were cut from the same bolt of cloth, and Sarno loved the novelty of the crowd-pleasing, giant one-armed bandit with its noise and excitement. Redd offered Sarno his standard Big Bertha deal for sizable properties: 60 percent of the take for the casino, and 40 percent for Bally Distributing. "You put it in here, if you want to," Sarno told Redd. "But, brother, you take 30 percent."[6]

Redd did some quick mental calculating. "OK, Mr. Sarno," he told him; "You have a deal."

Shortly after that, Redd got a call from a small downtown Las Vegas casino—"a hole in the wall," he described it—that had a Big Bertha in its doorway. The owner's wife worked at Caesars Palace and had told her husband about Sarno's deal. He seethed with anger: his deal was only a fifty-fifty split, so he thought Redd was cheating him. He called Redd and threatened to throw Big Bertha out unless he got Sarno's 70 percent split.

"Well, I'll tell you what I'll do," Redd told him, unfazed. "I'll give you 80 percent but my part, my 20 percent, [has to] equal at least 80 percent of what I'm taking out of Caesars's."[7]

The sawdust joint operator never complained again.

* * * *

In addition to Big Bertha, Frey and the other Bally Distributing Company's engineers spent time working on the company's bingo and horse race machines as well, but neither of which worked very well or found much public acceptance. Another machine the staff worked on was housed in a large yellow-orange fiberglass case, unofficially dubbed The Great Pumpkin. It turned out to be too big for most casinos, so Redd sold it to a Japanese game maker.

In 1973 Dale Electronics was forced into bankruptcy, and Frey was now free to begin working on an electronic poker machine for Bally Distributing. Just a year or so earlier Nolan Bushnell, an engineer-turned-entrepreneur, had founded a company named Atari in northern California's Silicon Valley. Copying an idea developed by Magnavox, Bushnell had designed a coin-operated ping-pong game named Pong, which displayed its images on a conventional television screen. The new game was so popular that Atari developed a home version of it. And in 1975, bolstered by a distribution agreement with Sears, Atari released it to the public with great success. Pong was the very first commercially successful video game.

"The game was basically a variation of a test board you used for TV . . . a pattern generator," Frey explained. "It was a pretty simple technology."

Given all his years' experience in the coin-operated amusement game industry, Redd immediately recognized the potential of this new technology. He suggested to Bill O'Donnell that Bally Distributing buy Atari, but O'Donnell nixed the idea. "Bally turned it down. I recommended that they buy Pong. . . . [W]e [Redd and Bally Distributing Company's engineers] saw what Pong could do as an amusement machine and we . . . could [en]vision doing the same thing with keno, poker or 21."[8]

Failing that plan, Redd asked Frey if he could build a gambling game using the Pong technology and a TV screen, and Frey began tinkering with the idea. "The twenty-one machines we had out on the routes were doing pretty good," Frey said. "I wasn't really trying to replace them; but I came up with a design for a twenty-one machine, a very crude one. I had no intention of ever building one; it was just my lab toy to get involved in this video business."

Frey showed the crude machine, sans case or embellishment of any kind, to Si Redd. Although it looked like some sort of electronic Rube Goldberg contraption, or a special effect for a Frankenstein movie, Frey said, "He [Redd] got very excited. I wasn't sure why, because compared to our beautiful [electronic] twenty-one machine, it was kind of nothing."

Bill O'Donnell was due to be in Las Vegas the next day, and Redd insisted Frey take his makeshift little machine down and show it to Bally's CEO. "That's very clever," O'Donnell said when he saw the machine. "But do me a favor; dump it in the trash."

Frey asked why. "You built that thing on a kitchen table," O'Donnell told him, "so anybody else who wants one can build his own. . . . A Bally slot machine can't be built by amateurs."

Dale Frey's prototype of a video twenty-one (or blackjack) game, dubbed "TV Twenty-One," in 1975, after he had built it into a cabinet. It was one of the world's earliest video slot machines. *Courtesy of Dale Rodesch.*

Embarrassed and chaffed at being called an amateur, Frey returned to Reno and reported his conversation to Si Redd. "Well," Redd drawled, "Bill isn't always right."

Atari had by now built a second video game, based on moving an object through a maze, but it had flopped badly. Redd purchased two dozens of the machines, which had cost Atari $900 each to build, for a mere $100 each. He asked Frey if he could build the electronics for a video twenty-one game into the Atari machine. Frey said he could do so for about $200 more, so Redd told him to convert one of the machines for a trial.

When the prototype was finished, Redd called his eastern Nevada slot route manager and asked if he thought the video twenty-one

An early A-1 Supply Company black-and-white video twenty-one (or blackjack) slot machine. These machines were sold to gray-area (non-gambling) markets, and the electronics in them were converted from a Pong game. *Courtesy of Dale Rodesch.*

machines would do well in his small town and rural territory. The man was very satisfied with the electronic twenty-one machines he already had on his routes, but he said he believed the games would be a big hit across the border, in Utah. Without a hopper installed, the machines were not technically gaming devices, so the men believed they could be put into private clubs in Utah as amusement games. Quasi-gaming devices such as these, when sent to nongaming jurisdictions for amusement use only, are known in the trade as gray-area games.

With the gray-area plan in mind, Frey adapted the two dozens Atari games into video twenty-one (or blackjack) machines, and off they went to Utah. After a couple of weeks, Redd wanted to see how the machines were doing, so he drove over to Utah and went to one of the locations. He handed the bartender a twenty-dollar bill and asked for quarters to play the twenty-one game that sat off in a corner, surrounded by a bunch of men. "Okay, here are your quarters, and your number. You're number thirty-seven," the bartender told Redd. There were thirty-six other players ahead of him.

Arguably the world's first video slot machine—although it was supposedly not being used for gambling—the twenty-one was a huge success. (Others credit Las Vegas–based Fortune Coin Company's three-reel video slot machine, also introduced in 1975, as the first video slot. But it is impossible to determine which one actually hit the market first.)

Everything worked out well with these gray-area games until another amusement route operator in Utah challenged that the video twenty-one games were, in fact, gambling devices, hopper or not. The laws governing such machines were vague in most states, including Utah, so when the state's conservative attorney general agreed with the complaining route operator, Redd had to withdraw all the machines. He stored them in Bally Distributing Company's Reno warehouse, where they would sit gathering dust for the next year or so.

Undaunted, Dale Frey continued to tinker with video games. "I had developed enough knowledge of the technology that I could put a decent looking picture on the screen," he said. In his earliest machines, he had been restricted to designing playing cards composed exclusively of horizontal or vertical lines. The letter K, for instance, denoting a king, looked more like an H, whereas a club was simply a number of boxes sitting atop one another. Of course, only black-and-white television tubes were being used; color was still a distant dream.

Although he had not figured out how to draw curves yet, Frey had learned to use diagonal lines. "I could now build a club that looked like a club," he said. "It might have 45-degree corners, but it was a good-looking image of a card." Although early video images were still very crude by current standards, little by little Dale Frey was learning to master the techniques. At the same time he was also beginning to experiment with microprocessors—the brains of a computer—and the possible use of this advanced technology for amusement games.

A 1974 sales brochure for Bally Distributing Company describes all the games the company had on its slot routes at that time. These slot machines were all known as "novelty machines," a category that included everything except a standard three-reel slot machine. They were: Winner's Circle, a horse-race betting machine; Computer 21, Computer Poker, and Raven Keno, acquired in the Raven Electronics purchase; and Bonus Bingo and Redd's Dice, both developed internally. Joining its staple Big Bertha in the oversized machine category was Constellation, whereas a futuristic-looking slot machine named Golden Eagle rounded out the offerings.[9]

Si Redd's personal message in the brochure summed up the company's objectives:

We continually must strive to anticipate the customer's desires. In this space age of electronics, television and computers, those desires require even more elaborate and unique amusements.

We have become the leader in our industry because we have successfully kept ahead of the customer's desires with more challenging and thrilling games of chance.[10]

Redd's concentration, however, was soon to be diverted from electronic and video games to another direction, and it would set him off on another, even more exciting and profitable path.

— CHAPTER 9 —

AN ACE IN THE HOLE

In mid-1975, Si Redd and Bill O'Donnell again began bargaining on a price for Bally Distributing Company. The firm had come a long way in the eight years since Redd had purchased controlling interest. He had started with three employees and 5000 square feet of warehouse space. The company now employed over one hundred people, and it had 88,000 square feet of warehouse, workshop, and office space. As Bally's only gaming machine distributor in the United States, the company was also becoming heavily involved in foreign sales.[1]

Redd began the negotiation with O'Donnell with the $9 million figure they had agreed to in 1972. However, O'Donnell said the company couldn't afford to pay that much. When Redd reminded him they had a prior agreement at $9 million, O'Donnell asked to see a copy of it. It immediately dawned on Redd why O'Donnell had never given him his copy of that contract. The negotiations continued, but Redd stood firm at $9 million.

"I refused to deviate from the nine million," Redd said. "I wouldn't take less. I'd go to court [if necessary]."[2] O'Donnell finally realized that Redd was adamant, and ratcheted his offer up to $7.5 million, but the negotiations stalled again at that point.

Finally, Redd played his ace in the hole. He reminded O'Donnell of the new video games that were being developed and that had not even been part of the 1972 agreement. "Those are worth $1.5 million all by themselves," Redd told O'Donnell, trying to sweeten the pot.

"If it's worth a million-and-a-half, you son of a bitch, you can just keep it!" O'Donnell thundered.[3]

So the deal was struck. O'Donnell would get $1 million from Bally Manufacturing for his personal 30 percent stake in Bally Distributing. His share was disproportionately low, because he insisted on a figure far below fair market value to avoid any possible claims of overcompensation. Redd would receive $7 million—$5.8 million in cash and 266.7 shares of Bally Manufacturing common stock—and exclusive rights to all the video games under design or production, except the video spinning reel games. O'Donnell had never seen the potential in video games, so he even agreed to a five-year noncompete clause for all but spinning reel video gambling games "anywhere in the world."[4]

In a long and illustrious career, this would turn out to be the biggest single misjudgment Bill O'Donnell ever made. At the same time, Si Redd refused to take credit for the brilliance of his bargaining position. "I realized it [video poker] was worth something . . . [but] settling with Bally for the million-and-a-half really was a face save," he said.[5]

Despite Redd's humble words, anyone who had ever sat across a bargaining table from the cagey old veteran never doubted for a moment that he knew exactly what he was doing. Thoroughly outfoxing an opponent, then innocently claiming he had been lucky, was a Si Redd trademark. Whether it was accidental or purposeful, however, Redd's secretary Barbara Rich said that the tale of how he had outmaneuvered Bill O'Donnell for the video game rights became a staple in Redd's storytelling arsenal for years to come.[6]

What cannot be disputed is that during the eight-year period from 1967 to 1975, Si Redd turned his $60,000 investment in Bally Distributing Company into a $9 million portfolio, a pretty hefty return for the crafty old sharecropper's son.

Redd also bargained to retain the rights to the Big Bertha games. The final condition of the sale was that Redd would stay on as president of Bally Distributing Company for three more years. Part of O'Donnell's insistence on this condition was probably spurred by his concern over Bally getting licensed. Although he had made substantial changes to the company since licensing had been denied three years earlier, he knew it would not be an automatic approval.

With a deal in hand, O'Donnell again petitioned for the necessary gaming license for Bally Manufacturing Corporation. However, a new problem surfaced. It seems that in 1972, following the earlier failed attempt to get licensed, an officer of Bally Manufacturing had gifted the family of one William Presser with $100,000 worth of Bally stock. Presser was a vice president and trustee of the Teamsters' Central States Pension Fund. When Bally was granted a $12 million loan from the fund eighteen months later, the smell of the deal wafted all the way to Carson City, Nevada.[7]

Based on that loan, and on ongoing concerns about Bally's past Mob affiliations, the Gaming Control Board continued to express serious reservations about the company. Eventually the board did agree to grant a probationary license, with the stipulation that Bill O'Donnell step down. Their decision then went to the Gaming Commission, the agency that had the final word on licensing. The commission, after a great deal of debate, approved the probationary license but removed the stipulation that O'Donnell must leave. Even at that, the license was approved not by the normally unanimous vote but by a simple majority. As for the probationary period, it was initially set at six years, but it would eventually be lifted after only four years.[8]

So on August 21, 1975, the transfer of the 70 percent interest (69.5 percent, to be exact) in Bally Distributing Company from William S. Redd and the trust of Ivy Lee Redd to Bally Manufacturing Corporation of Chicago, Illinois, was officially blessed, although by the very thinnest of margins.[9]

A scant nine days before the approval, hopeful that the deal would go through, Bill O'Donnell had had Bally Manufacturing listed on the New York Stock Exchange, the first gaming manufacturer to ever achieve such legitimacy. It had taken O'Donnell three years to acquire a Nevada gaming license for his company, and even at that, Bally had passed by only a whisker.

Despite signing off on the deal, and this time making sure to get a copy of the contract, Redd admitted he was disgruntled. "Bally didn't treat me right," he said. He also admitted to relearning a valuable lesson. "[T]hat background of my being a little careless and shooting from the hip, and not having a strong financial man. . . . We would have structured it a lot different," he said. "I really began, I believe, to use my experience, to see the necessity of hiring people like presidents, and vice presidents in charge of financing. More or less I think I went through a change in business [philosophy, as I learned] how to run a business. Instead of doing it all myself, [I'll] just let somebody else do it."[10]

Redd's final three years of running the company after Bally took over did provide him some satisfaction. "During those three years,"

Redd said, "the net profit that that branch office . . . made . . . went from two million to three million a year, then the third year they paid taxes on [net income of] sixteen million. They got all their money back in one year."[11]

* * * *

During that three-year period, Si Redd would have his hands full. By contract, he had to continue his duties as president of Bally Distributing Company, but now he would be taking orders from Chicago, at least to the extent that Si Redd *ever* took orders from anyone. On the other hand, he still had his own business interests to look after; and Si Redd being Si Redd, he was anxious to expand his own ventures as fast and as far as possible.

For the second time in less than a decade, Redd's personal enterprises had outgrown the facility that housed them. So he and his staff picked up and moved everything, this time to a much larger facility on South Rock Boulevard in Reno.

Initially they shared the facility with another company, but soon they had the vast space all to themselves.

Redd's secretary, Barbara Rich, remembered that the boss had come up with a special employee bonus at about this time that delighted everybody on the staff. About seventy miles east of Reno is the small farming community of Fallon. Farmers in and around the community raised a number of agricultural crops, but the area had become famous for one particular product: Hearts O'Gold cantaloupes. The fat, juicy, sweet melons were famous throughout the region, and they were shipped to restaurants and specialty grocers all over the country. Si Redd had tasted his first Hearts O'Gold melon in a Reno restaurant and couldn't wait to share it with friends and employees. So one spring day he drove to Fallon, loaded his car trunk with melons, and distributed them to all his employees. They caused such a stir that the following year—and a number of years thereafter—he would send a company truck to bring back an entire load to be passed out. "The office and production area smelled like a melon farm for a couple of days [after,]" Rich remembered. "Everyone enjoyed those melons."[12]

A-1 Supply Company was the corporate entity under which Redd held his personal enterprises: a couple of small casinos, the video games design and production venture he retained from the Bally sale, the Big Berthas, and a slot route operation. As part of the video games venture, he still had the two dozen video twenty-one games that had been removed from Utah and were gathering dust in storage. He wanted to get rid of those games and expand the sale of additional twenty-one games and others gray-area games into nongaming markets. Redd decided to hire someone to take charge of that task, and he had someone in mind: Dale Rodesch.

After his Dale Electronics had been forced into bankruptcy, Rodesch had forged a deal with Centronics Corporation. With Centronics money and Rodesch's expertise, they started a company called Gamex Industries in Las Vegas, with Rodesch as general manager. The firm developed the first widely available slot machines to feature a Stepper motor. But Rodesch had had a falling out with Centronics, and when Redd sought him out, he accepted a job to build a gray-area market for A-1 supply.[13]

In November 1975, only two months after he joined A-1 Supply, Rodesch and Si Redd traveled to Chicago for the annual AMOA show. The Amusement and Music Operators Association was the leading nongaming coin-op trade association, and the A-1 men would have an audience of route operators, manufacturers, and distributors from across the country. Redd wanted to find new customers so they could restart production on the gray-area video twenty-one games.[14]

Rodesch and the engineers had rigged one of the games from the warehouse with an RF modulator that allowed it to be connected to the TV set in Redd's suite for their demonstrations. Redd warned Rodesch that this was to be a secret operation: he wanted the route operators to see how great it was so they would add it to their product line, but he didn't want to tip his hand to the manufacturers or distributors in attendance.

"Si invited every coin machine operator he knew to come and have a look, but with an understanding of secrecy," Rodesch said.[15] At each meeting, a dozen or so operators were shown the machine, and everyone seemed very interested, many even offering to place immediate orders.

At one meeting, one of the operators told Redd he had already seen the demo in his own suite. "How is that possible?" Redd asked the man. These were the first demos of the twenty-one game. It turned out that the modulator had shown the demo on every TV set in the hotel. "Some secrecy," Dale Rodesch grinned. However, the men did return to Reno convinced that the video blackjack machine would be a winner.

Rodesch took subsequent trips to Tokyo and London to demonstrate the machines, and again they were well received. As a result of all these trips, A-1 produced about one hundred of the blackjack machines to meet demand. But Rodesch and Redd soon hit upon another idea. Rather than producing the machines themselves, they should take advantage of the huge number of Pong games that were now in storage around the world because of rapidly de-escalating demand. So the engineers designed a kit that could easily adapt a Pong game, or Atari's unsuccessful maze game that had followed it, into a video blackjack game for the gray-area market. The kit turned out to be another big winner.[16]

The early story of the development of Pong is touched upon briefly in Chapter 8. However, like most stories about the early years of video games and computer games—today a huge industry—it is a complex, multilayered story. Not surprisingly, Si Redd's name occasionally turns up.

The very first interactive electronic game goes all the way back to 1947, and for the next quarter century a number of pioneering engineers added this idea or that improvement to the process.[17] In 1971 Nolan Bushnell and a partner developed the first commercially sold, coin-operated video game called Computer Space. The game was housed in a funky-looking fiberglass cabinet—one video game historian compared its appearance, with tongue only partially in cheek, to a 1957 DeSoto. It had a black-and-white egg-shaped TV monitor, and was available in a number of futuristic colors: metal flake red, metal flake blue, and what was described by another critic as an ugly non–metal flake yellow. The Computer Space game board featured two alien spaceships battling gravitational inertia and each other. Although Stone Age technology by today's computer game standards, the game was so futuristic by early 1970s standards that it even won a small role in the futuristic 1973 movie *Soylent Green*.

Bushnell's own company, Syzygy Engineering, developed the game, and he had it manufactured by a Mountain View, California, firm, Nutting Associates, owned by Bill Nutting. Fifteen hundred of the games were produced, but only about half were sold.

Bushnell then developed Pong and offered to sell it to Nutting in return for a share in his company, but Nutting declined. That's when Bushnell founded Atari to manufacture and distribute his new game.

Nutting's company then fell on hard times, as many small technology firms did. Likely in 1977, Si Redd purchased Nutting Associates. By this time whatever rights Nutting may have retained for

Computer Space were worthless, as developing technology had far exceeded it. Dale Rodesch hired Bill Nutting to join A-1 Supply as production manager of his gray-area market amusement machine division.

"Si thought, with their Bay-area location, they might be a good 'cover' for the gray-area products going to California, Hawaii, and Guam," Rodesch said. "But [when] that didn't work out . . . I brought Bill Nutting (and a few of his people) into Reno."[18]

Dale Frey suggested another possible reason why Redd had bought Nutting Associates. Bill Nutting believed that Bushnell had stolen the Pong idea from his company. So, Frey said, Redd bought the company in order to get control of a lawsuit that Nutting planned against Atari and Bushnell.[19] At this time, it seemed that everybody in the video games business was suing somebody over who developed what and when, and who owned the rights to what and when. So Si Redd, an old hand at this kind of tactic, was probably trying to get his oar in the water along with everyone else. The Nutting lawsuit, however, never came to pass. Redd's purchase of the company never achieved either of the goals he hoped for.

Dale Frey, meantime, had been transferred from Bally Distributing Company to Bally Manufacturing Corporation, not physically but for payroll purposes. He now received his paycheck from Bally Manufacturing in Chicago, although he still received all his marching orders from Si Redd. Bally Manufacturing had two small engineering groups in Nevada, and Frey was made the manager of group 2, with the responsibility of developing video games for the company. This was rather strange, as Bill O'Donnell had little interest in video games, having even traded away the rights to the games to Si Redd.[20]

Dale Rodesch and A-1 Supply's gray-area games division still had those twenty-four video blackjack games from Utah in the warehouse, so Rodesch turned his attention to that matter. A San Francisco amusement game route operator bought the lot of them to install in gay bars. To circumvent the problem A-1 had had in Utah, the machines were sold as amusement games in Nevada, not in California. The route operator brought his own truck to Reno, paid for the machines there, and took them across the state line on his own, releasing A-1 from any potential licensing problems.[21]

The video blackjack machines were selling and performing so well in the gray-area market that Redd decided to have some manufactured for Nevada's gaming market.

He ordered 200 of the machines, with coin hoppers, from Bally Manufacturing. The machines were all produced in distinctive yellow and brown wooden cases, and they sold out quickly.

At the same time Dale Rodesch's gray-area market project for A-1 Supply was in full swing, and Rodesch's ex-partner Dale Frey, working in another building, was still tinkering with his video draw poker machine for Si Redd under the auspices of A-1 Supply Company, not for Bally Manufacturing Corporation.

A 1977 black-and-white video poker game built for the gray-area (non-gambling) markets. *Courtesy of Dale Rodesch.*

By July 1976 Frey had completed building his first prototype. The draw poker machine, like the video blackjack machine that was doing so well, used a black-and-white TV monitor. But another small Las Vegas start-up company, Fortune Coin, had recently released a video three-reel slot machine that used a color monitor. Si Redd purchased one and gave it to Dale Frey to dissect and study.[22]

Frey ordered another color monitor from a San Francisco company for $750, and began wiring it up. "I hooked it up to my black and white poker game, and lo and behold the damned thing was in color," Frey exclaimed.[23] The only problem with the device was that a color picture tube was much longer than a black-and-white picture tube, so it protruded out the back of the case through a hole Frey had to cut in it. That presented no problem with the poker machines because they weren't in production yet and the cabinets hadn't been built. But the tube was also too long for the blackjack machine for which hundreds of cabinets had been built.

"The fellows went out and bought a bunch of stainless steel dishpans and screwed them to the back of the case, covering the neck that was sticking out," Frey laughed. "And that's how we got started."[24]

Tyler Sciotto, who worked in executive-level positions at A-1 Supply and for more than a quarter century at IGT, remarked about the invention of video draw poker, saying, "Everybody had their fingers in it."[25] There were indeed a lot of men who came up with this schematic or that wiring diagram, including a number of engineers who worked for Si Redd. However, if one man is to be tabbed "the father of video poker," arguably it must be Dale Frey, the unassuming engineer who eventually put all the pieces together.

* * * *

Si Redd and other Nevada gambling executives had been following the news out of New Jersey about that state's possible entry into casino gaming for a number of years. In 1974, New Jersey's citizens had spurned a referendum to legalize state-run casinos, but in 1976 they approved another version to allow privately owned, state-regulated casinos. The new law restricted casinos to one city only, Atlantic City, once the tourism queen of the eastern seaboard, but now only a crumbling, poverty-stricken relic from the past.

Nevada's casino and hospitality industry leaders were understandably anxious over the coming of their first real competition since gambling had been legalized in the state in 1931. Si Redd, on the other hand, couldn't have been more pleased. A new gaming jurisdiction, just at the time his video gaming machines were beginning to win acceptance, would be huge.

It wasn't an easy transition for Atlantic City, and it certainly didn't go smoothly. But when Resorts International opened the first hotel casino on the famed Boardwalk on May 26, 1978, it marked the beginning of a new era in gambling in America, and it marked it with a splash! When the doors opened at 10:00 a.m., massive lines of eager gamblers stretched almost as far as the eye could see, and people waited for hours to get inside. Eventually the initial furor died down, but Atlantic City proved to be a monster success. However, the new competition Nevada casino operators had feared did not materialize. There were 15 million people living within a 100-mile radius of Atlantic City, and those day-trippers and overnighters were what made Atlantic City successful. It did not water down Nevada's customer base.

Ironically, however, Atlantic City also marked the end of an era for one gaming giant. When casino gaming was approved, Bally's Bill O'Donnell seized the opportunity to get in on the ground floor, not as a manufacturer but as a casino owner. In late 1978 construction began on Bally's Park Place Hotel-Casino. It opened in December 1979 under a temporary gaming license. But Bill O'Donnell's chickens all came home to roost, and the company was unable to get a permanent license with him as CEO. O'Donnell voluntarily stepped down from his post and left the company, allowing Bally to receive its New Jersey gaming license. He always yearned to return to the company he had helped build, but when O'Donnell died in 1995, he had not realized that dream.

Redd and O'Donnell remained close friends until the latter's death, despite their history of acrimonious dealings. Redd even thought O'Donnell had cheated him on a number of occasions, especially in the final sale of Bally Distributing Company. Despite that, the affable Redd never took those things personally. In his opinion, business was business, and winning—whatever it might take—was the ultimate goal. If he was ever outfoxed on a deal, Redd believed he only had himself to blame. It was never personal with Si Redd.

Pete Cladianos Jr., owner of Reno's Sands Regency Hotel-Casino, and both a friend and customer of Redd, said of him: "If Si saw a competitor that had something better than he did, he'd buy it if he possibly could, and if he couldn't buy him out, he'd run him out of business. He'd sue him. He'd tie him up in court. Si was a pretty ruthless guy, but he was very shrewd, and he had a lot of vision."[26]

His personal accountant added that Redd would often violate a contract when it came time to make good on a costly or inconvenient clause. When Redd was confronted, El Studebaker said, "Si's favorite saying was, 'Sue me; I'll bury you.'"[27]

As for Atlantic City, once all the kinks were worked out, it became the success New Jersey fathers had hoped for. At the close of 2007, despite witnessing its first ever annual drop in gaming revenue, Atlantic City's eleven hotel casinos grossed just over $4.9 billion. Nevada gaming revenues for the same period were nearly $11.8 billion. The early competitive threat that Nevada gaming moguls had expected from Atlantic City had never materialized. There was indeed room for both venues.

* * * *

In mid-1977, Dale Rodesch got a call to go see Si Redd in his office. Redd had maintained his personal office at Bally Distributing Company, and would continue to do so until his three-year contract with Bally expired in 1978.

"During my tenure at A-1 Supply, Si never had an office at any of the three successive facilities of A-1," Rodesch said. "When we met, we always adjourned to Si's Cadillac parked in the driveway next to his office. He was paranoid about Bally possibly bugging his office."[28]

Redd had surprising instructions for Rodesch: he told him to see if he could sell the company. Redd's second wife, Marilyn, had never liked Si's casino business. She felt it demeaned them. She also preferred to live in Las Vegas, but the business was headquartered in Reno. She had often begged her husband to retire. He was getting older—he had turned sixty-five the prior year—and the couple had all the money they would ever need.

It was obvious to Rodesch that Redd's order was half-hearted. He loved working, he loved the glamour and excitement of the business, the daily contact with so many interesting people. With Atlantic City shortly coming on line with casino gaming, and all the new games A-1 Supply was beginning to develop, Redd knew he stood at the cusp of an exciting new era in casino gaming. It seemed to Dale Rodesch and others that Si Redd was trying to placate his wife, and that his heart was not really in retirement at all.

A-1 SUPPLY, INC.

395 FREEPORT BLVD., SUITE 8
P.O. BOX 1826
SPARKS, NEVADA 89431 U.S.A.

TELEPHONE
(702) 358-1260

PRICE LIST

Our "21" games, which are based on Casino Blackjack and its many variations including Bonus Play, are priced as follows for the credit meter or amusement-only types:

Printed Circuit Board (only)	$ 600.00
Complete Conversion Kit (excluding monitor, cabinet and coin handling)	$1,200.00
Complete Machine, Wooden Console Model	$2,600.00
Complete Machine, Wooden, Cocktail Table Model	$2,600.00

The following prices apply for cash payout versions of various "21" games:

TV 21, Blue, Metal Case, Bench Type Cabinet	$3,500.00
TV 21, Wooden Console Model	$3,500.00
TV 21, Wooden, Cocktail Table Model	$3,900.00

In addition to machines based on the various forms of "21", we are also offering TV Draw Poker in the following cash-payout-only forms:

TV Draw Poker, Metal, Bench Type Cabinet	$3,800.00
TV Draw Poker, Wooden Console Model	$3,500.00

The above reflects our small quantity pricing, F.O.B. Reno. Delivery would be approximately 6 to 8 weeks after receipt of order. Terms of payment to be letter of credit.

5/26/77

An A-1 Supply Company price list from mid-1977 shows the products and prices for very early video slot machines. Note some of the games are nongaming machines, called gray-area games, whereas others are for gambling. *Courtesy of Dale Rodesch.*

Still, an order was an order. Redd told Rodesch he was willing to sell it for $250,000 plus the cost of the inventory. The first man Rodesch visited was Irwin Molasky in Las Vegas. Molasky was the most prominent developer in the city, builder of the city's first shopping mall, its first private hospital, its largest and grandest office buildings, and some of its earliest housing developments. Molasky and his partner, Merv Adelson, had negotiated with Rodesch for the acquisition of Dale Electronics a few years earlier, a deal that never materialized.[29]

Molasky passed on the A-1 Supply purchase. So did Nick Papolos, a Florida investor whom Rodesch had known for a number of years. Rodesch then traveled to London to see Marty Bromley, who had started the company that evolved into video game maker Sega. He also passed.

A-1 Supply's sales manager, Clint Shockey, was soliciting buyers from among out-of-state coin-op route operators and distributors, but also with no success. Hindsight is always 20/20, but as it would turn out the people Rodesch and Shockey approached missed out on one of the greatest opportunities of the twentieth century. As Rodesch was fond of reminding his friend Marty Bromley in London, "[You] could have had IGT for a quarter million."[30]

Rodesch returned to Reno with one more idea. He approached a group of doctors he knew who had some investment capital. They were interested, but the price Redd set for his existing inventory was a stumbling block, and the negotiations stalled. Then, suddenly, Redd withdrew A-1 from the trading block. He now had his eye on a much larger prize, one that reenergized him and convinced him, at least temporarily, to ignore his wife's wishes. It was called Fortune Coin Company.

Redd did make a concession to his wife, however. It's another great story that points to the bigger-than-life persona that was Si Redd.

Back in 1966, just a year before Redd discovered Nevada, an even bigger bigger-than-life character moved to the state: Howard Hughes.[31] The eccentric billionaire had decided he wanted to establish residence on the top floor of the Dunes Hotel in Las Vegas. Not just a room, mind you; he wanted the *entire* top floor. But the Dunes had a very successful restaurant up there, and the owners weren't keen on giving it up for anyone, not even Howard Hughes. So Hughes's go-to guy during this period, an ex–FBI agent named Bob Maheu, booked all the rooms and suites on the floor below, which seemed to satisfy the mercurial Hughes for at least a few days. But when the Dunes had to take back a few of the suites for some high rollers, Hughes—who still hadn't even arrived in Las Vegas—nixed the deal and told Maheu to try again.

Maheu next rented the entire top floor of the Desert Inn, promising management that they'd only need the suites for ten days. So, in late November, in the middle of the night, Hughes was spirited out of the Ritz Carlton in Boston, where he had been residing, tucked away on a train, and hustled to Las Vegas. At 5:00 a.m. on November 27, 1966, a few miles outside of town, he was taken off the train, comfortably settled in a van and driven to the Desert Inn, where he was whisked up a service elevator to his new home.

Thus began the historic four-year odyssey of Howard Hughes in Las Vegas. When Desert Inn management—personified by ex-rum runner and mobster Moe Dalitz—decided to oust his nongambling, germophobic guest from the high-roller suites, Hughes bought the hotel. Then he bought another, and another, and another, and another, and another.

The Desert Inn was the only Strip resort with its own on-site golf course. Bob Maheu and his family took up residence in the house on the golf course that had belonged to Dalitz so he could be at Hughes's constant beck and call. But the house was *too* close for Maheu's comfort, and he began badgering the reclusive old billionaire to allow him to build another home on the golf course, but farther away from the hotel and the Strip and all the noise and activity.

Eventually Hughes capitulated, at least in Maheu's version of the story. The version told by the Hughes Tool Company—which actually owned the new house—was that Maheu never received permission to build it, which was one of the chief reasons he was eventually terminated.

In any case, build it the vainglorious Maheu did, on two adjoining lots at a cost of over $600,000. According to Maheu, "The home was stately, pillared, and enormous—a French Colonial residence. . . . [W]e had room to entertain several hundred people at a time. The kitchen had five stoves, there were two magnificent staircases, six bedrooms, and as many baths." There was also a huge wine cellar.

Behind the sprawling two-story mansion was a swimming pool, deck, and entertainment area that put the Desert Inn Hotel to shame. So elaborate and extravagant was the huge house that Hughes's employees dubbed it "Little Caesars Palace."

In September 1969 the Maheu family moved in. Barely a year later, the Maheu family moved out. Bob Maheu had been fired, and when he filed a $50 million lawsuit against Howard Hughes for breach of contract, the family was evicted.

For the next several years the Hughes Tool Company retained the gigantic white elephant on the Desert Inn Country Club golf course. The Hughes gaming properties allowed entertainment headliners such as Debbie Reynolds and Bill Cosby to use the house during their

Las Vegas gigs. But what the company really wanted was another person with a splashy ego and flamboyant style to fall in love with Little Caesars Palace and buy it. In 1977 they found Si Redd.

Redd was nearing the end of his Bally Distributing Company operating contract. He had sold the company to Bally and was just awaiting the end of his three-year commitment. He had been trying to sell some of the company's dollar slot carousels to the six Hughes-owned Las Vegas casinos, but with little success. Then he had an idea, as he always did when someone said no to him.

Redd inquired how much Hughes Tool Company wanted for the Desert Inn Country Club mansion. In a tentative, hopeful voice the real estate agent told him they wanted $550,000 for the house. Then Redd talked to the Hughes gaming people and suggested a deal: he'd buy the house if they would agree to install a certain number of Bally dollar slot carousels on a participating basis in their properties. They liked the deal and agreed to three carousels, two for the Frontier Hotel and one for the Landmark.

But the crafty Redd wasn't quite finished finagling. He called Bill O'Donnell at Bally and said he could get a two-year contract from the Hughes' casinos, profits of which would more than pay for the Desert Inn house. He suggested Bally buy the house, and rent it back to him for $1,150 a month. O'Donnell agreed.

In typical Redd fashion, he had satisfied everyone. The Hughes Tool Company got rid of their white elephant; the Hughes gaming people got some very profitable dollar slot carousels that would help them offset their nagging gaming losses; and Bally got a large new customer and installed a lot of slot machines that would pay them a handsome ongoing percentage. Of course not to be forgotten, Redd too gained. He got a house that perfectly matched his grandiose style for the time he spent in Las Vegas, and he provided his similarly inclined wife with a place where she could entertain along with the best of the Las Vegas glitterati. To top it off, he said Bally gave him a ten-year option to purchase the house for only $375,000.

It was a consummate Si Redd deal.

* * * *

While his Little Caesars Palace gambit was unfolding, Redd was also pursuing an important business deal for his A-1 Supply Company. Fortune Coin was another small Las Vegas start-up company, owned by Stan Fulton. Its chief engineer was a brilliant, innovative man named Walt Fraley. In 1975 the company had introduced a black-and-white video three-reel slot machine, dubbed Fortune Coin. When it was introduced, however, it was not popular. It had no handle to pull, and players were skeptical about the virtual reels in place of the popular spinning reels of the mechanical era. The machine was soon scrapped. Two years later, having witnessed the popularity of A-1's video blackjack and video poker games—both with black-and-white monitors—Fortune Coin came out with a video poker game with a color monitor.[32]

Dale Frey related an amusing story about the first few weeks after Fortune Coin put their color video poker machines out for trial. A-1's machine, although black and white, had been out for many months. Frey and his engineers had spent quite a bit of time developing the payout table to be used for their machines, based on the mathematical probability of each poker hand occurring. For example, if a player bet one coin and ended up after the draw with two pairs, he would double his money; if his hand had three-of-a-kind, he would have three coins returned; if he had a flush, he would have seven coins returned, and so on, the payout getting larger with each improvement in the hand. If the player had bet two, three, or five coins, the payout would be two, three, or five times greater.

The Fortune Coin engineers decided to save some time and simply copy the payout table Frey and his men had developed, which was prominently displayed on every machine. But when one of the engineers went to a casino to copy it, he copied the table that represented a two-coin play, rather than a one-coin play. Using that table as their base payout, then multiplying by the number of coins played, Fortune Coin ended up with a payout table that was twice as generous as it should have been.

"They put it out in the field test with what was essentially a double pay, and they got wiped out," Frey laughed. "It was two or three weeks before they discovered the error, discovered that they were losing money terribly."[33]

Fortune Coin had also decided to sell their machines, not lease them as Si Redd was doing. This angered Redd, and he announced his intention to buy Fortune Coin to a few of his key employees. But when owner Stan Fulton turned him down flat, Redd decided to use the same ploy he had used successfully in acquiring Dale Electronics: he would hire away Walt Fraley, the chief engineer. Fraley agreed; after all it was Stan Fulton raking in all the money, not him. But he did have one condition: he wanted to be named general manager of

A-1 Supply and all its divisions. Redd agreed to the condition, and the deal was made.[34]

Dale Rodesch was not happy about this turn of events. He resigned from A-1 Supply to start Video Education, Inc., a company that developed video teaching machines for doctors. Si Redd's three-year management contract with Bally Manufacturing had ended at about this time and Dale Frey had now become solely an employee of A-1 Supply. Frey did not immediately resign, but he watched warily as Fraley came on board. By late 1979 Fraley had co-opted Frey's engineering responsibilities and stripped him of most of his duties, which made Frey resign.

Less than six months later, just as Redd had schemed, Stan Fulton sold him Fortune Coin for $1 million. Redd immediately began using the Fortune Coin platform for all their video poker machines, which they dubbed Fortune I Draw Poker. He transferred all video poker machine manufacturing to the Las Vegas facility he had acquired in the Fortune Coin purchase.

Walt Fraley had served his purpose well for Si Redd. Only a few months after Fulton sold out, Redd and Fraley decided to part company. What special consideration Redd gave Fraley was never made public, but it must have been substantial because Redd also cadged a multiyear noncompete clause out of his short-term general manager and chief engineer.

Si Redd now owned the only two companies in the world with the patents, background, technology, and expertise to manufacture video poker machines. He restructured his sales effort so he could either lease or sell the machines, at the customer's discretion, and he put an exorbitant $12,000 price tag on each machine that was sold. Nothing, however, was able to slow down the explosive growth and popularity video poker enjoyed over the next several years. By the time other companies were ready to launch their own version of the game, A-1 Supply and its successor companies had such a huge lead that they have never been caught, or even approached, in the thirty years since.

Very few men during the early experimental period of video poker, outside of the technology guys that were developing it, saw anything particularly noteworthy about the game. Bill O'Donnell of Bally certainly didn't, nor did the gaming entrepreneurial genius Jay Sarno. The one exception was Si Redd, the crafty old country boy from Mississippi.

Gaming pioneer Warren Nelson said, "Si turned the gaming industry upside down with his video poker machines."[35]

The Fortune I video draw poker machine, introduced in 1979 by Sircoma, the forerunner of International Game Technology, led the company to world dominance in slot machine manufacturing. *Courtesy of Marshall Fey.*

Pete Cladianos Jr., of the Sands Regency expounded on the point:

Si had the vision to see that video poker was going to be huge; Bally couldn't see that. As far as that goes, there weren't a lot of us around that *could* see that. . . . [W]e didn't visualize that anybody would play a video machine after having had reel machines all these years.

Si didn't care whether he sold them [or leased them]. He put the price up so high that not very many people bought them. He did the same thing with the Big Bertha machine. The first price on a Bertha was $40,000. Well, Bertha was probably the most profitable single machine around, but you couldn't run a bank of Berthas [due to their size]. You couldn't have thirty, forty, fifty Berthas, but you could have fifty video pokers.[36]

Despite the glowing praise for video poker, most of it was uttered or written after the game had achieved celebrity status. The earliest days, the first few months immediately after Redd put Fortune I Video Poker on the market, were far less dazzling. Most casino bosses still had their doubts. One of the game's earliest proponents was Boyd Gaming Group, headed by Las Vegas gaming legend Sam Boyd and his son Bill.

Sam Boyd had been a carnie man. During the Roaring Twenties he ran games of chance at the Long Beach Pike Amusement Park in California to help support his fatherless family. In 1941, he headed to Las Vegas with $41 in his pocket and big dreams in his head. He worked a number of casino jobs until he was able to buy a small interest in the Sahara Hotel-Casino that opened in 1952. His son Bill, a practicing attorney in the city from 1959 until 1974, joined his dad in the casino business when they opened the California Club Hotel & Casino in downtown Las Vegas in 1975. By 1979 they had built Sam's Town, the first of the city's casinos geared to locals.

"We got into video poker early on," Bill Boyd said. "One of the first games my dad dealt [in Las Vegas] was poker; he knew the game quite well, and he was really excited about video poker."[37]

Si Redd and Sam Boyd were almost the same age, and they had a similar pull-yourself-up-from-your-bootstraps type of history. They immediately became good friends, and Si and Bill later became close friends too. Bill Boyd related that video poker was an immediate hit at Sam's Town, but it took a little longer to catch on at the tourist-oriented California Club. However, within six months the game had taken off across the entire state, and nearly everyone jumped on the video poker bandwagon

With so many successful video slot machines rolling off the production line, Redd needed to increase the size of his slot route operation to place all those machines in casinos throughout Nevada and Atlantic City. In the early 1970s, he had loaned Bill Pennington and Bill Bennett $3.5 million to finalize their purchase of Circus Circus Casino from Jay Sarno. They had enjoyed such tremendous success in the hotel casino business since then that in 1978 they decided to sell off the lucrative slot machine route they had operated since 1971.[38] They approached Si Redd about buying it, and the timing was perfect. When he asked how much they wanted for the business, he was shocked—or at least he feigned shock.

"Three and a half million? You guys have to be nuts," he told them. "This may be worth three hundred, [but] I might [even] give you five hundred."[39] According to Redd's account, he eventually agreed to give them their full asking price, on one condition: he wanted to put one hundred video slots in their Las Vegas casino, and half that number when they opened a planned Reno property later that year. He would even put the slots in on a sixty-forty participating basis, he promised, with the larger number going to the casino. However, they would have to agree not to move the machines until his 40 percent take reached their $3.5 million asking price. The men agreed to the proposal.

Redd started a new company, Casino Services, for all his slot route operations. With the burgeoning success of video poker, the new company logged $7.8 million in revenue in 1979, and $18 million only two years later. In the same time frame it became the largest slot route operation in Nevada, operating 4800 machines. But the wily old businessman with coin machines coursing through his blood was far from finished.[40]

In late 1977 he formed another new division, The Antique Gambler, to renovate antique and collectible slot machines for resale. Dennis Salanti, an avid collector himself, was named general manager; and Redd appointed his wife Marilyn's son Roy Bunch as assistant general manager.[41]

Most coin-operated machine collectible companies were small, family-run operations. The Antique Gambler was far from that. The restoration facility included a dozen skilled technicians working in the mechanical department, wood shop, paint shop, parts department, remanufacturing workshop for making unavailable parts, and sales department. The business had been launched with the purchase of the inventory of a large, defunct Las Vegas slot machine manufacturer. It took four 40-foot semitrailer trucks just to haul all the parts up to Reno.

Salanti traveled the country buying old and abused three-reel slots, spare parts, repair manuals, and other equipment. Once back in Reno, every machine was expertly returned to original condition. Within a few years the business had over 1000 machines in stock or undergoing renovation. By 1980, Redd's stepson Roy Bunch had become general manager of the firm, and they had begun holding huge antique slot machine auctions annually.

In 1980 the three-day affair was held in the company's 115,000-square-foot facility in Las Vegas. Five hundred lots were on the auction block, including one hundred Grade 1 restorations of exceptional antique machines. A Nevada Gaming Control Board officer was on hand to ensure that every machine sold was legal in the state-of-residence of the buyer.

The star of the show was probably a Caille New Century Detroit slot machine from the turn of the century. It was completely restored inside and out, and authenticated as Grade 1 condition, the very best. It sold for $11,500.[42]

Given his broad and deep background with coin-operated machines, Si Redd personally became an avid collector of antique machines in the late 1970s. Tony Mills operated Mills Bell-O-Matic Corporation's large assembly plant in Reno. By the 1970s, Mills had assembled a prestigious collection of antique slot and amusement machines that was on display at his Reno factory. Si Redd approached Mills about buying the collection, which totaled about sixty machines. Mills agreed, and Redd paid him $90,000 for the entire collection.[43]

When Redd passed away in 2003, his collection, which he maintained at his home, was recognized as one of the finest in the nation.

* * * *

The decade of the 1970s ended with one more significant development for Si Redd and his growing enterprises. In 1979 he changed the name of his company from A-1 Supply Company to Sircoma. The name was an acronym for *SI Redd COin MAchines,* and had been conceived by his secretary, Barbara Rich. Around this time, he also took one more half-hearted stab at selling his company before the decade was out. But like so many Si Redd ventures, it failed when he pushed the envelope a little too hard.

Redd and his key people had been meeting with a small group of men from Chicago who represented a large Illinois conglomerate.[44] They were very interested in purchasing Sircoma, and the deal had advanced to the final stage. Over dinner at Carson City's finest restaurant, the last few details were worked out and the men shook hands on the agreement. It was decided they would all meet at Sircoma headquarters the next morning to sign the necessary paperwork.

Redd had recently hired a controller for Sircoma, Elwin "El" Studebaker, from Los Angeles. The next morning both men arrived early at the facility, and Redd called Studebaker into his office. "I'm going to try to get a new Cadillac every other year out of this deal," Studebaker recalled Redd telling him. The new controller advised against the idea, having had experience in such matters.

"We all shook hands on the deal, Mr. Redd," Studebaker said. "I think it's a big mistake to try for any more now."[45]

But Redd was adamant, saying that the additional cost of a few cars was puny compared to the multimillion-dollar size of the deal. "I'll blame it on Mrs. Redd if it's a problem," Redd said.

Later that morning the two teams sat down in the conference room, and Redd dropped his bombshell, ascribing the idea to his wife. But we had a deal; we all shook hands on it, the chief Chicago negotiator said, whereupon the entire Chicago team stood up and walked out of the room without another word.

"Si always wanted a little bit more than the figures would support," Studebaker said. That was the last serious attempt that Redd would make to sell his company for the next fifteen years.

One of the very first gaming people Redd had met in Reno was the Club Cal-Neva's managing partner Warren Nelson. The men had become good friends, and Redd invited Nelson to join Sircoma's board of directors and buy stock in the company. "I bought twenty thousand shares at five dollars a share," Nelson said. "[A year later] I bought another hundred thousand shares. It was definitely a good buy!"[46] Nelson's comment would turn out to be a colossal understatement.

The 1970s had been a very prosperous decade for Si Redd. Controller Studebaker said Redd's estate at that time was worth between $10 and $12 million, making it a good decade indeed. But the 1980s would be even better.

—— CHAPTER 10 ——

KING OF THE SLOTS

In 1980, an article ran in *Loose Change* magazine, one of the slot industry's leading journals, calling Si Redd "King of the Slots."[1] The recognition provided a level of fame and acceptance that the rarely bashful salesman reveled in. Newspaper stories, magazine articles, and TV interviews immediately began using the moniker whenever they referred to Redd, and he loved it.

Although the pithy sobriquet and its use in the mainstream media made Redd more recognizable to the general public, he was already a legend in the coin-operated amusement industry, even though he had abandoned that business for gaming more than thirteen years earlier. Randy Fromm, today publisher of *Slot Tech* magazine, was a young technical writer for another magazine in 1980, attending the AMOA Expo, the coin-op amusement industry's big annual trade show in Chicago. After a short walk to look at the exhibits, Fromm returned to his company's booth on the expo floor to find a stranger sitting in the booth surrounded by "a virtual parade of show-goers, all of whom seemed to know this guy," Fromm said. "It was like something from *The Godfather,* as folks were lined up to shake his hand."[2]

The visitor, Fromm would soon discover, was Si Redd. His boss explained that Redd still loved the business, and often stopped by to reminisce and chat with old friends. Fromm met Redd that day, and twenty-one years later would be one of the last media people to interview the then-ailing legend who was just shy of his ninetieth birthday.

Redd's nickname, "King of the Slots," would even be featured on a number of official proclamations. On November 14, 1981, Las Vegas Mayor Bill Briare proclaimed the day "Si Redd 'King of Slots' Day" in honor of Redd's seventieth birthday.[3] He was awarded similar proclamations from the state of Nevada and Clark County. All these honors were presented during a surprise black-tie birthday party at the swank Las Vegas Hilton. And was he surprised! Redd had been told to don his best tuxedo for a meeting with German government officials who were interested in his company's expansion plans. When he and wife Marilyn entered Dining Room A at the hotel, they were greeted with a raucous "Surprise! Happy Birthday, Si!" from the 250 assembled VIPs, dignitaries, and friends.[4]

Naturally, Redd had to endure a roast. "Si, you couldn't sell soup to the sick," Bob Cashell, master of ceremonies, chairman of the University of Nevada Board of Regents, and later multiterm mayor of Reno, scolded him in a good-natured way.[5] Later in the evening, to the cheers and applause of all the beautiful people in attendance, Marilyn Redd presented Si with a birthday gift. It was an announcement that a quarter-million-dollar donation had been made in his name to the University of Nevada–Las Vegas for construction of a boosters' lounge—the Si Redd Room—at the new UNLV 18,000-seat sports pavilion. It was a wonderful gift for a man who meant so much to the state; and it was just the first of many large donations the Redds would make to the Nevada university system.

Marilyn's generous gift to her husband also provided one of those it's-a-small-world moments for the couple. A few weeks after the birthday bash, UNLV Athletic Director Brad Rothermel phoned Redd and asked if he and Marilyn would accompany him to Reno for a formal acceptance of their gift by the university's Board of Regents. Redd accepted the invitation, and even volunteered they could take his private plane up to Reno for the ceremony.

Rothermel had never met Si Redd in person, although they had spoken on the phone a number of times. When they all met at the airport, it instantly hit Rothermel that he knew Redd from somewhere, but he couldn't put his finger on it. Comfortably seated in the plane, the two men began chatting about their backgrounds. When Redd mentioned that he had run some pinball machine routes in Illinois during the late 1930s and early 1940s, Rothermel thought, "That's it!"

In the spring and summer of 1942, nearly forty years earlier, five-year-old Brad often hung out in his father's gas station, Rothermel's

Si Redd clowns around on his seventieth birthday party in 1981. *Redd family photo.*

Highway Garage, in Monroe Center, Illinois, a small village near Rockford. The tiny Gulf Oil filling station had the only pinball machine in Monroe Center, and it had always fascinated the youngster. "I couldn't even see [the pinball machine]," Rothermel recalled. "[W]hen someone came in to play the pinball I had to get a chair . . . and stand on it just to [watch] the game."[6]

He clearly remembered that once a week a young man came in and emptied the coins out of the machine, and split them with his father. He also remembered that man was a much younger and stockier Si Redd. Si, Marilyn, and Brad all got a huge laugh out of the amazing coincidence. But what was even stranger was that a very similar incident happened a second time soon afterwards.

Mead Dixon, the highly respected gaming attorney who had a strong hand in running Harrah's following the death of Bill Harrah and who guided the company during its merger with Holiday Inns, had always admired the innovative vision Si Redd brought to the gaming industry. When Bill Harrah was alive, he had often thought of building his own slot machines, and in the late 1970s and early 1980s Mead Dixon contemplated buying Redd's Sircoma and its broad offering of video games for Harrah's casinos.[7]

Dixon and Redd had at least one thing in common. Dixon hailed from Springfield, Illinois. His father's family founded Dixon, Illinois, which is just a stone's throw up the Rock River from Sterling, where Si Redd had spent his years as a Wurlitzer jukebox route operator. In fact, Redd had run a number of successful jukebox routes in Dixon, and the two men knew many of the same stores and merchants on the main street.

The years leading up to the death of Bill Harrah had been lean years for the company. After Harrah's death, looking for ways to improve the company's financial picture, Dixon considered purchasing Sircoma. He went to the main facility at 520 South Rock Boulevard in Reno to have a look at the operation. Of that visit he wrote:

At Si Redd's plant, I saw all of these empty cases—housings—out back in the warehouse. It turned out that what Si needed for his video slot machines was a cathode ray tube—he needed a television screen. He was acquiring screens to put in his slot machines by buying televisions, throwing away the cabinets, receivers and controls, and keeping the boob tubes. I took one look at that and I thought, "What an opportunity there would be here just to buy the tubes instead." But I guess Si's numbers were strong enough that he hadn't bothered to find a contractor to provide the tubes. There was such a tremendous markup in his slots . . . that he could afford to buy televisions, keep the tubes, and throw the rest away.[8]

When Dixon presented his idea to buy Sircoma to the Holiday Inn brass, however, they thought it would be deviating from their principal business, and passed on the opportunity. Taking a longer view, Dixon said with a wry smile, "In hindsight, we made the wrong decision. Look at IGT today."

What was the magic in these new video slot machines, particularly the draw poker, that completely transformed the slot machine industry in the early 1980s, and made Si Redd a gaming legend and a wealthy man? Poker slots were certainly not new. In fact, the first poker slot preceded Charles Fey's invention of the traditional three-reel one-armed bandit by almost a decade. Fey's grandson, slot machine historian and author Marshall Fey, tabbed San Francisco as the "cradle of the slot machine." The City by the Bay was where his grandfather perfected his history-making machine, and where many other inventive souls came up with their own variations of coin-operated gambling devices.

But strangely, it was nearly 3000 miles east of San Francisco that the poker slot machine was invented. In 1891 Sittman & Pitt of Brooklyn come up with the first poker machine. It had five rotating drums, or reels, each carrying drawings of ten different playing cards on the face of the reels. The machines were called drop-card machines because two cards were dropped from each deck, usually the ten of spades and jack of hearts. This greatly reduced the chances of a player getting a royal flush, which paid the highest prize total.

A player would drop a nickel in the slot and pull a lever, setting the five reels spinning. When the reels stopped, the five cards showing in the window were the player's hand. On these early machines there was no opportunity for the player to discard and draw new cards. Despite that, the game proved to be so popular with gamblers that one would have been hard-pressed to find a bar in New York City that didn't have at least one poker machine beside the bar. There were no payoff mechanisms in the machines—the bartender would award the winning player a cigar or a free beer if he got a pair of kings or better.

It didn't take long for Sittman & Pitt's poker machine to make its way to the unofficial gambling capital of the wild wild West, San Francisco. Here inventors such as Charles Fey soon developed their own versions of the game. On many of these, actual playing cards were held by clips to the five reels, replacing Sittman & Pitt's painted cards. As the reels stopped, an actual card flipped up into place, providing a more realistic poker experience.

One of Charles Fey's early poker models held a sign on the front where the number of cigars a player could win was displayed:

FREE CIGARS

Royal Flush	100
Straight Flush	40
Four of a Kind	15
Full Hand	10
Flush	8
Straight	6

An 1897 Royal Perfection poker machine shows the cards being held by clips to the five rotating drums. Only fifty of the fifty-two cards were used, and the player had to play the initial hand without a chance to draw new cards. *Courtesy of Marshall Fey.*

Three of a Kind	3
Two Pairs	2
Pair of Kings, Aces	1[9]

San Francisco's notorious Barbary Coast and Tenderloin districts soon bristled with the new machines. Marshall Fey wrote, "By 1890 the city had 3,117 licensed establishments which sold liquor, amounting to one license for every 96 inhabitants. The sheer number of businesses selling spirits combined with disreputable city politics, made the wide open city a natural locus for nickel-in-the-slot machines."[10]

It was only a matter of time before these gambling devices would make their way across the Sierra Nevadas and into Nevada's many mining towns and camps. A February 21, 1895, item in the *Pioche Weekly Record* in southeastern Nevada announced, "N.P. Dooley arrived Thursday evening from San Francisco. He left on Monday's stage for DeLamar, and will take charge of his store there. He brought back with him a nickel-in-the-slot machine, and considerable sport has been the result of continually dropping of nickels in the slot."[11] The slot machine had found its natural home at last.

For the next eighty-five years, poker slots represented a very small percentage of overall slot machine production. Charles Fey's traditional three-reel one-armed bandit, Liberty Bell, was king and accounted for the vast majority of all slot machine production. All other slot machines, including poker, were considered "novelty" machines, and barely made a dent in the market.

All of that changed with Si Redd's video slots. There were a number of reasons why his video draw poker machines became such an instant hit with players. First, unlike other slot machines, in draw poker the player makes decisions that affect the outcome of each game. He decides which cards to hold, and which ones to discard, and his reasoning and skill have an impact on his chance to win. Real strategy is involved in the game, and the player is an active participant, not just someone who set the reels spinning. Strategy is so important in video poker that a handful of people who have mastered the game are even able to make a living—in some cases, a very attractive living—playing video poker professionally.[12]

William N. Thompson is a professor of public administration at the University of Nevada–Las Vegas, author of the book *Gambling in America,* and one of the nation's top gaming experts. He told the *Los Angeles Times,* "Video poker machines made amateur players think they were playing a casino game rather than just pulling a handle."

The second reason the draw poker machine became so popular was that it turned a competitive game into solitaire. Every large casino has a poker room where players can sit across from six or seven other players and play poker against one another. But there are millions of folks, many of them women, who are not comfortable playing against others. They don't have the skill, the knowledge, or the self-confidence to play head-to-head against another player. In video poker, it's just the player against the machine, and the machine is nonconfrontational. It never laughs at your mistakes, scoffs at your poor choice of discards, or curses angrily when you win a hand.

For this reason, video poker created an entirely new generation of players numbering in the millions who had never been regular casino customers. This fact was ultimately responsible for shifting the casino industry's reliance on a small cadre of high rollers who favor card games or dice to a mass market of small bettors who prefer video slot machines, primarily poker.

Si Redd voiced another reason for the game's popularity. "[W]hat makes the poker [machine] work is the fact that it is more . . . liberal as a slot machine. People play the same amount of money, but unknowingly at first, we made the poker machine different. There are more buttons to push. It takes you a little longer to play, [and] you're getting a better entertainment value."[13]

Redd and his key people did discover early on, however, that perhaps they hadn't made the machine quite liberal enough. In its earliest days, payoffs for Sircoma's Fortune I poker game did not begin until the player had achieved two pair; anything less than that was a losing hand. When the initial video poker craze began to pale, IGT quickly made two design changes. First, they began returning the player's money when he achieved a pair of jacks or better; and second, the machines were reprogrammed so they could accumulate credits, rather than returning coins after every break-even or winning hand. These two changes revitalized the game, and it continued its unbelievable growth.[14]

The final factor that led video poker in revolutionizing the slot machine industry was the growth of what are called neighborhood casinos in Nevada's gambling capital, Las Vegas. In the early 1980s, Clark County, Las Vegas' home county, had a population of 463,000 people. By 2006 that number had swelled to nearly two million, a staggering 432 percent increase. A few farsighted local gaming companies, most notably Station Casinos and Coast Casinos, believed this provided a huge untapped market. Many of these local residents, they reasoned, had a proclivity for gambling but would not venture out into the city's tourist-oriented gaming corridors to play.

The granddaddy of all Las Vegas' locals' casinos is Sam's Town, opened in 1979 by gaming pioneer Sam Boyd, now Boyd Gaming Corporation. Built on the Boulder Highway, in the eastern suburbs, the huge property has been a hit with local residents since it opened. Station Casinos' foray into the locals' market began with Palace

Station, which had its beginning in 1976 as Bingo Palace. Today Station Casinos owns all or part of eighteen locals' casinos, while Boyd Gaming owns four. A few other large properties under other ownership also serve primarily the locals' market.

Make no mistake: these locals' casinos are not small sawdust joints. They are huge, sprawling gaming-lodging-dining-entertainment complexes that feature such popular locals' amenities as excellent restaurants, multiscreen movie theaters, bowling lanes, arenas, concert venues, and hockey rinks. Although they all offer a full range of table and slot machine gaming opportunities, video poker machines are their bread and butter.

Professor Thompson said of Redd's video poker, "His machine became the most important device" in attracting players to the new neighborhood casinos.[15]

Even folks who wouldn't visit a casino under any circumstance could play the video poker machines. In Nevada, grocery stores, convenience stores, and drug stores all installed poker machines to attract players. And saloons, taverns and restaurants with cocktail bars filled their long, open expanses of bar tops with drop-in video poker games.

One additional factor spurred video poker's popularity also in the growing Atlantic City market. In New Jersey's early days of casino gambling, the casinos had no poker tables, so the video poker slots, which were approved for play in Atlantic City in 1981, provided an outlet for those who liked to play the game.

Other broader societal factors were also at play in the game's popularity surge: a new, technology-oriented society; increasing acceptance of gambling as entertainment; increased legalization of gambling nationally and worldwide; and the emergence of a young generation of video game players.

This latter factor would become even more important to casino video machines as the audience for video games continued to expand and to age. Like twins who are permanently separated at birth, video games and video slot machines moved down separate life paths, but never lost the DNA that tied them together. As each succeeding generation of youngsters learned as tots to play Odyssey, Pong, Asteroids, Missile Command, Donkey Kong, Super Mario Bros., Mortal Kombat, and so on, and as video games moved from the laboratory to the video arcade to the living room to the cell phone, one new generation of video slot machine prospects piled on another until they each, in their turn, began to reach the magic age of twenty-one. Video games, in effect, had become the farm system for future video slot machines, and despite the evils that might be inherent in such a system, it promised decades of prosperity for casino owners and for the leading maker of video slots, International Game Technology (IGT).

All of these factors coalesced at about the same time, creating a "perfect storm" opportunity for Sircoma and its successor, IGT. As Chuck Mathewson, then IGT's chairman and chief executive, told the *New York Times* in 1989, "The lowly slot machine is now the lifeblood of the casino industry."[16]

From a manufacturing standpoint too, video slot machines with microprocessors were superior to the old mechanical, electromechanical, and even electronic slots. With the older technologies, each type of slot machine required a different mechanism and cabinet, a practice that was both expensive and wasteful. With new microprocessors and a video tube, a reel-type, fruit-symbol slot machine could be transformed into a blackjack game, a dice game, a poker game, or almost any other game with only a few basic programming changes. This dramatically reduced manufacturing costs for Redd's company at the same time as the demand was skyrocketing.[17]

There were also a number of significant advantages in the new machines—in fact, in all slot machines powered by microprocessors—for the casinos too. The machines required less maintenance, slot machine cheating was vastly reduced, and individual machine and player tracking was made possible.

All of these factors contributed to the fact that in 1983 in Nevada, slot revenues exceeded table game revenues for the first time, a trend that has continued to this day. In 2007, for instance, slot revenue accounted for 65.8 percent of all statewide casino revenues.

Table 10.1 IGT 5-Year Financial & Performance Summary, Selected Categories* (Dollars in thousands)

	1979	1980	1981	1982	1983
Total Revenue	$18,683	$39,506	$61,510	$62,199	$60,032
Net Income	1,135	7,251	13,892	8,403	8,657
Stockholders Equity Per Share	0.31	1.70	4.62	5.31	6.52
Total Assets	17,244	31,144	51,316	62,535	77,951
No. Employees at Year's End	77	398	517	506	626

*(This table provides a look at selected Sircoma/IGT's key indicators during the five-year period from 1979 through 1983 and indicates the impact the severe recession of 1980–1982 and increased gaming machine manufacturing competition had on the company. *Source*: IGT Annual Report, 1983.)

Si Redd had learned his lesson of not trying to do everything himself. He had been burned badly on a number of occasions, and had resolved not to let it happen again. So in June1980 he hired a veteran Harrah's gaming executive, J. George Drews, to be president of Sircoma.

Drews was a native of Wilmington, Delaware. He had received a B.S. degree in engineering at the U.S. Coast Guard Academy, and later an MBA in business administration from Harvard Graduate School of Business. A serious, stern-looking young man, Drews entered gaming in 1971 as the controller for Harrah's, quickly rising to executive vice president of finance and administration. He was instrumental in taking Harrah's public in 1971 and having it listed on the New York Stock Exchange two years later. He also developed an outstanding reputation among Wall Street's leading financial institutions. But in 1980, when Holiday Inn took over Harrah's, Drews was forced to resign. Si Redd immediately offered him the position of president, chief executive officer, and director of Sircoma, retaining the title of chairman for himself.[18]

With Redd's backing, Drews had the company renamed in September 1981 to International Game Technology (IGT), and took the company public with a listing on the NASDAQ exchange.[19] Redd held on to just over half of the outstanding shares of the company in his name and the name of his deceased wife Ivy, in her trust.

By this time, Redd had elevated El Studebaker, who had been hired as Sircoma's controller, to the position of his personal accountant. At his own request, Studebaker fulfilled that position as a consultant rather than an employee. He recalled those days when IGT was first born. Redd himself had come up with the idea of using the acronym IGT, Studebaker said, because he thought it sounded a lot like IBM, which was the New York Stock Exchange's darling at that time.[20] Although his company was on NASDAQ, Redd was already looking forward to the day it would join industry leaders on the Big Board.

Drews built a solid management team over the next year or so that included Jon N. Bengston as vice president of marketing; Clarence Thiesen as vice president of finance; Robert Carabine as vice president of operations; Raymond Pike as vice president, secretary, and general counsel; and Robert Denz as vice president of lottery development. Like Drews, many on the team came from Harrah's.

In the earliest days of the company, these men had a tiger by the tail. In 1979 Sircoma had 12,000 video machines in gaming markets in Nevada and New Jersey. They had manufacturing or service facilities in Reno, Las Vegas, and Elko, Nevada, and Atlantic City, New

Jersey. They also had foreign plants in Great Britain and Australia. In the latter country they signed an agreement with Ainsworth Industries, manufacturers of Aristocrat gaming machines, in which each company would act as distributor for the other's products in its home country.[21]

Three years later, IGT had more than 20,000 machines placed worldwide. The company employed nearly 600 men and women and had over 300,000 square feet of facilities. Five years earlier, video slot machines had accounted for only 1 percent of the installed base of slots, but that figure had swelled to 20 percent, and IGT had supplied 80 percent of that number.[22]

A paragraph in the 1981 IGT Annual Report summed up the company's staggering growth: "[I]n the past four years, revenues have surged from $3 million to $62 million; net earnings have grown from $300,000 to $14 million; equity has increased from $250,000 to $34 million."

The fledging company had taken a towering stance in the gaming machine industry by the early 1980s, and it was beginning to garner national attention. *Inc.,* the national business magazine, ranked International Game Technology twenty-fourth in a 1982 list of the nation's fastest-growing publicly traded companies, and *Forbes* magazine named it on its list of "Up and Comers," the top 150 most promising small companies in the nation.[23]

This skyrocketing growth was the result of great timing and a superior product. In 1982 *Public Gaming* magazine asked Redd about the profitability for the casino industry of video draw poker versus regular slot machines. "We've got that down in black and white," IGT's chairman responded. "Poker machines are ahead 2-to-1 from the regular slot machines in Nevada."

"Here in Nevada," he continued, "people have been playing the slot machines for more than 50 years. It's something new to be able to sit down and make your own decisions playing poker. . . . They'll play them for four hours rather than one hour. We have some places that have 98 percent play . . . and that's 24 hours a day. It's unreal."[24]

Like any natural-born salesman, Si Redd was at his very best when he had a new product he firmly believed in. When he would begin talking about the video poker machines to a prospect, he could work himself into a lather in a matter of minutes. Mickey Roemer, who had been in sales at IGT before he was chosen to head the company's statewide progressive jackpot project, made a number of sales calls with Redd.

"Si was a remarkable salesperson, and to watch him work was really something," Roemer recalled. "[H]e was very flamboyant and wasn't afraid to ask for the sale. I've seen him swear on his mother's grave, and promise that this particular product is the best thing ever for the customer, and almost get down on one knee. . . . [Y]ou could almost see a tear in his eye."[25]

Redd was always ready to cut a deal in order to make a sale, Roemer said. "The accounting department even had a fulltime guy going along behind him to make sure all the paperwork was done correctly, so they could bill it out."

Dwayne Kling, then general manager of Reno's Horseshoe Club, recalled an incident when Redd made a sales call on him and the casino owner. The two men were waiting in the upstairs restaurant when Redd arrived, waving his arms in the air and talking in a high state of animation. "He moved around—he jumped around a lot—he was never still," Kling said.[26]

Redd sputtered, "You can't believe how many people I saw down there [on the slot floor] playing those IGT machines. You gotta get some more of my machines in there." Redd sat for a minute, sipped his coffee, then jumped up and ran back downstairs to check the machines again. In a few minutes he was back upstairs with another breathless update. "He was a pretty hyper fellow, pretty active," Kling smiled.

Rick Carter, who would partner with Redd in a failed Mississippi gambling ship venture in 1989, also enjoyed repeating stories about Si Redd's great salesmanship.

"He was sitting outside the office of a big casino operator one time, and he could overhear the conversation going on inside between the boss and one of his managers," Carter related.[27] The boss was telling his underling that he had to beat Redd down on his price for a big slot machine order they were ready to place.

"He's a tough negotiator, but I'm gonna show you how to work Si Redd," the boss said confidently, as Carter related the story.

Having overheard all this, Redd was ready when he was ushered into the office. Before anyone else could speak, he began apologizing. "I've got to apologize to you," he said pleadingly. "I've made a tremendous mistake and there's no way I can sell you those machines at this price. I have to go back and re-figure and re-bid it."

The boss was furious. "Doggone it, Si," he sputtered angrily, "there's no way you're going to do that. A deal is a deal, and I'm going to hold you to it."

After a few more moments of groveling, Redd finally relented and agreed to honor the earlier price. That was Si Redd when he knew he had a great product to offer his prospect.

In the 1990s, after an aging Si Redd had left IGT and become involved in a number of shaky business ventures, he still never lost his instinct for making the sale. Rhett Long, an executive who worked for Redd while he was developing Si Redd's Oasis Resort in Mesquite, Nevada, saw that Redd magic in action many times.

"Si . . . could sell ice to Eskimos," Long recalled. Remembering one of Redd's favorite gambits, Long said, "[He] always wore a fake Rolex watch, and he would say to a prospect, 'If I'm not telling you the truth, I'll give you the watch off my arm.'" Then he would strip the faux Rolex off, hand it to the prospect, and say, "That's how confident I am that I'm telling the truth."[28]

But just as in Redd's earlier days, Long contended he had to spend much of his time following behind the boss cleaning up his deal-making messes.

* * * *

Although IGT seemed to have everything going its way, dark clouds had begun to form over the casino industry. An October 1981 article in the *Nevada State Journal* was headlined "Tough Times Ahead for Reno."

Economic sluggishness will probably continue to repress business conditions in the Truckee Meadows during the next few months, a University of Nevada–Reno economist said Tuesday. Other business observers concurred.

Nationally, most economic analysts believe a recession is well under way. . . . "Without question, the economy has been slowing down here. And I would look for that to continue," [Thomas] Cargill said. "It's going to be a tough time for some gaming operators—no question about it," [Jerry] Higgins [executive director of the Gaming Association of Nevada] added.[29]

The recession of the early to mid-1980s turned out to be the most severe since the Great Depression, and it had a daunting impact on gaming and, therefore, on IGT. On top of that, the impact of new slot machine competition, both domestic and foreign, was beginning to become a problem for the men in IGT's executive offices.

Table 10.2 Nevada State Gross Gaming Revenue*

Year	Total Win (000)
1955	$ 108,173
1960	200,500
1965	321,331
1970	584,416
1975	1,127,738
1980	2,383,418*
1985	3,314,433
1990	5,459,411
1995	7,368,612
2000	9,589,510
2005	11,649,703

*In 1979 Sircoma introduced their Fortune I color video poker machine. (The impact of the broadening of Nevada's gaming base by video poker is shown in this table of Nevada's Gross Gaming Revenue, or the total amount of money won by all legal gaming properties in the state. Naturally there were also other factors at play, but most experts agree that video poker was the most significant factor in this growth. *Source*: Nevada Gaming Control Board.)

Si Redd had meant it when he hired George Drews as president and promised he could run IGT without interference. But as trouble set in, the old warhorse couldn't just sit back and watch everything he had spent more than a half century building simply fall to pieces. IGT's stock had opened at $11 a share in 1981, and had risen to $16, but by 1983 it had fallen back precipitously. So Redd began needling Drews, and once again taking a more active role in the company's day-to-day affairs.

It would be difficult to picture two more diverse individuals than George Drews and Si Redd. Drews was a university-trained engineer and businessman, an advanced-degree graduate of Harvard Business School and an expert in finance, administration, and Wall Street matters. He came to work in expensive, perfectly tailored suits, and could comfortably sip tea with the Queen of England if called upon.

Redd, on the other hand, often wore brightly colored shirts and an old-fashioned bolo tie, and could swap raucous stories with the best of them. His level of sophistication fell considerably south of the Mason-Dixon Line, and the Queen would probably not have consented to share even the same day of the week with him.

As their business became more of a dogfight than a stroll in the park, the two men grated on each other more and more frequently.

A number of IGT observers at the time said both men had tremendous egos, and did not get along well together. The two men also saw the direction in which the company should be heading very differently. Before Drews came on board, Redd had built a very strong slot route operation. Running routes was a business Redd understood, one he had been involved with in Mississippi, Illinois, and New England before he even came to Nevada. He believed route operations were an integral part of the company's future.

Drews saw it differently, and in the early 1980s he sold off some of the company's route operations to raise cash. Redd was furious. "He did it in order to feather his own nest," he charged. "Selling off my routes that I love and at the same time not treating the customer right. . . . [H]e did it for two reasons. He didn't understand it. He didn't like it."[30]

Redd's secretary, Barbara Rich, said Redd had grown unhappy and dissatisfied that he had ever agreed to take the company public. "He really didn't like the corporate world," she said. "He'd lost control, and he didn't like to lose control. His thing was being in control. . . . [I]t was his entrepreneur personality. [He] didn't want somebody, some board, telling [him] what to do."[31]

By the end of 1983 IGT had also entered the rapidly growing state lottery business.[32] Nearly twenty years earlier New Hampshire had become the first U.S. state to install a lottery, and by 1983 twenty-two states and Canadian provinces operated them, with aggregate annual sales over $7 billion dollars. The company owned 50 percent of IGT Nebraska, and it was conducting video lotteries for a number of Nebraska local governments, its test market for this new product line.

IGT's video lottery game terminals brought an entirely new gaming experience to lottery players, and the company's central lottery computers, tied to all video lottery terminals, provided complete tracking and reporting to lottery management. The company had also purchased an 80 percent interest in Electronic Display Technology, a manufacturer of large award systems and promotional displays for casinos. (This deal is discussed more fully later in this chapter.) And finally, IGT had introduced their new and improved Fortune II video slot machine product line.

Foreign sales were also becoming a larger part of IGT's balance sheet. President George Drews pointed out in a newspaper article that Nevada had only about 80,000 slot machines installed, and Atlantic City another 15,000 by the early 1980s. But the rest of the world had a whopping 700,000 machines in play. "We have done virtually zero in that market," Drews remarked.[33]

West Germany particularly looked promising. More than 200,000 arcade gaming slot machines were in play there, and a strange quirk in German law required that the machines be destroyed and replaced every three years. By early 1983 IGT had an application for licensing before German officials that would soon be passed, making the company the first American slot maker to enter the market. Deals in Japan, Spain, Australia, and Great Britain were also at various stages of development for IGT.

IGT was now manufacturing twelve distinct gaming machines, most in a number of different configurations, and four gray-area amusement games. But it had its eye on a number of new machines, particularly for the foreign markets. Innovation in product development had become the firm's corporate culture, and Si Redd spent more money on research and development than any of his competitors. He realized that with present technology, the only limit on the type of games IGT could produce was the limit of their own imaginations. For instance, video draw poker, by far the firm's most potent product line, now included regular draw poker, joker poker, two-handed poker, and drop-in bar poker, with a number of other variations under development. Big Bertha had given birth to Mini Bertha, and Mini Bertha had four variations, whereas video twenty-one, or blackjack, now came in standard twenty-one, live twenty-one, two-hand twenty-one, and players' edge twenty-one.

Si Redd also spent some of his time seeking new opportunities, both for the company and for his own personal portfolio of investments. A handful of plays that came up in the early 1980s showed great promise, he believed, and he pursued all of them in a manner that was purely Redd.

When engineer Dale Frey left Sircoma in the late 1970s, he and Dale Rodesch had decided to team up again. They started a new company called Dale Associates (not to be confused with the earlier Dale Electronics). Rodesch was working on a horse-racing game, and Frey's vision was to come up with a new version of draw poker, one that was different from anything currently on the market—"the Cadillac of draw pokers," Rodesch termed it.[34]

Frey drew up engineering specs for his new poker game, and the two men prepared a business plan and began soliciting financing. Si Redd heard about their plans and said he would be interested in seeing the specs for the poker game. Rather naively, given their past histories with Redd, they agreed and sent him the plans.

"The next thing we knew," Dale Rodesch said, "we were served with a lawsuit by Si, claiming Frey had appropriated the idea from Sircoma."[35]

Neither Rodesch nor Frey was ever deposed for the lawsuit, however, according to Rodesch, but it accomplished its purpose. "It prevented our getting third-party financing so long as the suit hung over our heads," he said. The Cadillac of poker was never produced.

Rodesch did proceed with his horse-racing game, and once again he received a phone call from Si Redd. "Boy," Redd said—using a moniker he often used with younger men, which wasn't a sign of disrespect; Redd simply had a faulty memory for names—"I understand you have a new horse race game and I'd like to come by and see it."[36]

Rodesch agreed, and Redd showed up a few days later with his chief engineer and a couple of other men. Rodesch's game featured a laser disc as a prerecorded source of actual race footage, and he showed the men his prototype. A few days later Redd called again and asked for another meeting. He asked Rodesch what kind of a deal he was looking for, and when Rodesch answered, Redd, feigning shock, said, "Boy, you must be crazy!"

Rodesch held his ground, and Redd left, probably calculating that eventually the stubborn man would have to relent. But Rodesch had not told him everything: he already had an agreement with Mickey Wichinsky in Las Vegas to buy and produce the game, and that deal went forward.

Rodesch and Wichinsky, who had both come out on the short end of previous dealings with Si Redd, must have appreciated the moment. It was a grand victory, evidenced by the fact that the game, Quarter Horse, has been in continuous production ever since, and is successfully operating in more than twenty countries around the world.

The second deal that Si Redd engineered was his purchase of another small but growing Las Vegas firm, Electronic Display Technology, or EDT.[37] John Acres, EDT's owner at the time, has gone on to become one of the most prolific and respected men in the development of casino games, slot player tracking systems, and progressive jackpot systems. But in the early 1980s his small company was devoted primarily to designing and building a progressive jackpot system for casinos. A progressive slot machine is one that is linked to other machines—either at one casino, or regionally at a number of casinos—to provide a bigger jackpot. A small percentage of each coin played is added to the progressive jackpot for all the linked machines, which results in a large, constantly growing jackpot. An electronic reader board is attached to each machine, or group of machines, and it constantly changes as the jackpot grows.

IGT had developed its own progressive system—they would later develop Megabucks, the world's largest progressive jackpot system—but in the early 1980s Redd was still searching for ways to improve IGT's progressive system. EDT looked like it could be the answer.

One morning, according to his account, John Acres received a phone call. "Well, hello, boy! I've heard good things about you. I'd like to come by for a visit," Si Redd greeted Acres. An hour later Redd arrived at Acres's office, full of Mississippi homilies and flattering platitudes about Acres and his progressive jackpot system.[38]

Acres felt his system was superior to IGT's, and cheaper to boot. "That might sound boastful," he said, "though we won every order on which we competed [against IGT]."

Redd visited for an hour, suggested the two men should look for ways to work together, then left. Acres didn't know what to make of the visit until he received a phone call about a week later from the Riverside Casino in Laughlin, Nevada, about an hour southeast of Las Vegas, where he planned to install one of his progressive jackpot systems.

"I listened quietly as the slot manager said he wanted to cancel the order because IGT had lowered their price," Acres said. When he reminded the manager that his system was superior, Acres couldn't believe it when the man said, "Yes, but IGT's price is free. You can't beat free!"[39]

When a number of similar calls followed, Acres angrily phoned Si Redd. "There must be something wrong on this end," Redd told him innocently. "Boy, I can't run a business giving stuff away for free." Redd promised he'd look into it and call Acres back.

A few days later Acres found himself sitting across from Redd while the older man, oozing his best country boy charm, proposed he'd help Acres out of his jam by buying 90 percent of EDT for a figure Acres described as "one zero shy of fair."

"Look, boy, this is how business is done," Acres said Redd told him. "If I were a mean SOB, I could just run you into the ground and leave you with nothing." "He'd won, and he clearly knew it," Acres said. "This was simply a test to see if I could muster the courage to ask for more."

Acres eventually agreed to sell 80 percent to IGT, and at a higher price, but he was, by his own admission, a beaten man. About two years later he sold his remaining stake in EDT and went on to a great career in gaming—a sadder, poorer, but wiser man.[40]

****

In addition to the recession that slowed casino earnings and IGT's sales during the early 1980s, the company would also face a much greater challenge, and a much more powerful opponent, only a short time later. In mid-1982 Bally Manufacturing Corporation introduced its own video poker machine and put it on trial at the Frontier Hotel-Casino in Las Vegas. When he discovered it, Si Redd was furious.

Bally had signed a five-year noncompete agreement with Redd for all video slot machines when the two had parted company in 1978. That agreement was not due to expire until May 1983; yet Bally was trying to fudge it by one year.

"We were becoming a huge monster against their competition," IGT chairman Redd said. "They took the gambling risk that they'd win the case, or we might not fight them. . . . [T]hey could have just broken me with lawyers' fees."[41]

What Redd was referring to was the fact that, despite their huge and growing success with video slot machines, IGT was still dwarfed by Bally Manufacturing Corporation. But Si Redd was not about to back down, even though there can be no doubt he admired Bally's aggressive bullying tactic. It was the kind of bold move he had perfected during his own career.

IGT sued Bally. They asked for an injunction against the company, plus damages. During a pretrial hearing IGT lawyers said the larger company intended to sell its video poker machines for substantially less than IGT's machines. The second-generation Fortune II Slots were priced at $8,000 to $10,000 each, and Bally would be selling its machine for $6,000. On top of that, Bally had already launched an aggressive sales campaign for their new machines.[42]

On July 12, 1982, Washoe County District Court judge William Forman granted the preliminary injunction until a hearing could be scheduled, which he said could take at least a year. In his finding, Judge Forman wrote that a contract dated October 31, 1978, between Redd and Bally was "valid and enforceable."

"The evidence indicates that until the summer of 1981 Bally never questioned the validity or meaning of its covenants not to compete with IGT in the video game business," Judge Forman wrote.[43]

Bally appealed the case to the Nevada Supreme Court, but in late December, the two parties agreed to settle out of court. Bally agreed to abide by the original contract, and further agreed to $2.5 million in damages. IGT's legal fees had amounted to nearly half that amount, but Redd said, "We won as far as the public is concerned. . . . [T]hey did us a lot of harm [, but] we are on the way to a very nice comeback."[44]

In an interview the following year with *Gaming Business* magazine, Redd vented a little of his anger toward Bally, at the same time making an unlikely prediction that probably even he didn't completely believe: "I never thought of this company [IGT] in terms of dollars or cents, or what you call gross volume or gross profit. The only thing that I do think of and I do believe in is that IGT will actually surpass Bally in its total volume . . . and profitability. I'm gonna be bigger than Bally."[45]

In May of the following year, when the noncompete clause finally expired, Bally did reenter the market with their video poker slots. But their launch met with lukewarm success, despite the price advantage on their machines. Bally's first poker machine had been specifically designed and engineered to look and perform differently than those of IGT. But the public was comfortable and accustomed to IGT's machines, and eschewed playing the new Bally machines.

"Eventually Bally figured out that they had better make their machines look as much like IGT's as they could," said Sands Regency's owner Pete Cladianos. "When it was harder to differentiate between the machines, then Bally started to do better."[46]

Still, it was a difficult mountain for the huge Chicago manufacturer to climb. Bill O'Donnell's failure to anticipate the positive market acceptance for video poker and other video-based gaming devices would cost the company dearly. Still, Bally did control a huge market share in the sale of traditional spinning reel slots. Although Bally knew IGT was working on its own spinning reel slots, when IGT was ready to enter the market the situation would be the exact reverse of the video poker scenario: Bally would be on top, and IGT would have a huge mountain to climb.

Whatever solace that fact might have provided in the executive corridors at Bally Manufacturing headquarters, it was very quickly dispelled when a new competitor arrived on the scene scant months later, putting both Bally and IGT on notice.

Universal Company, LTD., and its Nevada subsidiary, Universal Distributing of Nevada, Inc., located in Las Vegas, was a Japan-based game maker. The company had made its mark, and its fortune, on pachinko machines, those ubiquitous Japanese arcade games that had been popular since the 1920s. In 1983, while Redd and IGT were still trying to get their feet on solid ground, Universal entered the U.S. slot machine arena, and did so with a vengeance.

According to gaming studies author Jeff Burbank, Universal entered the spinning reel slot market with a few important technological advancements, and a bold new marketing strategy.[47] At the time, reel slot machines were programmed to provide a small win of a few coins every three or four pulls, and a large jackpot on a very infrequent basis. Universal's plan was to eliminate the small win every three or four plays and replace it with a larger win every twenty plays, and lose the infrequent huge jackpot and replace it with smaller but more frequent 1000-coin jackpots.

Initially the concept was slow to find acceptance with casino slot executives because the scheme lowered the machines' overall win percentage. But slot players loved it. As a result, within a couple of years the play on Universal's slots surpassed the play on Bally's machines, and the casinos were actually winning more money because of the increased play. Universal's sales manager Gary Harris estimated that by 1986, 75 percent of spinning reel slot sales was for Universal products.[48]

Just when Universal seemed to have the casino world by the tail, however, it all began to unravel. Universal had programmed a very unique feature into their slots, a device called a near-miss result. Because of the sophistication of their slots' computer program, they were able to stop the three or four reels on their machines so that it appeared to the player that he had barely missed winning the jackpot. This ploy generally excites a player and encourages him to continue pumping coins into the machine. Near misses, of course, occur naturally in slot play. So all Universal was doing, they claimed when caught, was helping it along a little.

The company had no reason to believe they were cheating. The near-miss feature had been used for years in Japan without any problems. And their slots, with the near-miss feature included, had been duly approved and licensed by the Nevada Gaming Commission.

Gaming regulators, however, were still operating under old, precomputer-era regulations, and didn't realize the ramifications of what they had set in motion.[49]

After IGT engineers developed and put into the marketplace their own spinning reel slots in the mid-1980s, Universal became a thorn in IGT's side as well. So IGT promptly engineered a near-miss feature into their reel slots, and in early 1988 they informed the Gaming Commission they would soon be seeking approval for the machines. Regulators realized they were in a bind, and in order to keep the situation from getting out of hand before they could study and change the regulations, they ordered Universal to stop the sales of its machines.

For the next ten months, charges and countercharges flew freely, and verbal jousting between all the involved parties continued. In an attempt to mollify regulators, Universal made a number of good-faith concessions, but officials refused to budge until they were ready. The key to the entire near-miss situation had to do with one of the basic tenets of slot machine regulation: randomness. The concept of randomness demands that each item in a set—like the different symbols on each reel of a slot machine—have an equal probability of appearing each and every time. The near-miss feature, charged regulators, interferes with that randomness.

On February 23, 1989, the Gaming Commission handed down its finding. Universal was ordered to remove the near-miss feature from its new machines and was given nine months to retrofit its 14,000 existing machines in Nevada.

It was a staggering loss for the Japanese company. They could easily have overcome the retrofitting costs, but the momentum they had lost when forced to stop selling their slot machines could never be recaptured. IGT had by then adopted the best of Universal's technology, so they could match the Japanese company feature for feature. As if to heap insult upon injury, IGT also filed a copyright infringement lawsuit against Universal for copying features of their Player's Edge video poker machines, causing Universal to stop producing those machines as well.[50]

For all intents and purposes, Universal was finished in the United States. Although Si Redd no longer had control of IGT by the time the Universal fight was over, his company's cagey maneuvering certainly made it seem as if his DNA was still firmly implanted in the company.

CHAPTER 11

A KALEIDOSCOPIC LIFE

Because Marilyn Redd spent much of her time in Las Vegas at the couple's swank Desert Inn Country Club house, Redd had given up his penthouse apartment at the Arlington Towers in downtown Reno and rented an apartment in another high-rise building about 2 miles upriver, at 1200 Riverside Drive. Like most second wives, Marilyn had never been happy sharing the apartment with the ghost of the first Mrs. Redd.

Marilyn Redd had established her residence on the second floor of the ex-Hughes mansion, whereas Si maintained his quarters on the main floor. To outsiders, it probably appeared as if the union was more a business partnership than a marriage, and many people in the know would have agreed.

Si Redd had also taken over the large office overlooking the pool used by Bob Maheu during his tenure with Howard Hughes. Redd had installed a number of large screen television sets on the wall so he could watch several football games at once, and he always had a couple of telephones in use for placing bets all across the country. On a large coffee table in front of his sofa he'd lay out all his betting paraphernalia, including a list of all the major games being played each week. His favorite football odds maker was an old buddy, Louis Boasberg, who owned New Orleans Novelty Company. The two men would spend hours talking about the latest odds, what players were injured, which teams were due for an off day, and so on. Then

Redd would get on the phone with the bookies he preferred to use and begin playing one against the other until he was able to pick up a half point or a point on the spread.

"He just loved the action," his son-in-law Alan Green said. "It used to cost him $350,000 to $500,000 a year [in losses], and that was [only] what he admitted to."[1]

Redd traveled frequently between Las Vegas' two major cities, for both personal and professional reasons. He purchased a business plane, a Beechcraft turboprop King Air that he dubbed Slot King, and maintained a pilot and crew to ease the rigors of those regular trips. The plane was also leased to IGT at a competitive rate for senior management travel.[2]

The Redds had also built a vacation home. They began by renting a condominium in Solano Beach, a small beach community just north of San Diego. They enjoyed the area, so they bought property and had a fine house designed and built right at the ocean's edge. Like the Desert Inn Country Club home in Las Vegas, the Solano Beach house was laid out for entertaining. Si and Marilyn loved to entertain friends, customers, politicians, VIPs, and other upper-crust guests at both houses. Invitations to their soirees were much anticipated. During the thoroughbred-racing season at Del Mar Racetrack, only a stone's throw from the Solano Beach home, the Redds were regular attendees, and before or after the races they often hosted get-togethers on their oceanfront patio.

Their parties and informal gatherings generally included a divergent group of people. It was rare that Redd would not mix business with pleasure, and a party would include a few people from each of the groups listed above. Redd was a great host, and a grand storyteller. He could schmooze those important to him—his customers and those politicians who could do things for him—so expertly that they rarely knew they were being schmoozed.

Redd's circle of close friends was small. He was generous with his friends, but anyone who wanted to buddy up to him had to accept his idiosyncrasies and occasional mean-spiritedness, which became more prevalent as he aged. On his best days, Redd was gregarious and fun to be around, an old-fashioned hail-fellow-well-met, chock-full of entertaining stories. On his worst days, he could tax the patience of his most forgiving allies. But his close friends knew the routine, and they either accepted him, warts and all, or avoided him when necessary.

Like many wealthy and powerful men with magnetic personalities, Redd could have easily attracted people to his inner circle. But he learned to be cautious of people, because many of them had ulterior motives in wishing to cozy up to him. In making close friends, he gravitated most comfortably toward his neighbors. He lived in upscale neighborhoods where men and women of similar economic status made their homes, so these people rarely had anything to gain by befriending him. It was easy to form comfortable, nonthreatening bonds in such a setting, and Redd did so in Sterling, Boston, Cape Cod, Reno, Las Vegas, and Solano Beach.

His acquaintances included a number of important politicians, both Republicans and Democrats, but they were rarely close friends of his. When asked in the early 1980s by his University of Southern Mississippi oral history interviewer to name some of his influential friends, he rattled off an impressive list of names: Bobby Kennedy, who had been a nearby neighbor on Cape Cod; Thomas "Tip" O'Neill, the powerful Massachusetts congressman who served as Speaker of the U.S. House of Representatives for over a decade; Nevada U.S. senator and ex-governor Paul Laxalt, one of President Ronald Reagan's closest associates; Nevada U.S. senators Howard Cannon and Chic Hecht, and Congressman Jim Santini; Congressman (now Senate Majority Leader) Harry Reid; Congresswoman Barbara Vucanovich from Nevada; and Nevada governor and future U.S. senator Richard Bryan.[3]

Redd had been acclaimed in the state and national press for a number of years for his contributions to the growth of gaming and for his generous support of Nevada's leading educational and charitable institutions. At wife Marilyn's urging, the Redds had become significant benefactors to the University of Nevada on both the Reno and Las Vegas campuses, donating millions of dollars over the years. They were also generous contributors to causes that advanced women's athletics and that worked toward curbing domestic violence, chiefly Marilyn's causes.

Marilyn generally took the lead in selecting the causes the couple would support. Years later, Redd's third wife, Tamara, assumed the same role, and the couple gave generously to a number of animal rights causes. But if his wives took the lead in selecting where the money would go, that did not diminish Si Redd's readiness to generously support worthy endeavors. He often remarked that he had been an extremely lucky man; and he was anxious to share his wealth with others less fortunate than himself.

Redd was widely recognized for his charitable contributions. The University of Nevada–Reno named the Redds "Distinguished

Nevadans." Si Redd was honored by the Nevada Easter Seal Society as the recipient of the annual Silver Lily award, was named Man of the Year by the Muscular Dystrophy Association of Nevada, and was awarded the National Jewish Hospital's Humanitarian Award, among many other such honors.

The Nevada press dutifully reported on each and every honor one of their leading citizens achieved, and Redd savored the recognition and the appreciation; in fact, he craved it. It seemed to say: what a fine, worthy citizen of our state you are, sir, and we thank you for it.

But it was the national press that truly lionized Redd for his business acumen, to his absolute delight. *Business Week, Inc., Fortune,*

A formal Si Redd portrait in the mid-1980s, while he was the majority owner, chairman, and president of International Game Technology in Reno, Nevada. *Used with permission.*

the *New York Times,* the *Wall Street Journal,* and an untold number of gaming industry journals all recognized the contributions the Mississippi sharecropper's son—they all loved that epithet—had made to the nation's fastest-growing recreational industry. On one occasion in 1994, to the surprise and dismay of his family, he even sat for an interview with the supermarket tabloid the *National Enquirer.* "Farm boy worked for a quarter a day—now he's worth $150 MILLION!" the story's headline trumpeted.[4] His family was embarrassed; Si Redd loved it.

One of Redd's employees related a story that indicated how powerful a man he had become. "We were coming down the stairs from the engineering department [at IGT headquarters] and in the lobby Governor [Richard] Bryan was sitting there, all by himself, waiting for Si to take him in. I thought, 'Here's the governor of the state of Nevada waiting for Si.' That kind of shows you how powerful Si Redd was."[5]

El Studebaker recalled a similar incident after Nevadan Harry Reid had become a U.S. senator. Studebaker met Reid at a shindig in which Redd was being honored. Later in the evening Studebaker overheard the senator telling someone why he had returned from Washington just for this party. "When Si Redd calls, you come," Reid said.[6]

Richard Bryan, who served six years in the Nevada Governor's Mansion and three terms in the U.S. senate, said he and Redd were only casual friends who had first met in the 1970s. But he admitted he really enjoyed being in Redd's company. "Si had an engaging personality; he just oozed charm out of every pore," Bryan recalled. "He was an energetic conversationalist . . . very animated . . . [and] he was the kind of guy you liked to spend time with. An evening with Si Redd was always fun."[7]

As sociable and friendly as Si Redd could be to his rich and powerful friends and allies, a few of his employees and virtually all of his competitors saw a far different person. He was disliked by some of those who worked for him and castigated by most of those he competed against.

Redd's employees, even some in key positions, found he could be hard, unyielding, unfair, and even scornful. Dale Frey, the engineer chiefly responsible for developing video poker, the foundation upon which Si Redd built his empire and his fortune, felt he was never rewarded amply for the game's development. When Redd hired him at A-1 Supply to develop video poker, Frey said Redd promised him

5 percent of all the profits generated by the sale of the machines. But according to Frey, when the task was accomplished, and Redd's huge success was launched on its back, he refused to give his chief engineer anything on top of his modest salary.

When Redd purchased Fortune Coin Company and made its chief engineer, Walt Frayley, A-1 Supply's general manager, he idly watched, even approved, when Frayley stripped Dale Frey of his title and responsibilities. Redd had bargained away Frey's ten years of loyalty and effective service as part of the terms of the agreement with Frayley, seemingly without a second thought.

Dale Rodesch—who worked for Redd for three years, and alongside him on special projects for many more—knew him as well as anyone. He was one of the few people who recognized and understood both the good and bad sides of Si Redd, and had no trouble balancing the two. Of Redd's treatment of Dale Frey, Rodesch said, "Si often told me that Dale Frey was like a son to him, and that Dale would be well taken care of. Was he ever!"[8]

A Sircoma/IGT sales executive who worked for Redd for four years and insisted on not being identified, called his boss abusive, nasty, cheap, and demeaning. "He never said a kind word to me in three years," the man claimed. When this sales executive brought in an unexpected $1.2 million–contract for machines to be installed in Boyd Gaming facilities in Las Vegas, he asked Redd for a raise on his $30,000 salary that had not been amended for three years. He said Redd snarled at him that he was already getting more than he deserved. When he then asked for a special bonus for the sale, Redd pulled a wad of bills out of his pocket, peeled off three dollars and threw them across the desk in his face. "Here. Take your wife out to dinner," Redd spat at him, he said.

One of the first engineers Redd hired at Bally Distributing when the company was just beginning to manufacture its own games was more generous in his assessment of the boss. Pete Mandas, another refugee from California's aerospace industry, joined Redd in 1971 and would remain with him for almost a decade.

"The way Si looked at employees," Mandas said, "he'd hire and nurture them until someone better came along. . . . [W]hat he liked most was people who dedicated their whole life to him. If you worked for Si, you worked seven days a week, twenty-four hours a day, then he loved you."

Mandas said Redd treated him well, although he had the same problem with hollow promises many other employees had. "Frey . . .

didn't get everything Si promised him. None of us did; but that's the way Si worked. He'd promise the world, then when it came time to deliver he'd renege on you. He did that to all his good people."[9]

El Studebaker echoed the same sentiment, saying, "He'd always promise you a big bonus, but when it came time to pay, he'd say, '[Business] just wasn't as good as I thought it would be this year. I can't pay you.'"[10]

Pete Mandas finally left Redd's employ in 1980, just before IGT went public, when Redd's promise of stock options failed to materialize. Today, Mandas owns P&M Coin Company, a holding company for a number of small casinos in Reno and Las Vegas.

Alan Green, an attorney and Redd's son-in-law, would also work for him from the mid- to late 1990s as president of the Oasis Hotel and Casino in Mesquite, Nevada. He explained that Redd was not the best judge of talent. He would often become enamored with a new employee and develop unrealistic expectations of the person. "[He'd] build them up with praise and responsibility only to determine later that . . . he'd put too high an expectation on someone . . . thinking that the person . . . could do anything."[11]

Feeling let down, Redd would then write the employee off and move on, often becoming downright mean and nasty to the person in the future for his inability to live up to the boss's expectation.

Many of Redd's shortcomings as a chief executive are typical of a person who possesses outstanding sales skills, as Redd certainly did. Many a company has promoted its best salesperson to a senior management position only to discover that the skills required of the two jobs are in stark contrast to one another. The outstanding salesman rises and falls on his own ability; the CEO or manager rises and falls on the abilities of his employees. Exaggerated promises are the good salesman's stock-in-trade, whereas for a manager, exaggerated promises create a hostile, untrusting work environment. The excellent salesman must have a narrow, self-centered perspective to excel: make this sale, or meet this month's sales goal. The outstanding manager must have a broad, selfless perspective: meet the company's objectives, whatever they may be.

Redd's extraordinary sales skills were his toolbox, and when he became a chief executive, he kept on using the same familiar tools to try to run an entire organization. Hyperbole, shallow flattery, assertiveness, and well-meant but soon-forgotten promises were his stock-in-trade. Although they served him very well when trying to convince a skeptical prospect to buy, they were the wrong tools for the CEO's office. Redd was not unaware of his shortcomings—he recognized them, and often spoke of his weaknesses. "I humbly admit I don't have a lot of intelligence. The secret to success, in my estimation, is hard work," he once told an interviewer.[12]

He employed the same self-deprecating language when explaining to another interviewer how he built Bally Distributing Company into such a force in the marketplace. "It just isn't true. I'm not the slot machine king," he said. "I will admit that I'm a hard worker . . . that I sold all the slot machines back there year in and year out. . . . However, they don't tell the whole story." The whole story, he laughed as he continued, is that "I didn't have any competition."[13]

These statements were probably as close to probing introspection as Redd would ever come. But like many men who have achieved a degree of wisdom over their lifetimes, he did recognize his faults. He knew he was particularly vulnerable on the legal and accounting sides of the business. But anything he may have lacked in basic business skills he compensated for with cleverness and sheer determination. Si Redd succeeded in business more by hard work and sheer instinct than by any special gifts he may have been born with, and for that he deserves high praise.

In many ways, Si Redd bore a striking resemblance to salesman George Babbitt, Sinclair Lewis's protagonist in his brilliant social satire *Babbitt,* published in 1922. Of course Redd was anything but the ultimate conformist that Babbitt was, but the two salesmen shared many of the same slightly warped principles when it came to their profession. Si Redd, like Babbitt, was an honest man, but as Lewis wrote, "not too unreasonably honest." And he understood the value of flexibility: "He advocated, though he did not practice, the prohibition of alcohol; he praised, though he did not obey, the laws against motor-speeding; he paid his debts; he contributed to the church, the Red Cross, and the Y.M.C.A.; he followed the custom of his clan and cheated only as it was sanctified by precedent; and he never descended to trickery—though, as he explained . . . 'I don't mean to say that every ad I write is literally true or that I always believe everything I say when I give some buyer a good strong selling-spiel.'"[14]

Even Redd would have likely agreed with this comparison. According to Chuck Mathewson, who succeeded Redd at the helm of IGT in 1986, Si often told him, "You know, I'm 90 percent honest."[15]

Si Redd's best friend, Bob Jones, and his son-in-law Alan Green disagreed with some of Redd's former employees' harshest criticisms.

They believed that many complaining employees simply thought they were entitled to more than they received, not an unusual expectation in any company. Jones pointed out that throughout his long career, Redd made a regular habit of loaning money to employees for any number of worthwhile purposes. The loans were usually at low or no interest, and were often not even repaid, Jones said.[16]

As an example, Jones said that when he worked for Redd in the early 1950s, the company loaned him $5,000 to buy his first house. After a couple of years passed and Jones had been unable to repay the interest-free loan, Redd told him they had to find a way to get the loan off the company's books. He said he'd increase Jones's salary by $100 a week—a very large amount given what Jones was being paid in 1954—and the additional salary could be paid back to the company to retire the loan in just a year's time. "That's what kind of an employer Si Redd was," Jones said.[17]

Redd did make many loans to his employees over the years, as Jones pointed out. Once he had obtained wealth, he considered himself an easy mark. "I am, no question, what you'd call a soft touch," he once remarked.[18]

Si Redd was that sort of fellow, a basket of contradictions. Although he may have had his shortcomings, he had his strengths as well. He was certainly a visionary, seeing what few other men could see. It was not an accident that he was on the cutting edge so many times during his career. He had a natural instinct for the marketplace, and he understood with total clarity what his customers wanted and needed. Richard Bryan said of him, "He captured the essence of the entrepreneurial spirit. He had an instinct and a sense for opportunity."[19]

Redd was, like many business geniuses, an avid risk taker. Risk did not scare Si Redd; if anything, it excited him, and propelled him to action. That was the gambler in his soul. Even during his earliest days in Mississippi, he was not hesitant to risk everything he had built on a large gamble. During his career, he often did so, and he was usually correct.

He grew up with another vital success skill, thanks in large part to his mother Nannie: an insatiable appetite for work. Work was Redd's life, from that first sales job when he was seven years old, selling salve and magazines to his rural neighbors. Although he often said that his first wife Ivy was the most important thing in his life, that statement bent the truth just a tad. Work was the most important thing to him, and it remained so until his mind and body deserted him late in his life. Si Redd never stopped working, nor did he have any desire to.

Redd also had the type of personal magnetism that few men possess. Dale Rodesch worked for or with Redd for nearly two decades. During that time, he admitted that he got burned on almost every deal he worked with the man, but he always came back for more. His last business encounter with Redd occurred in 1993, and ended in the same unsatisfying way as the others. Despite that, Rodesch said, "If Si were still alive and he called and said, 'Boy, come by and see me,' I would be there."

"That was the charm of Si Redd," Rodesch smiled.[20]

Few competitors, on the other hand, saw any charm in the man. Redd was cold and scheming with competitors and with other businesses that may have had something he wanted. And he was willing to do almost anything in order to get his way. "Si was a competitor," one of his key employees said. "He wanted the whole market, and he did whatever he had to do to get it."[21]

Even his very good friend and customer Bob Cashell, who ran a number of successful Reno casino operations, recognized and admired Redd's innate street smarts. "I was never his partner; we never went in business together," Cashell said. "But he was always saying, 'I want part of this,' and 'I want part of that.' He was very, very tough; and he could be ruthless if he wanted something."[22]

Ruthless was a word often ascribed to Redd by his competitors, but Barbara Rich, his secretary for twenty years, saw it another way. "Si didn't look at it that way," she said. "It was just his way of doing things for the good of the company. . . . [I]t was just what needed to be done."[23]

Redd was not unlike a lot of business leaders who cut their competitive teeth during the country's most challenging economic times. Born in abject poverty, Redd began his career in the poor rural South; then he spent the worst years of the Great Depression building a successful business in Illinois. In both situations, selling a product was a cutthroat business. There was a very limited number of prospects with money to spend, and the best businessmen quickly learned to use whatever tactics were necessary to succeed. Making a sale when a number of others were seeking the same piece of business often meant the difference between feeding your family or watching them go hungry.

As he moved on to Boston, then to Nevada, Redd's modus operandi to get what he wanted had been indelibly carved into his psyche. His background in the coin-operated machine industry had taught him that business was a tough battleground. Muscled by industry giants Wurlitzer and Seeburg, squeezed by Alabama and New England mobsters, and misled and cheated by his friend Bill O'Donnell at Bally, the old warhorse had learned the rules of the jungle the hard way.

At one point in his career, Redd's tactics did come back to haunt him. In the late 1970s, after he had sold Bally Distributing Company but was still running it for Bally Manufacturing, the federal government came after Bally and Redd for unfair competitive practices. J. P. Seeburg Corporation, the longtime jukebox and amusement machine manufacturer, had a brief but unsuccessful foray into the slot machine business in the early 1970s. By the late 1970s, with the advent of casino gambling in Atlantic City, they had secured a small but unprofitable slot machine market share competing against industry giant Bally Manufacturing.

At Seeburg's suggestion—some would say its urging—the government seated a grand jury in Chicago to investigate antitrust sale of slot machines in Nevada. At issue was Bally's practice, fueled by Redd's activities, of lending money at no or very low interest rates to casinos to ensure they would buy Bally slot machines. Also at issue was the company's longtime practice of installing slot machines at no charge on what was described as a trial basis.[24]

"We didn't know we were doing things that were violating the anti-trust laws," Redd explained. "We certainly didn't intend to. We were just trying to give the customers better service."[25]

Redd gave a deposition to the grand jury, as did a number of casino owners and managers who had been the beneficiaries of his largesse. In the end, nobody was indicted; but the money lending and free trial periods ceased in the future.

Throughout his life Si Redd drew sincere praise from some, and harsh condemnation from others. Few people ever met him who didn't have a passionate opinion one way or another about Si Redd. He truly did live what his University of Southern Mississippi oral history interviewer called "a kaleidoscopic life."

* * * *

Si Redd's responsibilities with the company he founded had changed with the addition of a professional management team. While running Bally Distributing Company, and later A-1 Supply, he had his finger in everything. He had always been a hands-on manager, but he had forced himself to change with Sircoma, then IGT.

"We do quite a number of things that I know nothing about," he admitted during IGT's initial growth spurt. "I have learned to delegate the authority. The only time I go back in production is just to try to meet the people and . . . let them know that I have a feel for them, particularly all of the old ones that I knew for years."[26]

That left Redd time to explore some new directions he felt would be beneficial to IGT in the long term. He had his eyes on one particular issue that he felt would be key to the company's future growth and prosperity: the spread of legalized gambling to other states and foreign jurisdictions. He saw a couple of opportunities in that growth. New legalized casinos meant a larger market for IGT's slot machines, and state-run lotteries using the company's new line of lottery machines also held promise.

Redd firmly believed that states where illegal gambling was prevalent—which included a number of states—would discover a tax revenue bounty by legalizing the practice within their borders. That's what had happened in Nevada. It would be an economic boon, he felt, and it would also be great for IGT. He was keen on contributing his own time and influence toward the development of these opportunities. "My contention, my belief . . . is . . . that most all of these states have all forms of illegal gambling—I mean, bookmaking and . . . horseracing," he told one interviewer.[27]

Likely foremost in his mind was his own home state of Mississippi. In 1951 a U.S. Senate committee investigating illegal gambling by servicemen at Keesler Air Force Base in Harrison County, home to Biloxi, counted 1257 illegal slot machines in the county. By the 1980s it's probable that number had grown considerably, and it generated no revenue for the city, county, or state.[28]

Toward that end, Redd spent a great deal of time traveling stateside and overseas, meeting with government officials, and trying to convince them that some form of legalized gambling would be beneficial. As it often turned out, Redd was a prophet before his time. Today all but two U.S. states—Utah and Hawaii—have some form of legalized gambling; and as of 2008, forty-six states had legalized casino gambling, either commercially or on Native American lands. Gambling has become legitimized, and today it is often referred to as America's favorite pastime.

Despite all the progress IGT had made in the early 1980s, the company was not firing on all cylinders. Si Redd knew it; George Drews undoubtedly knew it too. But neither man was quite able to put his finger on the problem. Sales were flat, earnings were flat, and IGT's stock price was falling. In 1982–1983 the company spent $1.6 million expanding its manufacturing and engineering headquarters in Reno, which was bursting at the seams, but that didn't help IGT's sagging fortunes.

Despite the problems, Redd and Drews knew the company had to continue spending money on research and development. That seemed to be one of the few things the two men could agree on. R&D had become IGT's corporate mantra; Redd's entire coin-op career had been based on bringing new and exciting products to the marketplace.

In 2009, Swedish economic researcher Mirko Ernkvist published the first academic study of the U.S. gaming machine manufacturing industry for his doctoral dissertation at the University of Gothenburg, Sweden. It is a fascinating look at the industry between the years 1965 and 2005, and it is of course replete with scholarly information about Si Redd, IGT, Bally, and other important people and organizations within the industry.

Ernkvist, in quoting IGT literature, wrote that when Redd's three-year management contract with Bally Distributing expired in August 1978, Redd entered into a consultancy agreement with the company. He was paid with Bally Manufacturing stock options, but one condition stated that as long as the agreement was in force, his companies could not compete against Bally in manufacturing video spinning reel machines.[29]

Redd realized that in order to grow, IGT needed to be able to offer this most basic of all slot machines to its customers. For a while, the company had had a joint distribution agreement with Ainsworth Industries of Australia, according to which it sold Aristocrat REEL slot machines. However, they could not get the Aristocrat machines licensed in New Jersey because of controversies involving the Australian company's management. So in 1981 Redd terminated his agreement with Bally Distributing so IGT could begin manufacturing its own spinning reel machines.

IGT's R&D people had been working internally to develop these machines, and they now shifted the effort into high gear. Tom Potts was the director of the Reel Slots Program at IGT, and he and others realized that the security of their microprocessor-driven technology could solve the major problem mechanical and electromechanical reel machines experienced: cheating. Wins were being rigged by slot cheats using wires, magnets, and other devices that altered the stopping positions of the reels. That was impossible with the IGT technology.

"We thought, what a great idea it would be to take the same concept and apply it to the spinning reel machine," Potts told a *Loose Change* magazine interviewer.[30] And so they did. The result was the IGT Fortune Reel machine, also called the M-Slots, which was followed soon afterward by the firm's S-Slot reel machines. Both machines employed traditional spinning reels, not video replications of spinning reels. There was also a handle to pull, and both advancements provided players with a more realistic and comfortable playing experience.

The difference was that in IGT's new machines the stopping pattern of the reels—the part most vulnerable to cheating—was done by random number generation within the built-in microcomputer itself, ensuring security. This breakthrough in reel slot machine technology had been developed by Universal, but now, when combined with the use of a Stepper motor, it gave IGT a leg up on their other competitors, Bally and Aristocrat.

IGT wasn't quite finished with its innovation. One additional program was being fine-tuned by the R&D folks, and when it hit the market, it would change the face of Nevada gaming. But to understand the program, it's necessary to step back in time nearly 400 years, to a much simpler time and place.

Lotteries have been used to finance worthwhile endeavors in America, either directly or indirectly, since the New World's earliest days.[31] When the Jamestown colony was struggling to establish roots in the New World in the early 1600s, the sponsoring Virginia Company petitioned the English Parliament for permission to conduct a lottery in England to fund the colonizing enterprise. Parliament members complied for a short time, until they discovered that the Virginia Company's lottery was interfering with their own, thus forcing the company to stop selling tickets. This was the first time the New World benefited from a lottery, but it would be far from the last.

Throughout the seventeenth, eighteenth, and nineteenth centuries in America, lotteries were commonly used to finance war, public interest projects, and education, particularly higher education. The University of Pennsylvania, Yale, Harvard, Columbia, and Princeton are among many prestigious colleges and universities that used a lottery to pay for needed buildings and programs early in their histories. War fits in because each time the federal government had to constrict state funding to fight a war, many states would make up the deficits by holding lotteries. That happened during the Revolutionary War and the Civil War. But then all lotteries were squelched in 1890 by federal legislation barring the use of the U.S. mail for lottery purposes.[32]

It remained that way until 1964, when the old law changed and New Hampshire launched the twentieth century's first state lottery. A few other northeastern states jumped on board, but the idea did not catch on quickly. Then war came along again, but this one was a different kind of war, the Cold War. The Reagan administration had a simple solution for defeating the Soviet Union and winning the war: outspend them. Huge military expenditures strained the federal budget, and the cost of many social services, including education, was passed back to the states. In response, a tidal wave of new state lotteries began in the 1980s, and by 2008 forty-three states allowed lotteries.[33]

For the state of Nevada and its casino gaming interests, the Big Bad Wolf came to the door in November 1984, with the launch of the California State Lottery. IGT would be ready, thanks in large part to chairman Si Redd's innovative spirit and the vision and expertise of two men. The first was IGT's initial board member Warren Nelson, of the Club Cal-Neva; the second was a brilliant Norwegian theoretical mathematician named Inge Telnaes.

Nelson had long harbored the idea for a large progressive jackpot system. "In the early 70s [at the Cal-Neva], we . . . created the Growing Jackpot machine, a predecessor to today's linked progressive machines," Nelson said. "Two of these complexes of linked slot machines were put on the floor, with shared jackpots of $64,000 apiece, recalling 'The $64,000 Question,' a popular television quiz program of the 1960s."[34]

Then, as now, from the casino's perspective, the appeal of offering a large jackpot to slot players is simple: in gambler-think, spending ten dollars for a chance to win a couple of thousand is one thing; spending a hundred dollars for a chance at millions is another, even if the odds are very, very long.

Soon after he had joined the IGT board in 1980, Nelson and other IGT executives became concerned when California officials began discussing the possibility of launching a state lottery to fund education. California was, and still is, Nevada's primary source of tourists, and anything that threatened that balance was a deep concern in the

Silver State. In 1984, when California voters approved the lottery, IGT decided to fight back.

Nelson dusted off his old dream and began pushing for a statewide system of linked IGT slots machines that could create multimillion dollar jackpots that would compete with those of California's lottery. Soon a team had been assembled within the company to design the program. "This was the beginning of Megabucks, one of the most fantastic things that ever happened to slot machines—they're a boon for every joint that takes them," Nelson said.[35] Si Redd agreed wholeheartedly. But it would not be as simple as the two nontechnically oriented men had anticipated.

The crux of the problem had to do with the laws of probability and the complex world of mathematics. Charles Fey's original slot machine had three reels with ten symbols—or stops—on each reel. Thus, there were 1000 possible combinations that could occur with each pull of the handle ($10 \times 10 \times 10 = 1000$). The law of probability states that each of the 1000 combinations has an equal chance to occur with every pull, and that over time, each one will occur as often as any other. Given that, it would not have been economically feasible to pay a large jackpot on odds of only 1000 to 1—IGT had to create odds of millions to one, and that couldn't be done with only three reels. Thus, to accommodate a large jackpot, the number of possible combinations, or stops, had to be increased so the jackpot would not occur too frequently.

Over the years manufacturers had already added to the number of symbols Fey had originally built into his machine until there were 22 on each reel, resulting in 10,648 ($22 \times 22 \times 22$) possible combinations. But that was still not nearly enough to create a really large jackpot, and manufacturers couldn't physically fit any more symbols on the 20-inch reels.

That was the dilemma IGT engineers needed to resolve. One early solution was to eschew three-reel slots and use the IGT keno machines that had been developed for the Nebraska lottery system; but that didn't work out. Then they thought that because they couldn't add any more symbols to the reel, perhaps they could increase the size of the reels. But that would mean increasing the size of the entire slot machine until every one was in the Big Bertha class—not a very practical solution. Another possibility was to increase the number of reels to four, five, or perhaps more, but experience had shown that slot players did not favor machines with more than three reels. Again, it was not an ideal solution.

Finally IGT's Megabucks technical team, headed by Peter Dickinson, vice president of engineering, decided to use the firm's video reel slots. Because these machines were computer driven, there was no limit to the possible combinations they could generate with the four-reel machines, which they decided to use. To slot players accustomed to traditional spinning reel machines, these new video devices looked odd, and the play felt different. However, because it was the best option available to IGT on the timetable they had set, they proceeded designing the software to link the video four-reel slot machines. Everyone realized it wasn't a perfect solution, but it was a way to get started.

As all of this was going on in the R&D department at IGT, the perfect solution was much closer than anyone would have guessed—in fact, right across town. A Norwegian theoretical mathematician named Inge Telnaes was living in Reno, having left IBM and accepted a job in 1974 with Bally in the city. For five years Telnaes had headed Bally's research center, but in 1979, amid an internal struggle within Bally, he struck out on his own. On May 15, 1984, Telnaes received a patent with a title that was enough to choke most nonmathematicians: "Electronic Gaming Device Utilizing a Random Number Generator for Selecting the Reel Stop Positions."

If the title sounds mildly confusing, how it works is downright baffling to all but experts in the field. The bottom line is that a random number generator in a slot machine's onboard computer chooses a random number that is used to select a *virtual reel,* which is mapped back onto the slot's physical reel. The virtual reel exists only in the memory of the computer. This mapping is done four times—once for each physical reel—and in that way millions of stops can be identified on the reels, rather than just the thousands on the physical reels themselves. Of course all of this is invisible to the slot player: he or she is playing against four random number generators while looking at the sort of old-fashioned mechanical spinning reels that seem to communicate a reassuring, physical limit to the odds.

The end result is that there were now enough possible stops on the reels to make huge jackpots possible, even if the entire idea of virtual reels was a sleight of hand. As we see in Telnaes's own words, taken from his patent application, "[I]t is important to make a machine that is perceived to present greater chances of payoff than it actually has, within the legal limitations [in which] games of chance must operate."

Back at IGT, as their progressive jackpot program had just begun to gather steam internally, Mickey Roemer had worked in sales for IGT for only nine months. Although he had earned a marketing and economics degree in college, Roemer had spent his early career as a musician. Following that, he spent time as a card dealer and keno writer, but IGT gave him his first big break when they hired him in sales. Roemer was plucked out of his sales job to head the progressive jackpot program. And while the engineers worked on perfecting the computer networking, Roemer began work on marketing, packaging, and preselling the program.

As the Megabucks system was originally designed, the participating casinos didn't have to put up any money, and they incurred no risk. IGT maintained the central computer that all of the individual participating machines were hooked up to, and bankrolled a percentage of every coin played to build the jackpot. In addition to the Big Prize—the jackpot itself, which IGT guaranteed to be at least $1 million—a player could also win smaller amounts, like on any regular four-reel slot machine.

Participating machines returned 88 percent to the player, Roemer recalled.[36] Six percent went toward building the progressive jackpots, 2 percent went to IGT for managing the program, and the remaining 4 percent went to the casino. When a player hit the jackpot by lining up four 7s on the bottom line of the reels (four 7s on the middle or top lines paid $25,000 and $50,000, respectively), IGT would take out the money that had been set aside and pay the winner in equal installments over twenty years. IGT's second revenue stream for running the enterprise came from the interest they earned on the money that would be taken out to pay the winners over the two decades.

Lotteries are forbidden by Nevada law. However, IGT had received approval for its statewide progressive jackpot system by U.S. District Court Judge Thomas Foley, who ruled that it did not fall within the definition of a lottery. Then, of course, the program had to pass muster by the Gaming Control Board and the Gaming Commission. Three test locations—one in Las Vegas, one in Reno, and one in Laughlin—were required to run for ninety days to prove the efficacy of the program to board members, who had never seen anything like it before. It did finally gain approval.[37]

Meanwhile, Roemer and IGT's executives had been searching for an appropriate name for the program. After rejecting a number of ideas, they decided on Megabucks, a name that had been used briefly for a multistate New England lottery program.

Everything, it seemed, was in place. Si Redd was excited about the new offering, and he was confident IGT had another winner on its hands. With the company stumbling financially, they badly needed another winner, he realized. But as Mickey Roemer began calling on potential casino customers, often with Redd in tow to make the introductions, they hit an unexpected snag. Casinos were openly skeptical. They did not cotton to the idea of cooperating with their competitors in a joint program, and they disliked the idea of sharing revenue and profits with a manufacturer such as IGT. Casino bosses also knew their slot players did not like to play the virtual reel machines IGT would be using for Megabucks.

By the program's planned March 1986 launch date, Roemer had signed up only nine casinos, with a total of 125 linked dollar slot machines. The group included the Boyd Group's California Club in Las Vegas, Warren Nelson's Club Cal-Neva in Reno, Harvey's at Lake Tahoe, and Karl Berge's Silver Club in Sparks, all old friends of Si Redd's and solid IGT customers. IGT kicked in $800,000 to get the initial jackpot started. Redd invited Nevada governor and friend Richard Bryan to make the ceremonial pull on the first Megabucks slot machine.[38]

One of the first players, a Concord, California, couple, fed a roll of silver dollars into a machine at the Club Cal-Neva. Their comments to a *Reno Gazette-Journal* reporter about the playing experience were lukewarm, and would offer a surprisingly prescient warning for the early days of Megabucks.

"This is nothing fantastic," the lady said. "It's a lot slower than other machines in paying off. I'm still going to play the [California] lottery."

Her husband added, "We visited several times a year before it [the lottery] started; now, very seldom. I like the old slot machines better. Heck, I've only seen one '7' come up and I've been here a half-hour."[39]

Many years later, Mickey Roemer confirmed the California couple's admonition. "During the first twelve to eighteen months, the program almost failed," he admitted.[40]

There were a number of early problems, most importantly the jackpot itself. It simply didn't hit. One of the initial participants in the program, Las Vegas' California Club, had also been one of the earliest adopters of Redd's video poker machines. Bill Boyd, executive chairman of the Boyd Gaming Corporation, offered another explanation for Megabucks slow start. "They didn't start with the jackpots very high," he said. "When they got it up to where people started saying 'Wow!,' then it really took off."

"We thought Megabucks was really a winner from the beginning. It was very important to our company, and to our industry," Boyd added.[41]

Once the first million-dollar jackpot did finally occur—about eighteen months after the launch, with all its attendant publicity—the game's popularity improved. Next, as casinos saw the potential of the game to draw players onto their slot floors, more of them came on board, creating a critical mass that aided the effort.

But one of the most important factors in the long-range profitability of the program for IGT came in 1989, when the company purchased Inge Telneas's random number generator patent for $375,000.[42] The staggering value of this purchase to IGT is seen in the fact that every slot manufacturer worldwide that wished to use Telnaes's virtual-reel system—and most did—had to license it from IGT. The company enjoyed large profits from the patent, and from the lawsuits they won protecting it, until it expired in 2002.

Warren Nelson's prediction about the ultimate success Megabucks would enjoy has come true in spades. Nelson died in 2004 at ninety-one years old, but he did live to see the largest Megabucks jackpot ever hit—and a world's record jackpot at that—a whopping $39.7 million payoff in 2003. It was won in Las Vegas by a twenty-five-year-old man who was in town for the NCAA Basketball Tournament. Nelson must have been very proud.

Today IGT has parlayed the progressive jackpot system into a dizzying array of games, including some for every coin denomination. Unbelievably, in 2007 a woman hit an $18.8 million jackpot on Penny Megabucks.

* * * *

With a team of professional managers running IGT—although he was constantly looking over their shoulders because of the souring economy and the company's slipping fortunes—Redd also spent time from the early to mid-1980s adding to his personal portfolio of gaming properties.

Seymore Husney of Las Vegas owned a small slot casino called Mr. Sy's Casino of Fun, at 3047 Las Vegas Boulevard South, across the Strip from the Stardust Hotel-Casino.[43] In 1979 Mr. Husney was caught in a dalliance with a hooker. Unfortunately for the casino owner, his paid paramour was only sixteen years old, a member of a child prostitution ring. Husney was sentenced to life in prison, a sentence that was ultimately reduced to only five years' probation through some legal quirk.

The Nevada Gaming Commission took a dim view of Husney's predicament and ordered that Mr. Sy's be sold. In August 1980 Si Redd bought the property for a price he said was "certainly more than a million—it was in the small millions."[44] Redd had no trouble getting licensed for the casino.

In 1982 Redd partnered with Warren Nelson in purchasing the Western Village motel and casino in neighboring Sparks. The third partner was Sid Doan, who had been operating the property. It did not turn out to be a successful marriage.

"Neither Si nor I could get anything done with Sid, who was basically a truck stop operator," Nelson said. "We wanted to loosen up the slot machines, but Sid was like a brick wall. It was too much trouble, and no fun."[45]

After eight months, Nelson took advantage of an escape clause in the contract and sold his stake to Redd, and Redd put the property under Peppermill management, the company that managed his other small properties.

The next year Redd bought the Rainbow Club, a small locals' casino in downtown Henderson, outside of Las Vegas, and Sierra Sid's truck-stop casino in Sparks, another property owned by Sid Doan.[46] Redd had a minor flap with Nevada gaming officials over these two purchases. IGT had loaned the two properties "several million dollars," and the Gaming Control Board was concerned that the IGT loans were too close to Redd's own personal efforts to buy the companies. Eventually, however, the problems were worked out to the Board's satisfaction.

Although all of the properties Redd had purchased since his arrival in Nevada were relatively small casinos or hotel casinos, by the mid-1980s the entire portfolio was financially significant.

Redd's financial success continued, but IGT's torpor worried the entrepreneur. Redd had founded a number of companies during his career—some small, some a little larger; some noteworthy, some not. But he had a special feeling for IGT that transcended the wealth it could bring him, or the notoriety it could earn him. He realized he had founded something extraordinary with this company, and he was not willing to let it simply slip into oblivion—but that was where it was probably headed, he reasoned. He was also likely aware that now, in his mid-seventies, this could be his final chance to build something important that would outlive him, that would allow him to permanently leave his mark on the business world.

Redd knew he was not personally capable of taking this very large, complex organization to the next level on his own shoulders. He would readily have admitted that he didn't even know what the next level should be. He had also come to believe that George Drews was not the man for the task. Quietly, sharing his thoughts with no one, he began to foment a plan.

CHAPTER 12

CRUISES TO NOWHERE

During his annual visit to the ultraswank Golden Door Spa in San Diego in 1985, a chance meeting provided a spark that ignited Redd's plans for the future. He met Charles "Chuck" Mathewson, a man he already knew by name and reputation. Two years earlier Mathewson had been in Reno playing in a golf tournament. While walking through the Reno Hilton's cavernous lobby area, he noticed a knot of people in the adjacent casino lined up to play one of the slot machines. He walked over to see what had attracted such a large crowd, and he saw a video poker machine for the first time. Mathewson checked the machine to see what company had manufactured it, and when he went back home he purchased 80,000 shares of IGT stock.[1]

Mathewson was raised in Long Beach, California, and as a young man entered the stock brokerage business as a clerk. He rapidly moved up in the financial world, becoming in 1962 a partner with a friend, Boyd Jeffries, in the Jeffries & Company investment banking firm. Seven years later, having grown at a staggering pace, Jeffries & Company was sold for $50 million, and Mathewson was set for life. A good friend and occasional bridge partner of legendary investor Warren Buffet, Mathewson continued to invest for his own portfolio, often betting heavily on small companies such as Reno's IGT.[2]

Now, as the investor was exercising at the Golden Door Spa, he met IGT's founder and majority stockholder, Si Redd, for the first time. During their time together at the spa, often spent hiking over the adjacent hills and trails, Redd told Mathewson about the expansion difficulties his company was experiencing. Later in the year Mathewson visited Redd in Reno. "I just came up there as a friend to talk to him," Mathewson said about the visit. "The next thing I knew, he said, 'Do you want to be on the board?' I said no, [but] they elected me anyway, and he's introducing me as a new board member. That's how Si worked."[3]

Mathewson began attending the board meetings and giving Redd advice, and he discovered he was enjoying it. He also became convinced that the small, foundering company had a lot of hidden potential. "They had a lot of vision, they had some good products and a decent balance sheet," he said. But he also observed that Si Redd had grown unsure of his company's future. "Si was very worried at the time," Mathewson explained. "You get older sometimes [Redd was in his mid-seventies] and you get frightened. He was frightened; he thought the company was going broke, and I didn't share that opinion . . . although things did look dismal at that time."[4]

So, Mathewson said, he offered to buy Redd out, to purchase his entire 52 percent stake in IGT in his own name, the names of sixteen key employees, and in the name of the company. Redd agreed, delighted to be "pullin' the fat from the fire," as he liked to say. Redd owned nearly 4.2 million of the company's 8 million outstanding shares in his name and in the name of his first wife Ivy's trust, according to the *Reno Gazette Journal.*[5] Redd received between $10 and $10.50 per share for the stock, which was selling over-the-counter at $10.125 at the time of the contract. The sale closed on December 31, 1986.

After the agreement was announced and Mathewson had taken over, he said of Redd, "This company is the most important thing to him. This is something Si wants to perpetuate. And that's exactly what he did." On a more personal note, he praised IGT's founder: "This will always be Si Redd's company. He's a super man and has the energy of someone 25 years younger."[6]

Echoing the same sentiments, Redd said, "I want to lay a cornerstone for perpetuating the company I began and to facilitate my estate planning. The success of the gaming industry and IGT remains my goal."[7]

Redd also agreed to enter into a five-year employment contract as chairman emeritus of the company, whereas Mathewson became president and chief executive officer. Mathewson immediately began firing some of the company's key personnel, including George

Drews, and bringing on some new executives he knew and trusted. He also eliminated many company perks, including ninety-four company cars, to cut expenses.

Mathewson quickly saw that the heart and soul of the company's product line was the software that drove its machines, so he began contracting out the manufacturing of dozens of hardware components that had always been made within the company.[8] He also saw the potential of the progressive jackpot system named Megabucks and threw all the necessary internal support behind its quick completion and introduction.

Within six years, the new management team would have IGT back on its growth track, and in January 1991 its stock was listed on the New York Stock Exchange (NYSE), a longtime dream Si Redd had nurtured. In that first year, it was the top-performing stock on the NYSE.

In 1986, the year Mathewson had taken over, fiscal year sales were $42 million, but the company lost $6 million. By fiscal year 1992 the company reported profits of $60 million on revenues of $345 million. IGT's per-share stock price had risen dramatically as well, skyrocketing from a low of ten cents a share in 1986 to $42 in 1992 (adjusted for splits). Chuck Mathewson had truly turned out to be the right person at the right time for Si Redd's struggling company.

Unfortunately, the old Mississippi sharecropper's son did not share to a full measure in the bonanza the company enjoyed in the late 1980s and early 1990s. The sale of his controlling interest in IGT when it was at a low point had still made him a wealthy man, and he made even more money on the stock options he received when he became chairman emeritus. But when he saw the unbelievable gains the company enjoyed under Mathewson's leadership, he often groused that the company had been stolen out from under him. Many of his friends and ex-employees wondered too if he had been forced out of the company he had founded. But Mathewson insisted that had not been the case. "I never forced him out," he said.[9]

Given Si Redd's admitted penchant for "shootin' from the hip," Mathewson's assessment is likely accurate.

* * * *

Despite Si Redd's genius, during his career he had exhibited faulty judgment in his business dealings on more than one occasion. In the past he had generally been able to overcome whatever problems

192 KING OF THE SLOTS

might have plagued his business ventures through good luck, hard work, sheer determination, or simply throwing more money at it. But as he entered his late seventies, and into his mid-eighties—a time by which most men have stopped working because of flagging mental and physical abilities—Redd's missteps became more frequent and more costly. A number of ventures he involved himself in faltered badly, or failed completely, and these failures would come to haunt and embitter the elderly entrepreneur.

Mississippians love to gamble. Long before the white man came, Choctaw and Chickasaw natives were fervent gamblers, a man often risking everything he owned on a game of stickball or some rudimentary game of chance. In the early 1800s the state embraced a number of legal lotteries, and later in the century riverboats along the Mississippi River gained fame as floating gambling parlors. From the 1920s through the 1950s back-room speakeasies proliferated along Mississippi's Gulf Coast, and by the late 1980s a man intent on wagering a few bucks on a game of chance could still find a honky-tonk or supper club in the Magnolia State if he looked, although gambling of all sort was still illegal throughout the state. Mississippians simply turned their heads the other way and allowed gambling in certain parts of the state, just as they indulged alcohol in the dry counties, just as long as neither activity was formally legalized.[10]

As Si Redd devoted his time and energy from the mid- to late 1980s to promoting the spread of legalized gambling to other jurisdictions, a bonanza fell in his lap in 1987. The U.S. Supreme Court affirmed the right of Indian tribes to participate and engage in self-regulated gambling in any state where such gaming was legal for any purpose. What it meant was that in any state where lotteries, bingo, pari-mutuel betting, card rooms, or any other type of gambling might be legal, Indian tribes in those states could also participate without state intervention. The next year Congress passed the Indian Gaming Regulatory Act, which opened up opportunity for the development of casinos on Indian reservations.

This was very bad news for commercial casinos, because it immediately opened the door for hundreds of new competitors. The trade group for tribal gaming estimates there are today close to 400 Indian gaming establishments in the United States, generating nearly $20 billion in revenue. As bad as this may be for commercial casinos, however, it was a boon to IGT and other gaming equipment manufacturers.

As Redd continued spreading the gospel of legalized gambling, it was only natural he would eventually turn his attention to his home state. Redd saw opportunity for IGT, but he also saw a personal opportunity. He knew his days with the company he had founded were limited: his five-year contract with IGT as chairman emeritus would end in 1992. Perhaps, he believed, entering the gaming business in Mississippi would be a fun and profitable diversion and allow him to keep his hand in the industry he loved.

The cagey old entrepreneur also had a selfless motive, and perhaps it was the strongest force behind his Mississippi business venture. If through his efforts he could help introduce some kind of legalized gambling in Mississippi, he knew it would create much-needed jobs as well as tourism and tax revenue to help solve the endemic economic woes of the nation's poorest state.

To accomplish all this, Redd had developed a grand plan. He wanted to operate a floating casino out of Mississippi's Gulf Coast into international waters, where gambling was legal. Since 1980, a gambling ship had been operating out of an American port to the Bahamas, so there was a precedent. Redd thought it was an excellent idea, but he wanted to put a Nevada-type spin on it. "All the cruise ships have a casino on board, but they don't do it Nevada style," he said. "They don't pay back enough. We're using machines . . . [that] pay back 97 percent."[11]

To put his plan in motion, he needed to assemble a team. He called an old hometown Philadelphia friend, Dick Molpus, who was then the Mississippi secretary of state, and asked for a referral to a good Gulf Coast lawyer. Molpus referred him to Gulfport commercial and corporate attorney Hugh Keating, who introduced him in turn to two up-and-coming young Gulf Coast restaurateurs, Rick Carter and Terry Green.[12]

These two lifelong Mississippians were also thinking about a riverboat. They only had one problem: they didn't have the money. When Redd called, it should have been a wish come true, but Carter and Green had never heard of Si Redd, despite his high profile. They decided to check him out. What they discovered wowed them: they had snagged a really big fish, as Terry Green put it.[13]

So Redd, Carter, and Green formed a partnership, Pride Cruise Lines Inc., with Keating serving as general counsel to steer them through the legal shoals. As Carter recalled it, he and Green invested only sweat equity in the project; Redd was the financier, holding 70 percent of the stock in the enterprise. Redd hired a

Las Vegas casino management firm as a minority partner to operate the venture.[14]

To fund the endeavor, Redd took out a sizable loan from People's
Bank in Biloxi. Chevis Swetman, president of the bank, and now
chairman, CEO, and president of People's Financial Corporation,
was more than anxious to make the loan. "He [Redd] had a financial statement that would choke a horse," Swetman said. "He put a
lot of his own money in it up front, and we bankers like to see a lot
of equity in a transaction."[15]

While Redd was putting his team together, a competitor emerged.
A Florida-based, Panamanian-registered gambling ship, *Europa Star,*
docked in Biloxi on December 19, 1987. The ship's presence was an
outgrowth of a Waterfront Master Plan the city had put into place
to bring such ships into their port to pick up passengers and ferry
them out into international waters, where they could gamble. After
a few hours at sea, the ships would return their passengers to Biloxi
from these "cruises to nowhere." And, the logic went, the visitors
would then spend their money in the city's hotels, stores, and restaurants. The ship offered wagering on roulette and bingo, and it had
slot machines on board. Despite carefully planning everything, the
ship owners made one blunder, but it was a colossal one.[16]

Mississippi Sound is a broad channel of water between
Mississippi's coastline and its outlying barrier islands that separate
the Sound from the Gulf of Mexico. The barrier islands are 10 to
12 miles south of the coastline. *Europa Star*'s owners believed they
only had to go 3 miles from the coastline to gamble in international
waters, but in reality they had to go 3 miles beyond the barrier
islands, which were within the state's boundaries. This put the entire
round-trip cruise at 26 to 30 miles from Biloxi and back, making it
an impractical venture from a financial standpoint. A great deal of
legal wrangling ensued, but in November 1988 the *Europa Star* left
Mississippi waters.[17]

While the *Europa Star* struggled with its mistakes, Si Redd and his
partners were moving forward with their plan. They were well aware
of the situation with the barrier islands and international waters, so
they avoided the pitfall that had sunk their competitor. Unfortunately, however, they would soon make mistakes of their own, and
be plagued by bad luck on top of it.

The first bad omen occurred when the Greek cruise ship they were
on the verge of purchasing had a collision at sea and sank. Carter
received word of the disaster just after he had held a press conference

announcing the partnership's plans, providing an ominous beginning for the venture.[18] Ignoring the dire sign, the men found another vessel they believed would suit their needs. The *Atlas* was also a Greek ship, but with a long and distinguished history. Her steel skeleton had originally been laid up in Holland in 1942 amid the Nazi bombing and pillaging of the country. After the war she was completed, and she launched in 1951 under the name *Ryndam*. In the 1950s and 1960s, based out of New York, she ferried cargo and passengers across the Atlantic for Holland America Cruise Lines. In 1972 she was sold to a Greek cruise line, and her name was changed to *Atlas*.

The replacement ship was bigger, older, and costlier to operate than the group's original choice. It was also a steamship. But Rick Carter said the ship's owner convinced them it would be a worthy choice for their needs. With no other fallback position available, and a tight timetable, the partnership agreed to purchase the *Atlas* for a sum Redd said was $11 million. Another $7 million was spent refurbishing her, and she was rechristened the *Pride of Mississippi*.

The ship, which would operate under a Bahamian flag, was a massive 500 feet long, and would have 100 to 150 slot machines and seven table games in her casino. She also had three swimming pools and a 300-seat theater, and could accommodate up to 900 passengers. Initial plans called for each of the two daily eight-hour "cruises to nowhere" to carry an average of 600 passengers, each paying about $60. That sounded like a cakewalk to the partners; in less than two months of operation, the *Europa Star* had boarded 6900 passengers

As the ship was being readied, Redd began the necessary process of securing approval from the Nevada Gaming Control Board and the Gaming Commission to enter gaming in another state. On January 11, 1989, he received an initial one-year conditional gaming license for the operation. To Redd's chagrin, the approval was passed by a 2-1 majority, rather than unanimously as was normally the case. He felt it was a slap in the face after all he had done for gaming in the state of Nevada.[19]

In February 1989 the *Pride of Mississippi* began operations from its dock in Gulfport. From the beginning, it was anything but smooth sailing for Redd and his partners. First, the group was surprised with a $900,000 use tax assessment by the state of Mississippi because the ship had been purchased out of state. After a lot of work, Keating was able to get the assessment lowered to less than $100,000. Then the old steamship—their original ship was diesel—was plagued with mechanical problems. Many of them were caused by silt being sucked into the engines while operating in the shallow waters off the coastline, but the ship's advanced age also caused numerous headaches. Next, because the ship was flying under a foreign flag, it was required by customs law to make a long voyage once a month to a foreign port, Cozumel, Mexico, which was a costly and wasteful proposition.[20]

But the problems didn't end there. Licensed harbor pilots were required to pilot the ship all the way out past the barrier islands, and they charged exorbitant fees for the service. The crew was another problem. The ship required a much larger crew than expected; and many crew members were from foreign countries, causing ongoing language hassles. Also, the management team Redd had hired made some costly errors, partly from inexperience with gambling ships, partly from the financial drain the venture was experiencing.[21]

The casino had no surveillance system installed for the first four or five months of operation, which is an absolute necessity in the casino business. "We'd fill the boat up and have a thousand people on the cruise," Carter said, "and when the boat came back nobody could tell me if we made any money or not."

"If we'd had the proper management and the proper checks and balances, we would have been successful in Mississippi," Carter added.[22]

So although the ship attracted the volume of passengers it had counted on, with costs much higher than anticipated, plus all the other attendant problems, the partnership experienced rough seas from the beginning.

The one thing that might have saved the enterprise was some sort of relief from the state in the form of a new, lenient gaming law. So the partnership aggressively pursued this last-chance option.

With Redd's authorization, Rick Carter and Hugh Keating developed a plan. With financing provided by Redd—a figure that eventually approached $80,000 to $100,000—Keating put together a legislative lobbying team that included himself, Carter, and professional lobbyists Scott Levanway and Buddy Medlin. Their goal was to promote legislation that would allow gambling to commence aboard a cruise ship as quickly as possible after departure from the dock. As it currently stood, about half of each eight-hour "cruise to nowhere" was spent getting to and returning from international waters, leaving a limited amount of time for gambling to occur.[23]

Even though gambling in the Magnolia State had been a de facto practice for centuries, that certainly didn't imply that legalized casino gambling would be universally acceptable in Mississippi. The lobbying team had their work cut out for them, and a very short time to accomplish it as the legislative session was nearing its end. Lawmakers for the state's heterogeneous population could never agree on anything, much less something as controversial as gambling. But the state's economic woes were the one consistent factor that would eventually win the day for legalized gambling proponents, although it would take a stalking horse to assist in their endeavor.[24]

That cover, ironically, was another form of gambling: the state lottery. While religious conservatives and lottery proponents fought a bitter, highly publicized battle over the necessary legislation to legalize a lottery, Keating's lobbying team and leading Gulf Coast businessmen, flying under the radar, were working feverishly toward legislative approval of a cruise vessel act to save the *Pride of Mississippi*.

In March 1989 Keating and his team came through; the Mississippi legislature approved a cruise vessel gaming act, the state's first gambling law. The act legalized casino gambling in state waters, including the Mississippi Sound, as long as the ship was heading for international waters or returning from them. Certain conditions were required: a casino gaming ship had to be at least 300 feet long, have a minimum draft of 15 feet, and be able to accommodate at least 400 overnight passengers. The *Pride of Mississippi* qualified on all counts.[25]

The battle had been too much for the elderly Redd. He had been suffering for years with headaches, and they had become debilitating by the early 1990s. His doctors had often suggested he get out of the stressful gaming business. In 1991, a small brain tumor would be discovered and removed, which offered him partial relief at best. Still, the tumor, which had probably been growing in Redd's brain for years, is one possible explanation for his growing paranoia and purposeful alienation of many of the people closest to him.

Because of the then-undiagnosed illness, Redd's wife Marilyn stepped in to take his place in the *Pride of Mississippi* venture. Those close to the situation said she was ineffective, confrontational, and counterproductive, accomplishing little good for the enterprise that continued to falter despite the new gaming law. Finally Redd appointed his son-in-law, attorney Alan Green, to step in as president of the company. It had become obvious that *Pride of Mississippi* had failed, and bankruptcy was the only viable option.

The cruises continued only until November—barely ten months in all—then Pride Cruise Lines, Inc., filed for reorganization under Chapter 11 bankruptcy law in Mississippi.[26]

Si Redd proved to be a stand-up guy in the unfortunate process. He personally paid in full every allowable debt the company was charged with under its bankruptcy filing, a rarity in such cases. "On a chapter 11, you're lucky to get twenty-five cents on the dollar," said banker Swetman, who had loaned Redd most of the money. "But with Mr. Si . . . it's banking the way it used to be when I first came into it. If a man said he was going to do something, he'd do it. Mr. Si was just a wonderful guy; I thought the world of him."[27]

The *Pride of Mississippi* was moved to Galveston, Texas, and renamed *The Slot King* in a last-ditch effort to make a go of it—and the star-crossed ship *almost* made it. "When we got to Galveston, we were doing fine," Rick Carter said. "We were making a lot of money."[28] Then in an unexpected move, the U.S. attorney in Galveston lowered the boom on the ill-fated ship. The courts decided to test a 1948 gaming ship act that had been designed to keep gambling barges off the coast of California. Pride Cruise Lines obtained legal opinions that *The Slot King* was not in violation of that law. But when the company received a target letter from the U.S. attorney saying the lawsuit would go forward, it was too much for Carter and Green. They resigned their 30 percent interest, and Redd was forced to put the company into a Chapter 7 bankruptcy filing, resulting in the liquidation of the company's assets.

According to Redd, his losses in the casino ship venture were close to $21 million. His personal accountant, El Studebaker, related a humorous story about the whole *Pride of Mississippi* venture, and Si Redd's own personal pride. When Redd first told Studebaker he was thinking of going into the deal, Studebaker said he tried to talk his boss out of it. He argued vehemently that it was a bad deal, until Redd finally told him to shut up and never mention it again. So, Studebaker said, he buttoned his lip. A year and a half later, after the venture had proven to be a disastrous mistake, Redd confronted his accountant. Wagging his finger in Studebaker's face, he shouted, "I can't believe you didn't argue harder!"[29] It was a typical Si Redd moment.

Rick Carter and Terry Green, however, were undaunted by the failure, mainly because it wasn't their money that had been lost. They returned to Mississippi and worked toward passage of a broader gaming law. In June 1990 the Mississippi legislature passed a gaming bill that allowed dockside gambling, which meant that casino ships could operate from a permanent mooring on the coast. It also created the framework for gaming oversight by the state. That law was a direct result of the economic improvements on the Gulf Coast that occurred because of the *Pride of Mississippi,* despite the failure of the venture for its investors.[30]

Carter and Green, meanwhile, developed a new plan once the dockside gaming law had been passed. They bought back *The Slot King* from the bankruptcy court, put it in permanent mooring in Gulfport, and had the first legal casino in the state. When they had approached Marilyn Redd with the idea, she flatly refused to participate. Si Redd, as it turned out, was all in favor of picking up where they had let off. But because of his illness he simply didn't have enough fight in him to overrule his wife.

Carter and Green arranged for other financing and repurchased the old ship themselves. They returned it to Gulfport, renamed it the *Copa Casino,* and opened for business in 1990. The *Copa* operated successfully until 1993, when the men sold it to another operator. But five years later they took it back, when their loan could not be met. Carter and Green operated it for two more years, then paid to have the old vessel scrapped. In what was perhaps a fitting end for the once proud steamship, she accidentally sank while the salvagers were towing her to India.[31] Today the two men own the 562-room Island View Casino Resort in Gulfport.

Although Si Redd's big plunge into Mississippi gaming did not work out well for him personally, it accomplished all he had hoped for his beloved Magnolia State. In 2007, Mississippi's gross casino gaming revenue was $2.9 billion, which generated $29.4 million (fiscal year) in taxes for state and local governments. Of course this does not even include other tourist-related revenue and taxes, or the thousands of jobs that have been created in Mississippi. All of this, most Mississippi experts agree, is thanks in large part to native son Si Redd.

Attorney Hugh Keating gave Redd all the credit for the events that led up to legalized gambling in Mississippi, saying, "It is reasonable to say that without the vision of Si Redd, the State of Mississippi would not be the outstanding gaming venue which exists today."[32]

Robert Engram, one of the state's initial gaming commissioners, agreed. Citing Redd's influence in getting the state's first gaming law passed, which was the precursor to dockside gaming, Engram said,

"That was the beginning of gambling as far as I was concerned in Mississippi."[33]

Finally, Redd's partner Rick Carter referred to Redd as the "Godfather of gaming in Mississippi."[34]

The state of Nevada was not as kind in its praise, a fact that wounded Si Redd deeply. When he sought to withdraw his gaming application for Pride Cruise Lines from the Nevada Gaming Control Board, it was granted by a 2-1 vote. However, the vote carried a demeaning "with prejudice" annotation.

Board member Jerry Cunningham said Redd "promised [to] make us proud. There's nothing here to make us proud. . . . [I]n my opinion, [Redd] really let us down."[35]

Redd himself offered the final word on the venture in a bruising mea culpa: "I thought I could do a great thing, [but] I completely fell on my ass. . . . [J]ust let me come home and do something that I do good."[36]

* * * *

Even as he was suffering one of the biggest financial failures and greatest disappointments of his life, Si Redd's spirits were buoyed by another event. In 1991 he was inducted into the American Gaming Association's Gaming Hall of Fame. Redd joined such distinguished gaming legends and good friends as Sam Boyd, Kirk Kerkorian, Bill Bennett, Bill Pennington, Bennie Binion, Jackie Gaughan, Barron Hilton, Jay Sarno, William Harrah, and Warren Nelson. It was a grand honor, and it indicated the height to which the sharecropper's son had risen in his chosen field.

In December 1991 Si Redd had completed his five-year term as chairman emeritus of IGT, and he was due to stand for reelection to the board of directors at the upcoming annual meeting. To the surprise of few insiders, Redd announced his resignation and total withdrawal from the company he had founded, citing health concerns including his recent brain surgery.

There was probably also some pressure from inside the company for Redd to withdraw. IGT had bid to supply video poker machines to the growing Australian gaming market. However, the gaming control commission in that country was set to disqualify the company because of their charge that Redd and IGT had earlier flooded Australia with illegal slot machines. When Redd resigned, IGT received the contract.

Si Redd and his second wife Marilyn are caught playing one of Si's Big Bertha slot machines at a gaming convention in the mid-1990s. Mrs. Redd would pass away a short time later. *Redd family photo.*

Regardless of the reasons for his resignation, it was undoubtedly a sad moment for the aging and ailing innovator, but he had known the handwriting was on the wall. The company was now completely in the hands of the professional managers he had installed. He no longer had a major financial stake, because he had sold the bulk of his shares five years earlier, and he was far removed from having any real say in how the company was run.

On the flip side, however, the company he had lovingly created in 1976 was now an industry giant, and its future was assured, as well as his own reputation as an industry giant. These facts gave Redd a great deal of satisfaction, but there was another thing too: Redd wanted to get back into the thick of the action. A few years earlier, he had told a newspaper reporter, "Now I'm chairman emeritus, and you know what that means. What it REALLY means is 'Keep your nose out of the business.'"[37] He knew he could no longer make a mark at IGT, but there were still opportunities aplenty for a gaming innovator of his reputation, despite his flagging, age-related abilities. His last venture, the *Pride of Mississippi,* had been a dismal failure from a personal standpoint, but he did not want—nor would he allow—his legendary career to end on a failing note. As always, the cagey veteran had a couple more aces up his sleeve.

When he had sold the majority of his IGT stock in 1986, Redd had also signed a six-year noncompete agreement with the company. By 1992 that agreement had run its course, and anybody who knew Si Redd knew he'd be back. First and foremost in his mind, now that he was free to get back into the gaming equipment manufacturing business, was International Technical Systems (ITS), a new company he launched.

"We will attempt to do everything IGT does," Redd told a news-paper reporter in announcing his new company. "Not necessarily to be as large, but to do all over again what I did accomplish with IGT—engineer, manufacture and lease gaming machines all over the world."[38]

It was a bold statement. IGT manufactured 75 percent of the new gaming machines sold in the United States at the time, and 35 percent—and growing fast—of those sold internationally. But Redd had never been shy. He told another reporter from his home state he thought it was possible that the new company could bring in as much as $38 billion in revenue. "So I'm wrong, 50 percent wrong," he boasted, "that's still $19 billion." Shrugging his shoulders, Redd added, "[If] I'm wrong again by 50 percent, that's still $9 billion."[39]

Redd and his employees—he had twenty of them working at ITS by 1994—had a ten-year strategic plan already carefully crafted. According to Redd, he had poured more than $20 million of his money into ITS by that time. The Mississippi Gaming Commission had just recently licensed some ITS machines in that state, as had the Nevada Gaming Commission, and ITS had sold about 2,500 machines by then, Redd claimed.[40]

The company's core products were different from traditional slot machines. One was a video touch-screen machine that offered a choice of eight games, including various forms of poker, bingo, and spinning reel slots. They had also developed a keno machine that had already passed the Nevada Gaming Commission's muster, following a test at the Railroad Pass Hotel-Casino in Henderson, outside of Las Vegas. ITS also planned to build and sell video lottery terminals and slot accounting and player tracking systems.[41] To further expand his product line, Redd turned to an ex-employee from his A-1 Supply Company days, Dale Rodesch.

"After having little contact with Si for nearly a dozen years, I received a phone call from him in 1993," Rodesch related. "He asked if I could come [to his house in Solano Beach] for a chat."[42]

Rodesch could never resist his old boss, despite the disappointing nature of many past encounters, so he headed for Solano Beach. Redd asked Rodesch if he'd be interested in developing a new video slot for ITS. Although Redd never told Rodesch where the new game would be sold, Rodesch guessed it was for emerging Indian tribal casinos because the two men made a number of subsequent visits to those casinos in New Mexico.

A contract between the two men followed, and Rodesch subcontracted a number of experienced gaming engineers to develop the video slot game. "When the game was nearly complete," Rodesch said, "Si called and said he wasn't going to proceed with his plans for ITS." Although he was disappointed, Rodesch was not surprised; the same thing had happened a number of times before.[43]

At a follow-up meeting, Redd agreed to pay the balance he owed Rodesch in return for the game's technical documentation. Redd waved a check at Rodesch, but insisted he first sign a paper saying he would never compete with Redd again in the coin machine business. "I tore up the agreement and handed it back to him," Rodesch said, smiling. "I never got the balance owing, and Si never got the final documentation."[44]

Redd had also pitched his son-in-law Alan Green on ITS, and had him set up a New England subsidiary, International Technical Systems of New England, that would market video lottery terminals in that region. Green and other company officials began lobbying the Massachusetts legislature to approve the machine for statewide use. Legislators were interested, but asked to see a model of the lottery machine before approving it. But there was no model; a prototype hadn't even been built yet. When Green questioned Redd, he was told not to be concerned: when the time would come for the legislation to pass, a model would be available, Redd said. For Green, it was a chicken-and-egg situation: he couldn't get legislative approval without a prototype, and Redd wouldn't build a prototype until he had legislative approval.[45]

Green also began promoting the machines in other New England states, while Redd tried to convince IGT to partner with him and manufacture the lottery terminals. Then on September 23, 1993, the ITS New England house of cards came tumbling down. A large article about the casino industry appeared in the *Boston Globe,* the region's newspaper-of-record, revealing a few shady facts about Redd's background and writing, "Although ITS is a shell company that has never built a video poker machine, it describes itself as a 'worldwide provider of video gaming systems.'"[46]

That was all it took for jittery legislators throughout the region to say, No thanks! Redd ordered Green to close up shop in Boston, but ITS continued pursuing sales for its multigame touch-screen machine that had so far sold moderately well. However, by 1996 the bloom would be off that rose too. After years of bending Nevada's gaming regulations with his loose style of deal making and of having his hand slapped repeatedly, Redd had finally gone too far. The Gaming Control Board came down hard on the King of the Slots.

Redd was accused of sending ITS slot machines to places where they should not have been going, a major breach of gaming regulations. Because Redd was such a revered figure in the gaming industry, the Gaming Control Board tried not to be overly harsh with him. He was told that a hearing would be held to determine his suitability to continue holding his gaming licenses, a hearing that almost certainly would go against him. If so, it could also have forced the sales or closure of the large operation he had built in Mesquite, the Oasis Casino Resort.[47]

"Si was in denial, or confusion," Alan Green said. "He was insistent that he . . . didn't do anything wrong."[48] As he had often done in the past when confronted with his mistakes, Redd blamed others around him: his attorneys, his employees, his auditors.

Alan Green went to Las Vegas to see if he could save his father-in-law's sagging fortunes. He was able to get ownership of the Mesquite operations transferred to the Redd Family Trust, and he applied for a gaming license so he could take over the Mesquite property and see to its orderly disbursement. The Gaming Control Board agreed to stall their hearing until Green could be investigated and licensed, a process that took about six months. Then Redd was allowed to voluntarily surrender his gaming licenses, with his agreement not to interfere with the family trust or the operation of the Mesquite properties.[49]

When ITS finally closed down, Redd took a philosophical approach to the failure, along with his customary humbling mea culpa. "We tried to manufacture something new; but I was all over the country promoting and didn't pay enough attention to it. The engineers were not good enough; I hired friends instead of the best."[50]

* * * *

Building ITS, the Oasis Resort, and Mesquite Vistas master-planned community in the first half of the 1990s was plenty to keep a young man busy. But at an age when most folks are just happy to wake up in the morning, Si Redd was just getting warmed up. In an interview with a business magazine in 1994, when he was eighty-two years old, he outlined all the other ventures he had purchased, or optioned to purchase:

- The Lodge at Brian Head, a Utah ski resort he was remodeling for timeshare ownership;
- an option on a riverboat 70 miles south of St. Louis;
- North American rights to market Casino Keno, an online keno system, and a comparable lottery system from an Australian manufacturer;
- a North American distributorship from Nevada and Australian companies to sell a casino player tracking system;
- a Tennessee video gaming design and manufacturing company; and
- a 30 percent ownership in a retail merchandising company that sold collector series prints.[51]

Remarking on all the balls he had in the air, Redd explained, "The whole world is becoming a big casino; it's such a tremendous opportunity. I guess it's just in my blood."[52]

Unfortunately, many of these enterprises did not end well. Redd still loved the art of the deal; wheeling and dealing was one of the few joys left in his life. But like so many times in his past, he made spur-of-the-moment decisions that were not carefully studied or thoroughly thought out. When the deals went sour, he turned them over to his employees to straighten out, or he simply bailed out. If he lost a few million dollars here and there, it wasn't really a big deal to him. He still had plenty of money to finance his dreams.

Despite his sixty-five years of experience in the coin-operated machine business, and the many dazzling successes he had achieved, the splashy old entrepreneur never learned from some of his most common mistakes.

── CHAPTER 13 ──

AN OASIS IN THE DESERT

The small desert town of Mesquite, Nevada is nestled in the Virgin Valley, about 80 miles northeast of Las Vegas. The town is located near the three corners where Nevada, Arizona, and Utah meet. About a stone's throw down the road lies the town of Bunkerville. In the late nineteenth century, when the two Mormon settlements were first planted, the towns were friendly rivals in almost every way.

In the early 1960s, the Nevada Department of Highways announced its plan to build an interstate highway across the state into Utah. All of a sudden the friendly rivalry turned into something much nastier as each town tried to ensure the interstate would go through their respective community. In 1963, when the final decision was announced, Mesquite was the big winner. Today, it is a bustling, growing little resort city, whereas Bunkerville is still a small agricultural village.[1]

By the mid-1970s, it was a short drive from the center of Mesquite to four national parks, five state parks, and dozens of historical sites. Despite that and the presence of Interstate 15, the town was still just a roadside motel stop with no appreciable tourist base. A parsimonious agricultural base, composed primarily of large dairy herds that supplied Las Vegas with its dairy products, provided employment for most of the 800 small-town folks who chose to live there.

Recognizing the area's potential, Si Redd had purchased the small Western Village Truck Stop in Mesquite in 1976. In addition to the truck stop and its gasoline pumps, there was a coffee shop, twenty-eight basic motel rooms, and twenty-three slot machines. In later years, when he often spoke of those early days in Mesquite, Redd related that half of the slots didn't work, to the delight of his good Mormon neighbors who didn't want to encourage gambling anyway. In spite of that, and in typical Si Redd fashion, he saw opportunity where few others did. "Years ago," he boasted to a reporter in 1990, "I could see the potential for Mesquite."[2]

Not too long after his original purchase of the property, Redd had decided to travel to the town and look over his operation. As he always did wherever he went, Redd immediately made friends. He took to one fellow in particular who would play an important role in his future Mesquite plans. Jimmie Hughes was a fifth-generation Virgin Valley rancher. His great-grandfather, he proudly related, was only the fourth white child born in the Valley. Hughes ran some cattle on his 600-acre spread, the Arvada Ranch, just across the state line, in Arizona. Hughes and Redd were simpatico, and they immediately bonded. Hughes said, "Si often told me, 'You know, you and me are a lot alike; I'm just an old Mississippi plowboy, and you're just an old Arizona cowboy. We get along good.'"[3]

After he purchased the Western Village, Redd employed a succession of men to run the small operation for him, and because it was just a sideline he paid little attention to what was going on in the small desert community more than 400 miles from Reno. Because he was never a whiz at analyzing numbers, Redd wasn't even alarmed by the negative financial reports sent to him by a succession of general managers.

But after a few years he did begin to question the numbers. They just didn't look right for some reason. Next time he saw his friend Bob Cashell, who was then running a casino management firm in Reno, Redd asked him if he would go down to Mesquite and see if he was being cheated by his on-site managers and employees. Redd offered the use of his plane, and Cashell and a couple of his employees flew down to Mesquite.[4]

When they returned, Cashell phoned Redd. "You're right, Si; they're ripping you off," he told him. "I could see it the minute we walked into the restaurant."[5]

So in 1981 Redd leased the property to the Reno-based Peppermill Company, which was already leasing a number of his other small casinos. In his 1984 University of Southern Mississippi oral history interviews, he described the lease contract he had negotiated.

"[I] leased it to the Peppermill Company for fifty-five years—a tremendous proposition. I think I get over a million dollars a year just from the net profit," he said.

"I put a value on that place of eight million dollars. I owned it outright. I paid two million, more or less," he continued. When Redd and the Peppermill operators finally agreed to four million in value, he said, "I'll lease it to you for twenty percent of four million a year. . . . I got sixty-two thousand or whatever a month. That's two thousand dollars a day. I know it's better than sharecropping," he laughed.[6]

That was the deal for the first year only. After that, according to Redd, he was receiving a small percentage—2 or 3 percent, he believed—of the gross revenue. It was obvious even this early that Si Redd had big plans for the little truck stop: "[I]t looks like together with my help [financially] . . . they will put up a tremendous place that will be successful," he said of the Peppermill management.[7]

The expansion began almost immediately. The Peppermill executives, with Redd's money, began enlarging and remodeling the property. Over a twelve-year period, from 1981 to 1993, the Western Village Truck Stop would become the Peppermill Oasis Resort, with 728 rooms, a 24-hour casino, four restaurants, six swimming pools, the 18-hole Palms Golf Course, and the Western-themed Arvada Ranch Gun Club and recreational facility.

On March 9, 1984, following a vigorous campaign by a committee of leading Mesquite citizens, the town was granted a charter as a "third-class city." Clark County politicos were skeptical; the new city had only 1200 people living in approximately 440 homes, and the prevailing wisdom held that there was too small a tax base to make self-rule viable. Despite that, the citizens had won their fight.

The first mayor of the new city was Jimmie Hughes. In a big celebration held in the community center, Hughes threw a damper on the proceedings when he told the assembled crowd that the infant city was broke. Soon afterwards, Hughes traveled to Carson City, the state capital, and managed to get a $43,000 state appropriation to get things started.[8]

About this time, Si Redd showed up in town to inspect the construction going on at his property. Mayor Hughes made a call on Redd. He told the casino owner that the struggling little city needed some help. Mesquite had a volunteer ambulance service, Hughes said, but their only vehicle was a tired old station wagon. Redd promised help, and in short order he presented Hughes with a block of his IGT shares, which, when sold, netted the city $40,000 for a brand new ambulance.[9]

In 1988 Redd made another trip to inspect the growing resort. Once again, he and his cowboy buddy Jimmie Hughes—who was still Mesquite's mayor—got together. This time, however, Hughes's problems were more personal. He was having financial problems with his 600-acre Arvada Ranch. The recession of the early 1980s had hurt him badly, and he had a hefty mortgage with an eastern insurance company. He was raising alfalfa on the ranch, and had also taken to pig farming.

"They [the pigs] ate my lunch," the old cowboy told Redd. "Those hogs taught me one thing: there's only one thing dumber than a hog and that's the guy that raises 'em."[10]

Hughes also had an idea to try out on his friend. He suggested that the Oasis Resort really needed a fine golf course in order to compete more effectively with nearby Las Vegas and its burgeoning golf course development. On a collection of drawing papers Hughes had sketched out the layout for a golf course on a piece of his Arvada Ranch. He showed Redd the hills and the swales, and where they could locate the fairways and the greens and water hazards.

Hughes also described a little side business he had built up, where parties from town were being bussed to the ranch for hayrides and steak fries, horseback riding, and a petting zoo. He suggested he could also build a fine gun club and a rodeo grounds on the property and create a real western-themed cowboy experience for folks who stayed at the Oasis Resort.

Redd loved both ideas and offered to buy 250 acres of the ranch to implement Hughes's plans. First, however, they needed to take care of that pesky mortgage. A few days later Redd handed Hughes a cashier's check that amounted to about fifty cents on the dollar on the outstanding loan on the ranch. "Next time you go to Hartford to visit these folks," Hughes said Redd told him, "you just kind of slide this check across the table and see if they'll take it."[11] That's exactly what Hughes did, and after a lot of grumbling and gnashing of teeth, the lender accepted the check as payment in full for the loan.

Redd was now the owner of 250 acres of Arizona ranch property, and he immediately hired Hughes to implement all the plans they had made.

* * * *

For the next few years, as Si Redd devoted most of his time and energies to his *Pride of Mississippi* venture, the city of Mesquite and the Oasis Resort continued to grow. The "modern era" of the Las Vegas megaresort was launched in 1989 with the opening of Steve

Wynn's Mirage Hotel-Casino. When it opened, the Mirage was the most expensive hotel casino ever built—at a cost of $630 million—and Wynn is today considered the father of modern Las Vegas. But the Mirage was not alone. More than a dozen other megaresorts followed over the next decade, and today the city entertains nearly thirty-eight million visitors a year in its 141,000 hotel rooms.

Naturally, a lot of this visitor traffic trickled down to outlying resort areas, and by the early 1990s the Peppermill Oasis Resort Hotel-Casino was doing pretty well. As had often been the case, Si Redd had been proven correct about his vision for Mesquite. One of the key executives at the Oasis, Rhett Long, said business was negatively impacted during the early 1990s, however, because there was always construction going on. The Peppermill management, he said, was investing for the future—with Si Redd's money, of course, because he owned the resort. Among the plans was the formation of a company named Grand Destinations, which would sell part of the Oasis' room inventory as time-shares, an idea initially put forth by Redd's accountant El Studebaker. Rhett Long had originally been hired to launch that endeavor.[12]

According to Long, there was an excellent team in place at the time. Si Redd had hired a New York attorney, Bob Stander, to serve as CEO of all his outside interests, which had been put under an umbrella called WSR, Inc. One of the Peppermill partners, Bill Paganetti, ran the Oasis Resort, with Long backing him up. Stander had done most of the work assembling the land that was necessary to expand the resort and build its golf courses. Much of that land Redd bought from the federal government's Bureau of Land Management, for which he paid anywhere from $32,000 to $100,000 per acre.[13]

By early 1993, Redd was completely divorced from IGT and was still licking the financial wounds he had suffered in Mississippi. He had recovered from the large but benign brain tumor that had been removed a few years earlier; and at eighty-two years old, although he had slowed both mentally and physically, he was still not ready to retire. Among the many diversions Redd enjoyed was deep-sea fishing, and he often flew down to Mexico to spend a few days trying his luck.

But nothing could detract the man for long from whatever his latest project might be. He arranged to buy back the Oasis lease from the Peppermill people and took charge of the operation himself. He dropped the Peppermill name and the resort became the Oasis Resort Hotel-Casino, and he named Rhett Long general manager of the property. Because Redd's gaming license was clouded by his ITS

An avid fisherman, with his own large fishing boat, Si Redd made this
catch in Acapulco in the early 1990s. *Redd family photo.*

activities, Long served as the "key employee" for the resort for the
purpose of licensing.

"I want Mesquite to be the end of the rainbow for me," Redd told
a newspaper reporter. "I want to make Mesquite a big city. I hope
the day comes when it will be as big as Reno."[14]

During his tenure at the Oasis, Rhett Long became quite close to
Redd. "He always treated me with great respect," Long said.[15] Redd
also trusted his young general manager, enough so that he often sent
him on bizarre assignments that weren't directly related to the Oasis
Resort. Once, he asked Long to take a flight in his private plane to
Colombia to collect a delinquent debt for some ITS slot machines he
had sold to the nephew of Colombia's president. Long's vision of trying
to strong-arm the leader of the cocaine capital of the world did not give
him any comfort. "If you make me go," Long told his employer, "that'll
be the shortest trip ever. You'll never see me or the airplane [again]."[16]

Another time Redd sent Long to Sainte Genevieve, Missouri, about 50 miles south of St. Louis, on the Mississippi River, to prepare his latest venture for opening. Redd had purchased, sight unseen, an old paddleboat that he planned to renovate and turn into a floating casino on the river. According to Long, Redd paid "a couple of million dollars" for the boat. When he arrived, Long found a decrepit old wooden vessel mired deeply in the muddy bottoms next to the river.

After consulting with a number of maritime experts, Long estimated it would cost $8 to $9 million to renovate the old wreck, and even then it would not be sturdy enough to withstand the Mississippi River's strong currents. "Si was sold a bill of goods," Long laughed.[17]

Despite his boss's faulty judgment, Long felt kindly toward the legendary gaming innovator, who seemed to realize that he wasn't as sharp as he had once been, and often treated it with a sense of humor. "He had a wooden kid's chair next to his desk," Long recalled. "It was painted pink, and it had a giant [stuffed] white rabbit in it . . . about five feet tall." Any time Si didn't want to take responsibility for some blunder he'd made, Long said, "He'd look at the rabbit and say, 'Harvey, did you do that?'"[18]

It seems Harvey made a *lot* of mistakes. Redd was always lending money to people who came to him with bizarre stories about great investment opportunities they had to offer. Because he had so much money by the early to mid-1990s—his accountant, El Studebaker, estimated his wealth at this time to be about $240 million—he never thought twice about lending out $50,000 or $100,000, like it was penny candy. The only thing Redd insisted on in granting these loans was that he would receive a high rate of interest. But, as Studebaker pointed out, the interest rate was usually a moot point because the majority of the borrowers had no collateral, and when their harebrained schemes failed, Redd would lose all his investment capital.[19]

At one time, in order to make this point to his boss, who seemed oblivious to the losses, Studebaker totaled all the loans Redd had outstanding, and 80 percent of them were delinquent. Still, that never slowed Redd down. If he thought something was a good idea, he invested.

* * * *

Within a couple of years of Redd's arrival, the Oasis was joined in Mesquite by the 724-room Virgin River Hotel—which had a convention center, an18-hole golf course, a bingo parlor and twin movie theaters—and the first phase of Resort International's Player's Island

The Oasis Resort, Hotel and Casino in Mesquite, Nevada, grew out of a 28-unit motel and truck stop Si Redd purchased in 1976. He was the first to see the potential for the small town. *Courtesy of the Las Vegas News Bureau.*

Resort-Casino. Redd had added a recreational vehicle park and a 325-room annex across the street called the Oasis Annex. Mesquite was fast becoming exactly what Redd and the city fathers had envisioned.

But Redd was not as strong physically as he believed he was, and after a short time he found it necessary to again dispatch his wife Marilyn to run the operation. Unfortunately, the situation turned out to be a *Pride of Mississippi* revisited. Marilyn Redd, with her haughty demeanor and confrontational style of management, became a thorn in everybody's side. "She caused a lot of hate and discontent; things were rocky for everybody," said one of Redd's key managers in Mesquite.

Jimmie Hughes, who had done an admirable job building Redd's Arvada Ranch property into everything the two men had envisioned, resigned. Others followed. Redd fired his CEO, Bob Stander, and at the end of 1994 he fired Rhett Long as well, although Long felt certain Marilyn Redd was behind both dismissals. The next year he fired El Studebaker, who had been given the additional position of chief financial officer at the Oasis Resort. Studebaker had been by his side for sixteen years. For the next two years, a succession of chief executive officers, general managers, and financial officers came and went at the Oasis. Still, the resort prospered in spite of its internal chaos.

According to one of the Oasis's key executives, it wasn't fair to put the entire blame for the company's internal problems and staff turnover on Marilyn Redd. David Humm had been a star quarterback during the powerhouse years of the University of Nebraska in the early 1970s. The school's first and only 5000-yard passer, Humm still holds many team records for the school. At graduation he was drafted by the NFL's Oakland Raiders, where he played for five years and won a Super Bowl ring. He then spent a year with the Bills in Buffalo and two with the Baltimore Colts before being traded back to the Los Angeles Raiders for his final two years, where he won another Super Bowl ring.

In 1995 Humm was in a medical rehab center in Las Vegas for an old football injury when he met Marilyn Redd, who was also there for injury rehabilitation. They took a liking to one another, and when Humm was released, Mrs. Redd asked him to join her for a visit to the Oasis. When he was offered a position as director of marketing for the resort, he accepted.[20]

Humm had a great deal of respect for Marilyn Redd. "She knew what she wanted. She was strong-willed [and] she had no fear of anyone," he said. "She was forceful when she wanted something, and she was as generous as could be."[21]

During his short tenure with the Redds, Humm spent a lot of time alone with the couple, and he did not believe that the Redds' marriage was one of convenience. "[T]here was care there," he said. "Whatever it was, there was a love. . . . [T]here was a magnetism between the two of them."[22]

The couple also liked and admired Humm. When Marilyn Redd passed away, Si asked Humm to give the eulogy at her funeral. He would leave the Oasis after only a year and a half, following Marilyn Redd's funeral and Si's retirement from active participation in the business.

****

Si Redd's vision for Mesquite was not limited to a successful resort hotel. He went into partnership with a local man named Dennis Rider, and the men purchased 2200 acres of land with plans for a mixed-use, master-planned community named Mesquite Vistas. It was the largest development the small city had even seen, and it would eventually grow to 5000 acres.

The nucleus of the project was to be two 18-hole golf courses designed by Arnold Palmer. By 1994 the first one, the Oasis Golf Course, was under construction. It would be a 158-acre facility with a par 72 layout of 6932 yards. It would also include a clubhouse and restaurant, and the nation's third, and the West's only, Arnold Palmer Golf Academy, which provided instructional programs for individuals and groups, The year after it was completed, the Oasis Golf Course was rated by *Golf Digest* magazine as one of the top five new courses in the nation.[23]

In describing the importance of the new courses, Redd pointed out that in 1993 his Peppermill Palms course—the one initially envisioned by Jimmie Hughes—had hosted 56,000 rounds of golf, and was forced to turn down another 50,000 rounds. "A lot of our customers play golf and subsequently play the friendly slot machines and table games," he explained.[24]

Mesquite Vistas was designed to include retail and commercial sites, office space, churches, a tennis and swimming complex, parks, jogging paths, a nature trail, and of course, a wide variety of housing options. When the community celebrated its grand opening in

The Arnold Palmer–designed Oasis Golf Course in Mesquite, Nevada, was the centerpiece of Si Redd and his partner's 5,000-acre Mesquite Vistas mixed-use community, which began development in the mid-1990s. *Courtesy of the Las Vegas News Bureau.*

early 1996, nearly 20 percent of the 1900 first-phase homes had already been sold. Dennis Rider said the typical buyers were retirees and young professionals from Las Vegas, Utah, Montana, and Idaho. Eventual plans called for 5000 home sites, ranging from condominiums to million-dollar estates.

Cindy Risinger, a licensed Nevada real estate agent, moved to Mesquite in early 1995 to sell homes in three of Mesquite Vistas new home neighborhoods. The infrastructure had been mostly completed, as had the Oasis Golf Course, and many lakes and green belt areas had sprung up from the desert sand like—well, like an oasis. Risinger recalled that longtime residents of Mesquite, often somewhat standoffish, had taken immediately to the new development. They had been offered a chance to get in on the ground floor of the championship golf club and were delighted at what was happening to their small city.[25]

Potential buyers were excited too at what they saw, although the lack of adequate shopping and health care facilities was a stumbling block for some. But the small-town environment, excellent year-round weather, long-range profit potential, and fabulous golf opportunities won many of them over.

In 1995, Marilyn Redd discovered she had cancer. She was only fifty-nine years old. Mrs. Redd could be a difficult person to work with, but that could not diminish the fact that she was a hard-working, self-motivated, self-made woman. Like her husband, she had succeeded in business the hard way, beginning with nothing. She had willingly shared her financial success with Nevada's university system, and just months before her cancer was discovered she had been inducted into the University of Nevada–Las Vegas Athletic Hall of Fame as a distinguished contributor. She was also a significant major benefactor to many worthwhile women's programs.

The Redds' marriage had often been a rocky one—Si Redd had even contemplated divorce, according to his family. Following her death in April 1996, a trust Marilyn had established made life unpleasant for her husband because it tried to divert much of his wealth to individuals and charities of her choosing. He told his *Pride of Mississippi* partner Rick Carter that he had even had to sell his plane and the Howard Hughes mansion in Las Vegas just to stay afloat, although he was probably exaggerating the seriousness of the situation.[26] Eventually, however, because Nevada is a community property state, the assets were equally divided between the two sides.

During their nearly twenty-year marriage, Si often disparaged Marilyn privately to close friends and family. Despite that, he never had a bad word to say about her in public, and even continued to give her a large share of the credit for his significant business achievements. He treated his wife, her memory, and their life together as a courtly Southern gentleman would have done, despite whatever differences they may have had.

Si Redd purchased a home in Mesquite from Cindy Risinger after Marilyn's death. It was a large home overlooking a lake and the fairway on the 18th hole of the Oasis Golf Course, with a view of the Virgin Valley Mountain Range in the distance.[27]

It was at this time that Redd was forced to surrender his gaming license because of his illegal activities with ITS. That, coupled with Marilyn's passing and his own age-related physical and mental health issues, made it apparent that time had finally caught up with the indefatigable gaming legend. The contagious enthusiasm and vigor that had long marked his gaming endeavors had mostly ebbed away. He would become his old robust self on occasions, but mostly in short bursts. Then he would revert to the mental and physical faculties of the eighty-five-year-old man that he was.

Based on his ITS debacle, Redd announced his retirement from business and his plan to turn over control of all his Mesquite operations to his son-in-law Alan Green. Green was named president and sole director of the Oasis, and Redd's daughters Sherry Green and Vinnie Copeland were named trustees of the William S. Redd Family Trust. The Greens had by this time also moved to Mesquite.

Redd instructed his son-in-law to sell everything: the resort, the Arvada Ranch and other parcels in Arizona, and the Mesquite Vistas project.[28] It would not be an easy or a quick task for Green, who found himself in the middle of an appalling mess. "When I got there," he said, "the hotel didn't even have a budget. They just paid the bills when they came in." Complicating matters, Green's father-in-law, in true Si Redd fashion, continued to stick his finger in everything, despite his agreement with the Gaming Control Board to stay out of the operation. He also displayed the growing paranoia that had set in as he aged.[29]

As one example, Green hired Deloitte & Touche, the large accounting and auditing firm, to help him put all the financial affairs and business operations in order. Then the company would value the property and help Green market and sell it. A two-person team from the firm was assigned to go to Mesquite. The lead accountant's assistant happened to be a very attractive, but well-qualified young lady. After one meeting, Redd called Green aside and told him to fire the firm immediately. He charged that the lead accountant was only using the assignment as an excuse to bed his pretty assistant, although nothing had occurred that pointed in that direction. Green argued strongly, but eventually capitulated when the old man would not back down.[30]

Every time Redd interfered with the orderly operation of the properties, Green was forced to remind the old man that he was legally obligated to inform the Gaming Control Board of the incidents.

Si Redd was the front man and greeter at his Oasis Hotel and Resort in Mesquite, Nevada, in 1996, when he was in his late eighties. *Redd family photo.*

Though he never followed through on the threats, it did keep his father-in-law at bay, but it also further alienated Redd from other family members.

Kept away from the important decisions, Redd spent his time as a front man and greeter for the resort, a task he enjoyed and was still very good at. In his retirement announcement in the newspaper, he said, "Expect to see me, for I will be back greeting our guests and all the employees."[31]

In a promotional video put together by marketing director Humm and the resort's advertising agency and released in 1997, a happy, smiling Si Redd, bedecked in a pink shirt, red sport coat, and western bolo tie—an outfit he often wore in public—talked about his favorite subject: customer service. "Customer service is absolutely number one. . . . [N]ever mind all the buildings and the structures and the golf courses, without that smile employees give to the customer, we don't have anything. It's the cornerstone of our prosperity."[32] It was a mantra the elderly entrepreneur had completely believed in since the days of his very first used Bally Goofy pinball machine.

Alan and Sherry Green would eventually remain in Mesquite for nearly five years while Alan unraveled all the complex deals his father-in-law was involved with. A buyer for the Oasis Resort, the Palms Golf Course, and the Arvada Ranch property was finally found. It was gaming entrepreneur Randy Black, who had built the Virgin River Hotel-Casino a few years earlier. The *Los Angeles Times* reported that the Oasis had been sold for $31 million.[33] El Studebaker opined that Redd funneled a total of $55 million into all his Mesquite ventures, but because the late 1980s and 1990s were outstanding years, he had realized a significant return on his investment, probably more than enough to cover all the losing schemes he had participated in.[34]

The Mesquite Vistas master-planned community was eventually sold off to individual developers, which had been the plan all along. Green agreed with El Studebaker that his father-in-law had realized a very good profit on all his Mesquite enterprises. The family still owns some of the land and the Oasis Golf Club.

—— CHAPTER 14 ——

ACES AND EIGHTS

The twilight years of Si Redd's life were subdued compared to the frenetic pace he had set during his first eighty-five years. One thing, however, had not changed: his need for companionship. After Redd's second wife, Marilyn, passed away in early 1996, he began splitting his time between his Mesquite house and a home in Las Vegas. His daughter Sherry and her husband Alan Green were also living in southern Nevada while Green tried to wrap up Redd's business affairs. Green related another amusing Si Redd story.

At his Las Vegas home, Redd had noticed a nice-looking middle-aged woman, a practical nurse he would soon discover, walking an elderly neighbor slowly past his house every day. Redd wanted to meet her, but with uncharacteristic timidity he wasn't sure how to approach the woman. "He was like a little schoolboy asking what he should do," Green said.[1]

Green suggested he don his sweats and sneakers and "accidentally" run into the nurse and her patient as they walked by, and ask if he could walk with them. When that had been accomplished, the suddenly bashful octogenarian asked his son-in-law what he should do next. "I suggested he ask her . . . if she would care to come back [to his house] and have coffee," Green offered.[2]

Green was up to his ears dissolving Redd's varied business ventures, and he didn't see his father-in-law for some time after that. However, the family was secretly planning a surprise birthday party for Redd, which was to be held at his Las Vegas home. Come the day, family and friends were secretly assembled inside the house awaiting the arrival of the guest of honor. Redd walked in the front door, and everyone jumped out and yelled "Surprise!" But family and friends were the ones in for the surprise. Si Redd introduced everybody to his new wife, Tamara, the practical nurse who was about half his age.

It was obvious that Redd's sense of humor hadn't deserted him. About his July-to-December romance with Tammy, he later enjoyed telling people that because he was getting old, "I decided to buy myself a nurse."[3]

Randy Fromm, publisher of *Slot Tech* magazine, scored one of the last interviews with the old warhorse when he was just shy of his ninetieth birthday. Fromm had contacted Redd personally, but Redd told him that everything about his life had already been written, and that he would send him a package of material. But when Fromm said he wanted to discuss the service side of Redd's career, the old man couldn't resist.[4]

After a comfortable hour chatting about the industry at Redd's Solano Beach oceanfront home, Fromm asked Redd about servicing his slot machines, and about customer service in general. Redd shared one of his rare stories that hadn't been around the block a

Si Redd and his third wife, Tamara, a practical nurse, in 1999. Of his July-to-December relationship, Redd quipped, "I decided to buy myself a nurse." *Redd family photo.*

dozen times before, but a story that neatly encapsulated how important service had been to the Redds' successful seven-decade career.

Somewhere back in the 1970s, Redd said, his delivery truck had
dropped off a Big Bertha slot machine to a small casino in rural
Nevada, about 150 miles from Reno. But the deliverymen had forgotten to leave the key that opens the machine. There was a minor mal-
function a short time later, and when the casino manager couldn't get
inside to fix it, he called Reno to complain. "This thing was there on
participation. We had to get the machine up as soon as possible," Redd
told Fromm. So Redd immediately rented a large airplane at the Reno
airport, loaded another Big Bertha on board, and flew it up to the
stranded casino boss. That was Si Redd's brand of customer service.[5]

Later in his life, Redd became an avid dog fancier, adopting Pekingese
and Rottweiler dogs and donating large sums of money to rescue
kennels. *Courtesy of* Slot Tech *magazine © 2001.*

Redd's last media interview occurred in late 2001, when he met with a reporter from *Las Vegas Life* magazine for a feature called "Flashback." The Redds were now living in a home in Las Vegas Country Club Estates that the writer described as a modest-for-the-neighborhood house. He wrote that despite his ninety years, Si Redd "now appears an alert and erect Southern gentleman. Though [his] back has stiffened, his demeanor had not. . . . [H]e seems at ease with himself, taking pride in his life's accomplishments."[6]

Si Redd apparently had at least one more grand scheme on his mind, despite his nonagenarian status. He told the reporter about Noah's Ark, an animal preserve he planned to build on 1500 acres of land south of Las Vegas. It would be, the article related, "a preserve for endangered and threatened species that will feature time-share villas, an amphitheatre, theme park and two research facilities to collect and store animal genomes." It would have sounded like a pipe dream coming from anyone else, but if he had lived long enough, Si Redd might just have pulled it off.[7]

Just weeks before his death, and well aware that his time on earth was coming to an end, Redd asked his wife Tammy to contact Rick Carter, his young partner in the failed *Pride of Mississippi* venture a dozen years earlier. "Ask him if he'll come see me here in Solano Beach," Redd instructed Tammy.[8]

Carter hurried to the old man's bedside. When he arrived, Redd was going in and out of consciousness because of heavy medication, so Carter settled into a local hotel to wait for a good time. After a few days, Tammy called Carter to say that Redd was awake and alert and would like to have him visit.

When Carter arrived, he said Redd was jovial and upbeat, the same happy, funny, determined fellow he had gotten to know so well during their business venture. "I've just got one question I have to ask you," Redd said, according to Carter. "Are you making any money, Son?" Redd was referring to the renamed *Pride of Mississippi,* now permanently moored dockside in Gulfport, which Carter and his partner were operating.

"I told him we were making a lot of money," Carter said, "and then he patted me on the leg and said, 'Attaboy.'" Then Redd put his head down and went back to sleep.[9]

Carter said it was very touching that one of the last things the man he considered his mentor was worried about was whether he, Carter, had turned their failed venture into a business success.

Carter also found Si's wife to be a pleasant surprise. "She really took care of Si; she really cared for him," he said. "When I went in to see him, she propped him up and gave him a big hug and kisses, and you could see then that it wasn't fake. She really cared for this guy. She really impressed me a lot."[10]

* * * *

On Tuesday, October 14, 2003, at his summer home in Solano Beach, William Silas Redd passed away at ninety-one years old. His third wife, Tammy, was by his bedside.

The title of this chapter, "Aces and Eights," is a tribute to Si Redd, and one that certainly would have given him a chuckle. Aces and eights are known in poker lingo as the "dead man's hand." It comes from the life of another legendary figure, Will Bill Hickock, and it is presumably the poker hand he was holding at the time he was shot in the back in a saloon in Deadwood, South Dakota.

Si Redd was a legendary figure in his own right. His obituary ran in newspapers across the nation, and those who knew him best praised the man and his many accomplishments, both in his obituaries and in earlier statements they had made about him:

"He had gaming machines in his blood. He was a great salesman [and] an inspirational man. Very few figures in our industry are bigger than life. Steve Wynn is one. Si Redd was another" (Chuck Mathewson, Chairman of IGT).[11]

Of gaming legends Si Redd, Steve Wynn, Kirk Kerkorian, and Jay Sarno, "Each is a seismic figure. Each is worth his own book" (U.S. Senator Harry Reid of Nevada).[12]

"The great thing about Si is he had it his way for 92 years. Si could sell you everything, and the thing is, it usually worked for you" (Steve Wynn, Chairman of Mirage Resorts).[13]

"I think he has probably had more impact on changing the slot machine business than anybody else in our industry" (William S. "Bill" Boyd, Chairman of Boyd Gaming Group).[14]

"His business influence and his dedication to civic responsibility have placed Redd at the pinnacle of society. His entrepreneurial spirit and enterprising skills have made him a leader in the business community" (Nevada Governor Bob Miller).[15]

"Si is simply one of the industry's true 24-carat characters. . . . [O]ne of his strengths was his instinctive ability . . . to grab people by the heart" (Phil Hevener, *Las Vegas Sun* gaming writer)."[16]

Perhaps Si Redd had best summed up his own life a few years earlier, on the occasion of his retirement from business, when he said simply, "I'm the luckiest guy in the world. I believe it was the fun of the journey that I enjoyed the most."[17] Of course, another statement he had made years earlier goes hand in hand with the prior one: "I've been very poor, and I've been kind of rich. I'd have to say kind of rich is better."[18]

Of all of his accomplishments, Redd was most proud of founding IGT and of its growth to a position of world leadership in slot machine manufacturing, networking systems, and Mega-jackpot systems. Today the company is licensed in more than one hundred legal gaming jurisdictions in North America, Europe, Latin America, Asia, Australia, and South Africa. As of 2007, the company employed 3400 men and women worldwide.[19] Naturally, the deep worldwide recession of 2007–2009 hit IGT and the gaming industry, as it did all major business segments, but the company has bedrock fundamentals and will recover with the rest of the economy.

IGT focuses on a broad range of products, including slots, video slots, poker, lottery games, Mega-jackpots, central determination systems, network systems, table solutions, and Internet gaming, according to the company's 2007 Annual Report. The company has designed nearly 1000 games.

IGT's 2007 revenues were $2.6 billion, with gross profit of $1.5 billion, a gross margin of 56 percent.

IGT is indeed a grand legacy for any man to have left behind.

NOTES

Abbreviations: IGT–International Game Technology; *JCL–Jackson (MS) Clarion-Ledger; LAT–Los Angeles Times; LVRJ–Las Vegas (NV) Review-Journal; LVS–Las Vegas (NV) Sun; NSJ–(Reno) Nevada State Journal; REG–Reno (NV) Evening Gazette; RGJ–Reno Gazette Journal;* UNOHP–University of Nevada Oral History Program; USMOHP–University of Southern Mississippi Oral History Program.

CHAPTER 1

1. Description of the early days of the Neshoba County Fair, Steven H. Stubbs, *Mississippi's Giant Houseparty*, ix, 3–8; Florence Mars, *The Fair: A Personal History*, n.p.

2. Stubbs, *Mississippi's Giant Houseparty*, 8.

3. William Alexander Percy, *Lanterns on the Levee*, 249–250.

4. Stubbs, *Mississippi's Giant Houseparty*, 159–164.

5. Jenelle B. Yates and Theresa T. Ridout, *Red Clay Hills*, 106.

6. Stubbs, *Mississippi's Giant Houseparty*, 160.

7. William Si Redd, USMOHP, 1–2.

8. Reed Bingham, "Living Legends," *Comstocks Northern Nevada*, Winter 1998, 54.

9. William "Si" Redd, USMOHP, 2.

10. The Redd family genealogy comes from Redd, USMOHP, 1–2; and the 1900, 1910, and 1930 U.S. Federal Census Reports, State of Mississippi. In both of his oral histories, done in later years, Si Redd refers

to his mother as "Nancy." However, all official records, including her husband Marvin's own handwritten World War I Draft Registration, refer to her as "Nannie." It is probable she changed her first name, just as she eventually changed the family's last name, so it would sound less "country."

11. Redd, USMOHP, 1.

12. Yates and Ridout, *Red Clay Hills,* 214.

13. Bingham, "Living Legends," 54.

14. E-mails from Dr. Harold Graham and Ralph Gordon, 05/19/2008.

15. Yates and Ridout, *Red Clay Hills,* 10, 18.

16. A. J. Brown, *History of Newton County,* 55.

17. Percy Brooks, USMOHP.

18. William S. Redd, interview by Byron Liggett, June 23, 1994, UNOHP, 1:15 [NOTE: indicates Tape 1, page 15.]

19. John L. Smith, "To the End," *LVRJ,* 10/15/2003.

20. Redd, interview, June 23, 1994, UNOHP, 1:2–3. Years later, Redd admitted he had heard the story about the Lord speaking to a preacher somewhere else, had liked it, and began using it to speak of his own father.

21. Redd, interview, June 23, 1994, UNOHP, 1:13.

22. Ibid., 1:14.

23. Redd, USMOHP, 4.

24. Meridian, Mississippi, official Web site.

25. Redd, USMOHP, 2.

26. http://www.carolshouse.com/places/neshoba.

27. Redd, USMOHP, 2–3.

28. Ibid., 4–5.

29. Ibid.

30. World War I Draft Registration.

31. Yates and Ridout, *Red Clay Hills,* 234.

32. Ibid., 5; Redd, interview, June 23, 1994, UNOHP, 1:2.

33. Brown, *History of Newton,* 289.

CHAPTER 2

1. Florence Mars, *Witness in Philadelphia,* 2.

2. Ibid., 2–3.

3. Ibid., 3, 6.

4. Redd, interview, June 23, 1994, UNOHP, 1:17.

5. Robert Macy, "Gaming Pioneer," *LVRJ,* 01/10/1996.

6. Ibid., 1–18.

7. Ibid., 1–22.

8. Ibid.

9. Randall Lane, "Back into the Breach," *Forbes,* 96.

10. Eudora Welty, *One Time, One Place,* 3–4.
11. Jonnie McClanathan, interview with the author.
12. Ibid.
13. *Metro Business Chronicle.*
14. Redd, USMOHP, 68.
15. Redd, interview, June 24, 1994, UNOHP, 3:9.
16. Redd, USMOHP, 7.
17. Redd, interview, June 23, 1994, UNOHP, 1:26–27.
18. Ibid., 27; Redd, USMOHP, 7.
19. Redd, interview, June 23, 1994, UNOHP, 1:28.
20. Ibid.
21. Daniel R. Mead, "Si Redd," 11.
22. Redd, USMOHP, 8.
23. Mead, "Si Redd," 11.

CHAPTER 3

1. Redd, USMOHP, 8.
2. Ibid., 14.
3. Lee Ragland, "Pinball Wizard," *JCL,* 03/13/1995.
4. Redd, USMOHP, 9.
5. Ibid.
6. Mark Fierro, "The King of the Slots" video.
7. Redd, interview, June 23, 1994, UNOHP, 1:29.
8. Redd, USMOHP, 9–10.
9. Ibid., 11.
10. Redd, interview, June 23, 1994, UNOHP, 2:1.
11. Early history of the jukebox, Kerry Seagrave, *Jukeboxes,* 1, 5, 22, 39, 41; Vincent Lynch and Bill Henkin, *Jukebox,* 7.
12. Mead, "Si Redd," 12.
13. Ragland, "Pinball Wizard," *JCL,* 03/13/1995.
14. Redd, USMOHP, 24.
15. Ibid.
16. Ibid., 16.
17. Ibid., 14.
18. Mead, "Si Redd," 11.
19. Ibid.
20. Robert M. Jones, interview with the author.
21. Mead, "Si Redd," 11.
22. Ibid.
23. Redd, Promotional Video.
24. Redd, USMOHP, 14.
25. Lynch and Henkin, *Jukebox,* 20.

CHAPTER 4

1. Description of northern Illinois in the 1930s, Harry Hansen, *Illinois,* 590–591.
2. Redd, interview, June 24, 1994, UNOHP, 3:26–27.
3. Redd, USMOHP, 15.
4. Jones, interview with the author.
5. Redd, USMOHP, 15.
6. Jones, interview with the author.
7. Sherry Green, interview with the author.
8. Jones, interview with the author.
9. McClanathan, interview with the author.
10. Seagrave, *Jukeboxes,* 111.
11. Ibid., 50.
12. Ibid., 92, 111.
13. Redd, USMOHP, 22.

CHAPTER 5

1. Redd, USMOHP, 22.
2. Ragland, "Pinball Wizard," *JCL,* 03/13/1995.
3. Mead, "Si Redd,"13.
4. Story of the Cocoanut Grove fire, Redd, interview, August 17, 1994, UNOHP, 6:4.
5. WPA, *Massachusetts,* 137.
6. McClanathan, interview with author.
7. Redd, interview, June 24, 1994, UNOHP, 2:3.
8. Redd, *USMOHP,* 17.
9. Rodesch, Dale, interview with the author.
10. Mead, "Si Redd," 13.
11. Redd, interview, June 24, 1994, UNOHP, 4:10-11.
12. Redd, *USMOHP,* 18.
13. Works Progress Administration, *Massachusetts,* 299.
14. Robert Cashell, interview with the author.
15. Harry Reid, *The Good Fight,* 267.
16. Alan Green, 08/07/2008 e-mail to the author.
17. Jones, interview with the author.
18. Seagrave, *Jukeboxes,* 164–165.
19. Seagrave, *Jukeboxes,* chs. 5–6, passim.
20. Ibid., 223.
21. Redd, USMOHP, 22.
22. Jones, interview with the author.
23. Richard Olsen, interview with the author.
24. Ibid.
25. Mead, "Si Redd," 13.

26. Ibid., 14.

27. Redd, USMOHP, 24.

28. Don Lynch, "How I Became King," 32.

29. Olsen, interview with the author.

30. Estes Kefauver, *Crime in America,* 138.

31. Shuffle-Alley history and description, Marvin Yagoda, "Marvin's Marvelous," www.marvin3m.com/bowl, accessed 08/12/2008.

32. Ibid.

33. Alan Green, interview with the author.

34. Ibid.

35. Mario Machi, "American Mafia.com," http:www.americanmafia.com/cities/New_England-Boston.html.

36. Christopher Hagen, "Quarter Master," n.p.

37. Alan Green, interview with the author.

38. Hagen, "Quarter Master," n.p.

39. Jones, interview with the author.

40. Mead, "Si Redd," 14.

41. Redd, USMOHP, 28.

CHAPTER 6

1. Basil Nestor, "Ten Most Influential," *Strictly Slots* online archive; *New York Times,* W. T. O'Donnell obituary, 07/14/1995.

2. Redd, USMOHP, 28.

3. Zilker v. Klein.

4. Ibid.

5. Background of Dick Graves; Dwayne Kling, *Rise of Biggest Little City,* 58.

6. *Time,* "Las Vegas: 'It Just Couldn't Happen.'"

7. Zilker v. Klein.

8. Marshall Fey, *Slot Machines,* 197.

9. Warren Nelson, *Always Bet on the Butcher,* 137.

10. Lynch, "How I Became King," 90.

11. Redd, USMOHP, 29.

12. Macy, "Gaming Pioneer," *LVRJ,* 01/10/1996.

13. Mead, "Si Redd," 14.

14. Lynch, "How I Became King," 32.

15. Story of the invention of the slot machine, Fey, *Slot Machines,* 37–41.

16. Lynch, "How I Became King," 90.

17. Early history of Reno, Holly Walton-Buchanan, *Historic Houses and Buildings,*" xi–xv.

18. "Betting on Nevada," *Nevada Magazine,* 8.

19. Kling, *Rise of Biggest Little City,* 123.

20. Eric N. Moody, "Early Years of Casino Gambling," 113–114.

21. Silvio Petricciani, *Evolution of Gaming,* 47.

22. Max Miller, *Reno,* viii.

23. Joseph E. Stevens, *Hoover Dam,* 48–49.

24. Jeff Burbank, *License to Steal,* 6.

25. *Time,* "Las Vegas: 'It Just Couldn't Happen.'"

26. A. D. Hopkins and K. J. Evans, *First 100,* 117, 121.

27. Ibid., 121.

28. Ibid.

29. "Hotel El Rancho Vegas," Center for Gaming Research, http://gaming.unlv.edu/ElRanchoVegas/index.html.

30. Hopkins and Evans, *First 100,* 287.

31. *LVS,* 01/02/2000.

32. Lynch, "How I Became King," 32; Redd, interview, September 15, 1994, UNOHP, 7:15.

33. Lynch, "How I Became King," 32.

34. Nelson, *Always Bet on the Butcher,* 135–136; Kling, *Rise of Biggest Little City,* 114.

35. Nelson, *Always Bet on the Butcher,* 136.

36. Ibid.

37. Mead, "Dick Raven Story," 32–33.

38. Ibid.

39. Redd, USMOHP, 26.

40. Fey, *Slot Machines,* 187.

41. Ibid., 17.

42. Mead, "Si Redd," 14.

43. Redd, interview, September 15, 1994, UNOHP, 7:16.

44. Redd, *USMOHP,* 63.

45. Macy, "Gaming Pioneer," *LVRJ,* 01/10/1996.

46. Hagen, "Quarter Master," n.p.

47. Ragland, "Pinball Wizard," *JCL,* 03/13/1995.

48. Hagen, "Quarter Master," 28.

49. *Public Gaming,* "Si Redd," 44.

50. Ragland, "Pinball Wizard," *JCL,* 03/13/1995.

51. Jones, 09/28/08 interview with the author.

52. Tony Mills, interview with the author.

53. Cashell, interview with the author.

54. Chevis Swetman, interview with the author.

55. Bingham, "Living Legends," 54; *Nevada Portraits,* n.p.

56. Redd, interview, June 24, 1994, UNOHP, 4:17.

57. Kling, *Rise of Biggest Little City,* 147; Bingham, *Nevada Portraits,* 82.

58. Pete Cladianos Jr., *My Father's Son,* 118–119.

59. Mead, "The Experimental," 37–39; Mead, "Harrah's Secret Slot Shop," passim.

60. Mead Dixon, *Playing the Cards*, 190–191; Kling, *Rise of Biggest Little City*, 76.

61. Ibid., 193.

62. Ibid.,

63. Ibid., 119.

64. Mills, interview with the author.

65. John Ascuaga, interview with the author.

66. Redd, interview, September 15, 1994, UNOHP, 7:16.

CHAPTER 7

1. Alan Green, e-mail to the author.

2. Ibid.

3. Ibid.

4. Jones, interview with the author.

5. Rich, interview with the author.

6. Fey, *Slot Machines*, 179–180.

7. Jack Douglass, *Tap Dancing on Ice*, 158.

8. Lynch, "How I Became King," 33–34.

9. Ibid., 92.

10. Ibid.

11. Kling, interview with the author.

12. Nelson, *Always Bet on Butcher*, 138.

13. Ibid.

14. Alan Green, 09/24/2008, e-mail to the author.

15. Hood, *Whatever It Takes*, 175.

16. Kling, *Luck Is the Residue of Design*, 264.

17. Lynch, "How I Became King," 36.

18. Ibid.

19. William R. Eadington, "Economic Trends in Gaming," 30, 31.

20. Hagen, "Quarter Master," 28.

21. Ibid., 33.

22. Ibid.

23. Redd, USMOHP, 39.

24. Redd's and O'Donnell's negotiations, Redd, USMOHP, 31–41.

25. Redd, USMOHP, 31.

26. Ken Miller, "How Bally Manufacturing Cleaned Up Its Act," *RGJ*, 03/30/1986.

27. Jerome H. Skolnick, *House of Cards*, 347; Redd, USMOHP, 40–41.

28. Kefauver, *Crime in America*, 229.

29. Background on Nevada gaming regulations, William N. Thompson, *Legalized Gambling*, 96–98; Ronald Farrell and Carole Chase, *The Black Book*, 28–31.

30. Redd, USMOHP, 31.

31. Barbara Rich, interview with the author.

32. Ibid.

33. Ibid.

34. Redd, USMOHP, 41–42; Redd, interview, September 15, 1994, UNOHP, 7:25–26.

35. *NSJ,* 01/23/1972, 04/18/1972; Redd, USMOHP, 41.

36. Redd, interview, September 15, 1994, UNOHP, 7:27–28.

37. Redd, USMOHP, 25.

38. Ibid.

39. Ibid.

40. Warren Nelson and his Spot Slot keno machine; Nelson, *Gaming from the Old Days,* 141–142.

41. Ibid.

CHAPTER 8

1. Mead, "Dick Raven Story," 30–33.

2. Ibid.

3. All quotes from Dale Rodesch and Dale Frey in this chapter, and their accounts of their development of video poker, are from a 09/06/2008 interview and numerous e-mails from Rodesch to the author; and 09/14/2008 and 04/01/2009 interviews by Dale Frey with the author.

4. *Guinness Book of World Records,* 623.

5. Alan Green, interview with the author.

6. Redd, interview, June 24, 1994, UNOHP, 4:25.

7. Ibid., 4:25–26.

8. *Public Gaming,* "Video Market Fertile," 34.

9. Bally Distributing Company, 1974 sales brochure.

10. Ibid.

CHAPTER 9

1. *RGJ,* 02/23/1979.

2. Redd, USMOHP, 44.

3. Lynch, "How I Became King," 94.

4. Zilker v. Klein. (Author's note: As a matter of fact, the 70/30 Bally Distributing Company ownership ratio discussed is not accurate. Redd owned 69.5 percent and O'Donnell owned 29.5 percent The other 1 percent was owned by an unnamed shareholder whose identity the author has not been able to determine.)

5. Redd, USMOHP, 44.

6. Rich, interview with the author.

7. Skolnick, *House of Cards,* 302, 348.

8. Ibid.

9. E-mail to the author dated 09/15/2008 from the State of Nevada Gaming Control Board, Tax and License Division.

10. Redd, USMOHP, 33, 31.

11. Ibid., 32.

12. Rich, interview with the author.

13. Rodesch, 09/12/2008 e-mail to the author.

14. Ibid.

15. Ibid.

16. Rodesch, 09/07/2008 e-mail to the author.

17. Background story about Pong; Rodesch, 10/08/2008 e-mail to the author; Frey, 09/14/2008 interview with the author.

18. Rodesch, 10/08/2008 e-mail to the author.

19. Dale Frey, 09/14/2008 interview with the author.

20. Frey, 04/04/2009, conversation with the author.

21. Frey, 09/14/2008 interview with the author.

22. Ibid.

23. Ibid.

24. Ibid.

25. Tyler Sciotto, conversation with the author.

26. Cladianos, *My Father's Son,* 120.

27. Elwin Studebaker, interview with the author.

28. Rodesch, 09/19/2008 and 09/12/2008 e-mails to the author.

29. Ibid.

30. Ibid.

31. Story of Redd's purchase of Desert Inn house; Robert Maheu and Richard Hack, *Next to Hughes,* 173–176, 241; 10/15/2008 e-mail from Hughes's author Geoff Schumacher; Redd, interview, December 19, 1994, UNOHP, 9:25–26; Redd, USMOHP, 65.

32. Fey, *Slot Machines,* 213–214.

33. Frey, 09/14/2008 interview with the author.

34. Ibid.

35. Nelson, *Always Bet on the Butcher,* 139.

36. Cladianos, *My Father's Son,* 120–121.

37. William Boyd, interview with the author.

38. Redd, interview, June 24, 1994, UNOHP, 3:1–2; 4:31.

39. Ibid.

40. Fey, *Slot Machines,* 214.

41. Mead, "Antique Gambler," 18–21.

42. Mead, "Antique Gambler Auction," 19–23.

43. Mills, interview with the author.

44. Story of selling Sircoma, Studebaker, interview with the author.

45. Ibid.

46. Nelson, *Always Bet on the Butcher,* 139.

CHAPTER 10

1. Lynch, "How I Became King," 32.
2. Randy Fromm, *Slot Tech*, July 2001, 28–29.
3. City of Las Vegas Proclamation Certificate, in author's possession.
4. *RePlay*, 12/18/1981, 14.
5. Ibid.
6. Brad Rothermel, interview with the author.
7. Dixon, *Playing the Cards*, 1, 193–194.
8. Ibid.
9. Fey, *Slot Machines*, 5.
10. Ibid., 13.
11. *Pioche Weekly Record*, 02/21/1895, 4.
12. Dennis McLellan, "William Redd," *LAT*, 10/19/2003.
13. Ragland, "Pinball Wizard Hits Jackpot," *JCL*, 03/13/1995.
14. Robert N. Geddes, "Video Draw Poker," 12–13.
15. McLellan, "William Redd," *LAT*, 10/19/2003.
16. Richard Stevenson, "Slot Machine Maker Hits Jackpot," *NYT*, 09/12/1989.
17. Bob Carabine, "Those Video Slot Machines," 21.
18. Kling, *Rise of Biggest Little City*, 42.
19. IGT Annual Report, 1983.
20. Studebaker, interview with the author.
21. Tim Anderson, "Electronics Come of Age," *RGJ*, 05/31/1981.
22. Ibid.
23. Tim Anderson, "Video Gaming Firm's Future," *NSJ*, 05/29/1982; "IGT an 'Up and Comer,'" *NSJ*, 11/14/1982.
24. *Public Gaming*, March 1982, 46.
25. Mickey Roemer, interview with the author.
26. Kling, interview with the author.
27. Rick Carter, interview with the author.
28. Rhett Long, interview with the author.
29. Anderson, Tim, "Tough Times Ahead for Reno," *RGJ*, 10/21/81.
30. Redd, interview, September 16, 1994, UNOHP, 8:22.
31. Rich, interview with the author.
32. IGT Annual Report, 1983.
33. Voyles, Susan, "Slot company's Prospects Bright," *NSJ*, 03/03/1982.
34. Rodesch, 09/15/2008 e-mail to the author.
35. Ibid.
36. Ibid.
37. John Acres, "IGT's Open System," http://www.slotmanager.net/Articles/Departments/ BNP_GUID_9-5-2006_A_.
38. Ibid.
39. Ibid.
40. Ibid.

41. Redd, USMOHP, 44.

42. Voyles, "Judge Tells Bally," *REG*, 07/13/1982.

43. Ibid.

44. IGT, 1983 Annual Report; Redd, USMOHP, 45.

45. *Gaming Business,* April 1982, as quoted in Ernkvist, "Creating Player Appeal," 131.

46. Cladianos, *My Father's Son,* 122.

47. Story of Universal's entry into Nevada, Burbank, *License to Steal,* 104–127, passim.

48. Ibid.

49. Ibid.

50. Ibid.

CHAPTER 11

1. Alan Green, 02/06/2009 e-mail to the author.

2. IGT, 1983 Annual Report.

3. Redd, USMOHP, 53.

4. *National Enquirer,* 02/15/1994.

5. Roemer, interview with the author.

6. Studebaker, interview with the author.

7. Richard Bryan, interview with the author.

8. Rodesch, 09/15/2008 e-mail to the author.

9. Pete Mandas, interview with the author.

10. Studebaker, interview with the author.

11. Alan Green, 10/29/2008 e-mail to the author.

12. Mead, "Si Redd," 17.

13. Redd, interview, September 16, 1994, UNOHP, 8:1.

14. Sinclair Lewis, *Babbitt,* 38–39.

15. Charles Mathewson, interview with the author.

16. Jones, 11/03/2008 interview with the author; Alan Green, 10/30/2008 e-mail to the author.

17. Jones, 11/07/2008 interview with the author.

18. Redd, USMOHP, 62.

19. Bryan, interview with the author.

20. Rodesch, 09/17/2008 e-mail to the author.

21. Mandas, interview with the author.

22. Cashell, interview with the author.

23. Rich, interview with the author.

24. Redd, USMOHP, 44.

25. Mead, "Si Redd," 17.

26. Redd, USMOHP, 45–46.

27. Ibid., 47.

28. Ben C. Toledano, "Mississippi Gambles," 1.

29. Mirko Ernkvist, "Creating Player Appeal," 271 (n.101).
30. Mead, "How IGT Spells Success," 12–14.
31. Richard McGowan, *State Lotteries,* 3–14.
32. Ibid.
33. Ibid.
34. Nelson, *Always Bet on the Butcher,* 138.
35. Ibid., 140.
36. Roemer, interview with the author.
37. Mead, "Megabucks," 15.
38. Mike Henderson, "Casinos Launch $1 Slot," *RGJ,* 03/07/1986.
39. Ibid.
40. Roemer, interview with the author.
41. Boyd, interview with the author.
42. Ernkvist, "Creating Player Appeal," 169.
43. Clyde Weiss, "Redd Completes Purchase," *LVRJ,* 08/29/1980, 3A.
44. Ibid.
45. Nelson, *Always Bet on the Butcher,* 196.
46. *REG,* "Redd's Purchase Application OK'd," 07/22/1983.

CHAPTER 12

1. Richard W. Stevenson, "Slot Machine Maker Hits Jackpot," *NYT,* 09/12/1989.
2. William J. O'Neill, , *Business Leaders & Success,* 101–104.
3. Mathewson, interview with the author.
4. Ibid.
5. Voyles, "'Slot King' Sells Control," *RGJ,* 12/19/2006.
6. Ibid.
7. Redd, IGT Press Release, 12/17/1986.
8. Lane, "Back into the Breach," *Forbes,* 96.
9. Mathewson, interview with the author.
10. Background on gambling in Mississippi; Denise Von Herrman, *Resorting to Casinos,* 12–23.
11. Lynch, "How I Became King," 35.
12. Hugh Keating, interview with the author.
13. Jere Nash and Andy Taggart, *Mississippi Politics,* 216.
14. Carter, interview with the author.
15. Swetman, interview with the author.
16. Thomas B. Shepherd and Cheryn L. Netz, "Mississippi," in *International Casino Law,* 72.
17. Ibid.
18. Carter, interview with the author; Ragland, "Pinball Wizard," *JCL,* 03/13/1995; Burbank, "IGT Founder 'Sy' [sic] Redd," *LVS,* 01/12/1989.

19. Burbank, "IGT Founder 'Sy' [sic] Redd, " *LVS*, 01/12/1989.

20. *RGJ*, 01/11/1990; 12/14/2008 e-mail and interview with Hugh Keating.

21. Carter, 01/08/2009 interview with the author.

22. Ibid.

23. Keating, interview with the author.

24. Von Herrman, *Resorting to Casinos*, 26–28.

25. Shepherd and Netz, "Mississippi," in *International Casino Law*, 72.

26. Keating, 12/14/2008 e-mail to the author.

27. Swetman, interview with the author.

28. Carter, interview with the author.

29. Studebaker, interview with the author.

30. Carter, interview with the author.

31. Ibid.

32. Keating, 12/14/2008 e-mail to the author.

33. Ragland, "Pinball Wizard," *JCL*, 03/13/1995.

34. Nash and Taggart, *Mississippi Politics*, 216.

35. *LVS*, "Redd Loses Fortune on Gambling Ship." 01/11/1990.

36. Ibid.

37. Barbara Land, "The Slot Machine King," *RGJ*, 02/25/1989.

38. Jamie McKee, "'Video Poker King,'" *LVBP*, 11/07/1994.

39. Ragland, "Pinball Wizard," *JCL*, 03/13/1995.

40. Ibid.

41. Ragland, "Pinball Wizard," *JCL*, 03/13/1995; *LVRJ*, "In Brief Business Notes," 02/23/1995.

42. Rodesch, 09/17/2008 e-mail to the author.

43. Ibid.

44. Ibid.

45. Alan Green, 02/13/2009 e-mail to the author.

46. Doug Bailey and Mitchell Zuckoff, *Boston Globe*, "Gaming's New Face Has Corporate Profile," 09/28/1993.

47. Alan Green, 02/12/2009 e-mail to the author.

48. Ibid.

49. Ibid.

50. *Las Vegas Life*, November 2001.

51. McKee, "Video Poker King," *LVBP*, 11/07/1994.

52. Ibid.

Chapter 13

1. History of Mesquite; James L. Scholl, "Mesquite, Nevada," 89.

2. Lynch, "How I Became King," 35.

3. Jimmie Hughes, interview with the author.

4. Cashell, interview with the author.

5. Ibid.
6. Redd, USMOHP, 37.
7. Ibid.
8. Scholl, "Mesquite, Nevada," 93–96.
9. Hughes, interview with the author.
10. Ibid.
11. Ibid.
12. Long, interview with the author.
13. Doug McMillan, *RGJ*, "Nevada Land Swap," 03/30/1986.
14. Macy, "Gaming Pioneer," *LVRJ*, 01/10/1996.
15. Long, interview with the author.
16. Ibid.
17. Ibid.
18. Ibid.
19. Studebaker, interview with the author.
20. David Humm, interview with the author.
21. Ibid.
22. Ibid.
23. Gloria Savco, "Mesquite: A Sleepy Town," *LVRJ*, 12/17/1995.
24. Marcia Pledger, "Golf, Gaming," *LVRJ*, 07/10/1994.
25. Cindy Risinger, e-mail to the author.
26. Carter, interview with the author.
27. Risinger, interview with the author.
28. Alan Green, 01/27/2009 e-mail to the author.
29. Ibid.
30. Ibid.
31. Caruso, Monica, "Gaming Pioneers," *LVRJ*, 10/16/1996.
32. Fierro, "Slot Machine King" video.
33. McLellan, "William Redd, 91,"*LAT*, 10/19/2003.
34. Studebaker, interview with the author.

CHAPTER 14

1. Story about Redd's third marriage; Alan Green 04/04/2009 e-mail to the author.
2. Ibid.
3. Ed Koch, "Gaming Pioneer," *LVS*, 10/15/2003.
4. Fromm, *Slot Tech,* July 2001, 28–29.
5. Ibid.
6. Hagen, "Quarter Master," 28–30.
7. Ibid.
8. Carter, interview with the author.
9. Ibid.

10. Ibid.
11. Koch, "Gaming Pioneer," *LVS*, 10/15/2003.
12. Reid, *The Good Fight*, 269.
13. Jones, "Slot Machine King," *LVRJ*, 10/15/2003.
14. Ragland, "Pinball Wizard," *JCL*, 03/13/1995.
15. Thompson, "A Si of Relief," *LVS*, 10/16/1996.
16. Ibid.
17. Macy, "IGT Founder Finds New Challenge," *LVS*, 01/14/1996.
18. Lynn Waddell, "It's a Redd Letter Day," 11/15/1991.
19. IGT, 2007 Annual Report.

BIBLIOGRAPHY

BOOKS, NEWSPAPERS, MAGAZINES, MANUSCRIPTS

Abbreviations: IGT–International Game Technology; *JCL–Jackson (MS) Clarion-Ledger; LAT–Los Angeles Times; LVRJ–Las Vegas (NV) Review-Journal; LVS–Las Vegas (NV) Sun; NSJ (Reno)–Nevada State Journal; REG–Reno (NV) Evening Gazette; RGJ–Reno Gazette Journal;* UNOHP–University of Nevada Oral History Program; USMOHP–University of Southern Mississippi Oral History Program.

Acres, John. "IGT's Open System—A Freeway to the Future or a Toll Road to Hell?" *Slot Manager* magazine Web site. http://www.slotmanager .net. Las Vegas: BNP Media, Inc.

Adams, Frank. *Wurlitzer Jukeboxes, 1934–1974.* 3rd edition. Des Moines, IA: Jukebox Collector Magazine, 1997.

Anderson, Tim. "Electronics Come of Age in Casinos." *RGJ,* 05/31/1981.

———. "IGT an 'Up and Comer.'" *RGJ,* 11/14/1982.

———. "Tough Times Ahead for Reno." *RGJ,* 10/21/1981.

———. "Video Gaming Firm's Future Is Competitive." *RGJ,* 05/29/1982.

Bailey, Doug, and Mitchell Zuckoff. "Gaming's New Face Has Corporate Profile." *Boston Globe,* 09/28/1993.

Bally Distributing Company. Sales brochure. Reno, NV: 1974.

Bally Technologies. http://www.ballytech.com.

Beazley, Jim. "Reno Firm Now Ships 'Slots' Around World." *RGJ,* 02/23/1979.

Bingham, Reed. "Living Legends, William Si Redd." *Comstock's Northern Nevada,* Winter 1998.

———. *Nevada Portraits.* Reno: Nevada Museum of Art, 2004.

Brooks, Percy. *Oral History of Percy Brooks.* Mississippi Oral History Program of the University of Southern Mississippi, Hattiesburg, Vol. 273, part 1, 1999. Online at http://www.lib.usm.edu/~spcol/coh/cohbrooksp .html, accessed 05/20/2008.

Brown, A. J. *History of Newton County, Mississippi: From 1834–1894.* Rep., Decatur, MS: Melvin Tingle, 1964.

Burbank, Jeff. "IGT Founder 'Sy' [sic] Redd Gets Initial Approval for Cruise Ship Gaming." *LVS,* 01/12/1989.

———. *License to Steal: Nevada's Gaming Control System in the Megaresort Age.* Reno: University of Nevada Press, 2000.

Carabine, Bob. "Those Video Slot Machines." *Loose Change,* Nov. 1982. Long Beach, CA: Mead Publishing Co.

"Carols House." http://www.carolshouse.com.

Caruso, Monica. "Gaming Pioneers Retire from Industry." *LVRJ,* 10/16/1996.

Cladianos, Pete Jr. *My Father's Son: A Gaming Memoir.* Reno: University of Nevada Oral History Program, 2002.

Dixon, Mead. *Playing the Cards That Are Dealt.* Reno: University of Nevada Oral History Program, 1992.

Douglass, Jack. *Tap Dancing on Ice.* Reno: University of Nevada Oral History Program, 1996.

Eadington, William R. "Economic Trends in Gaming Related Tourism in Northern Nevada." Paper 79-1, Bureau of Business & Economic Research. Reno: University of Nevada, 1979.

Ernkvist, Mirko. "Creating Player Appeal: Management of Technological Innovation and Changing Pattern of Industrial Leadership in the U.S. Gaming Machine Manufacturing Industry, 1965–2005." PhD diss., University of Gothenburg, Goteborg, Sweden, 2009.

Farrell, Ronald, and Carole Chase. *The Black Book and the Mob: The Untold Story of Nevada's Casinos.* Madison: University of Wisconsin Press, 1995.

Fey, Marshall. *Slot Machines: A Pictorial History of the First 100 Years.* 5th ed. Reno, NV: Liberty Belle Books, 1997.

Fieldler, Alvin Sr. *Oral History with Alvin Fieldler.* Mississippi Oral History Program of the University of Southern Mississippi, Hattiesburg, Vol. 709, 1998. Online at http://www.lib.usm.edu/~spcol/coh/ cohfieldera.html, accessed 05/20/2008.

Fierro, Mark. "The King of the Slots." Promotional video recording and interview tape prepared by Shonkwiler Marcoux Advertising, Las Vegas, for Si Redd's Oasis Resort Hotel-Casino, Mesquite, Nevada. 1995.

Fromm, Randy. "Slot Tech Magazine Visits Si Redd." *Slot Tech,* July 2001. El Cajon, CA.

Geddes, Robert N. "Video Draw Poker . . . America's Coin-Operated Gambling Craze." *Loose Change,* May 1990. Long Beach, CA: Mead Publishing Co.

Guinness Book of World Records, 1983. New York: Bantam, 1983.

Hagen, Christopher. "Quarter Master: Si Redd, Legendary Developer of Video Poker and Megabucks, Built His Legacy One Coin at a Time." *Las Vegas Life,* November 2001. Las Vegas: Greenspun Media Group.

Hansen, Harry, ed. *Illinois: A Descriptive and Historical Guide.* Works Progress Administration, Federal Writers' Project. Rep. New York: Hastings House, 1974.

Henderson, Mike. "Casinos Launch $1 Slot Machine Network." *RGJ,* 03/07/1986.

Hood, Jeanne. *Whatever Will Help: A Woman's Rise to the Top in the Gaming Industry.* Reno: University of Nevada Oral History Program, 2006.

Hopkins, A. D. and K. J. Evans. *The First 100: Portraits of the Men and Women Who Shaped Las Vegas.* Las Vegas: Huntington Press, 1999.

"Hotel El Rancho Vegas." Center for Gaming Research, University of Nevada, Las Vegas, Virtual Libraries. http://gaming.unlv.edu.

IGT. Annual Reports, 1981, 1983, 2007, Reno, NV.

———. "Short History of Gaming Machines." https://www.igt.com/Content/base.asp?pid=8.17.36.15.

———. Various press releases, as indicated in the notes.

Jackson Clarion-Ledger, Jackson, Mississippi. (See Ragland, Lee.)

Jones, Chris. "'Slot Machine King,' IGT Founder Dies at 91." *LVRJ,* 10/15/2003.

Kefauver, Estes. *Crime in America.* Garden City, NY: Doubleday, 1951.

Kling, Dwayne. *Luck Is the Residue of Design.* Reno: University of Nevada Oral History Program, 2000.

———. *The Rise of the Biggest Little City: An Encyclopedic History of Reno Gaming, 1931–1981.* Reno: University of Nevada Press, 2000.

Koch, Ed. "Gaming Pioneer Known for Invention, Generosity Dies." *LVS,* 10/15/2003.

Land, Barbara. "The Slot Machine King." *RGJ,* 02/25/1989.

Lane, Randall. "Back into the Breach." *Fortune,* 11/09/1992. New York: B. C. Forbes Publishing Co.

Las Vegas Business Press, Stephens Media Group, Las Vegas, NV.

Las Vegas Life, Greenspun Media Group, Las Vegas, NV.

Las Vegas Review-Journal, Stephens Media Group, Las Vegas, NV.

Las Vegas Review-Journal. "In Brief Business Notes: 'Gaming Board OK's Keno System Sales.'" 02/23/1995, 1D.

Las Vegas Sun. "Red Loses Fortune on Gambling Ship." 01/11/1990. Greenspun Media Group, Las Vegas, NV.

Lewis, Sinclair. *Babbitt.* New York: Harcourt & Brace, 1922.

Lynch, Don. "How I Became King of the Slots." *Nevada,* May–June 1990.

Lynch, Vincent, and Bill Henkin. *Jukebox, The Golden Age.* Berkeley, CA: Lancaster-Miller, 1981.

Macy, Robert. "Gaming Pioneer Says It Was 'the Fun of the Journey.'" Associated Press, *LVRJ,* 01/01/1996.

———. "IGT Founder Finds New Challenge in Tiny Mesquite." Associated Press, *LVS,* 01/14/1996.

Maheu, Robert, and Richard Hack. *Next to Hughes: Behind the Power and Tragic Downfall of Howard Hughes and His Closest Advisor.* New York: HarperCollins,1992.

Marfels, Christian. *Bally, the World's Game Maker.* Las Vegas: University of Nevada–Las Vegas, International Gaming Institute, 1998.

Mars, Florence. *The Fair: A Personal History.* Philadelphia, MS: Stribling, 2001.

———. *Witness in Philadelphia.* Baton Rouge: Louisiana State University Press, 1977.

McGowan, Richard. *State Lotteries and Legalized Gambling: Painless Revenue or Painful Mirage.* Westport, CT: Praeger, 1994.

McKee, Jamie. "'Video Poker King' Starts All Over Again." *LVBP,* 11/07/1994.

McLellan, Dennis. "William Redd, 91, Gambling's Visionary, 'King of Video Poker.'" *LAT,* 10/19/2003.

McMillan, Doug. "Nevada Land Swap: Public Seen Taking Financial Bath." *RGJ,* 03/30/1986.

Mead, Daniel R. "The Antique Gambler." *Loose Change,* July 1978. Long Beach, CA: Mead Publishing Co.

———. "The Antique Gambler Auction." *Loose Change,* June 1980. Long Beach, CA: Mead Publishing Co.

———. "The Dick Raven Story." *Loose Change,* Jan. 1986. Long Beach, CA: Mead Publishing Co.

———. "The Experimental." *Loose Change,* Jan. 1986. Long Beach, CA: Mead Publishing Co.

———. "Harrah's Secret Slot Shop." *Loose Change,* Feb. 1986. Long Beach, CA: Mead Publishing Co.

———. "How IGT Spells Success: S-S-L-O-T-S." *Loose Change,* June 1986. Long Beach, CA: Mead Publishing Co.

———. "Man with a Mission." *Loose Change,* Oct. 1996. Long Beach, CA: Mead Publishing Co.

———. "Megabucks, a New Idea for Nevada." *Loose Change,* Apr., 1986. Long Beach, CA: Mead Publishing Co.

————. "Si Redd: The Slot Machine King." *Loose Change,* Sept. 1980. Long Beach, CA: Mead Publishing Co.

Meridian, Mississippi, Official Web site. http://www.meridianms.org/com_history.html.

Metro Business Chronicle, Jackson, Mississippi. www.metrochronicle.com.

Miller, Ken. "How Bally Manufacturing Cleaned Up Its Act." *RGJ,* 03/30/1986.

Miller, Max. *Reno.* New York: Dodd, Mead, 1941.

Moody, Eric N. "The Early Years of Casino Gambling in Nevada: 1931–1945." PhD diss., University of Nevada–Reno, 1997.

Nash, Jere, and Andy Taggart. *Mississippi Politics: The Struggle for Power, 1976–2006.* Jackson: University Press of Mississippi, 2006.

Nelson, Warren. *Always Bet on the Butcher: Warren Nelson and Casino Gaming, 1930s–1980s.* Reno: University of Nevada Oral History Program, 1994.

————. *Gaming from the Old Days to Computers.* Reno: University of Nevada Oral History Program, 1978.

Nestor, Basil. "The Ten Most Influential People in the History of Slots." *Strictly Slots.* http://www.strictlyslots.com/archive/0407ss/SS0704influential.pdf, accessed 12/29/2008.

Nevada Commission on Tourism, State of Nevada, Carson City. *Nevada.* "Betting on Nevada." January–February 1991.

Nevada State Journal. "Tough Times Ahead for Reno." 10/21/1981.

O'Neil, William J. *Business Leaders & Success: 55 Top Business Leaders & How They Achieved Greatness.* New York: McGraw-Hill, 2004.

Percy, William Alexander. *Lanterns on the Levee: Recollections of a Planter's Son.* 1941. Rep. Baton Rouge: Louisiana State University Press, 1984.

Petricciani, Silvio. *Evolution of Gaming in Nevada: The Twenties to the Eighties.* Reno: University of Nevada Oral History Program, 1978.

Pioche Weekly Record. Microfilm #0369. Library of the University of Nevada–Reno.

Pledger, Marcia. "Golf, Gaming Make Perfect Playmates." *LVRJ,* 07/10/1994.

Public Gaming. "Si Redd: Pioneer in the Video Slot Machine Industry." March 1982. Kirkland, WA: Public Gaming Research Institute International.

————. "Video Market Fertile Ground for IGT." February 1983. Kirkland, WA: Public Gaming Research Institute International.

Ragland, Lee. "Pinball Wizard Hits Jackpot with Slot Innovations." *JCL,* 03/13/1995.

Redd, William Si. *An Oral History with Mr. William "Si" Redd.* Orley Caudill, Interviewer, 04/15/1983 and 04/19/1983. Mississippi Oral

History Program of the University of Southern Mississippi, Hattiesburg, Vol. 257, 1983.

Redd, William S. Interviews by Byron Liggett. 23 June 1994; 24 June 1994; 17 August 1994; 15 September 1994; 19 December 1994. Unpublished transcripts in research files, University of Nevada Oral History Program, Reno, Nevada.

———. Promotional Video on the Life of Si Redd. Owned by the Redd Family. Produced by Shonkwiler/Marcoux Advertising, Las Vegas, NV, circa 1996.

Reid, Harry, with Mark Warren. *The Good Fight: Hard Lessons from Searchlight to Washington.* New York: Putnam's Sons, 2008.

Reno Evening Gazette. Reno, NV.

Reno Evening Gazette. "Redd's Purchase Application OK'd." 07/22/1983.

Reno Gazette-Journal. Reno, NV.

Reno Gazette-Journal. "Redd Loses Fortune on Gambling Ship." 01/11/1990.

RePlay. RePlay Publishing Co., Tarzana, CA.

Savco, Gloria. "Mesquite: A Sleepy Town Awakens." *LVRJ,* 12/17/1995.

Scholl, James L. "Mesquite, Nevada: From Farm Hamlet to Resort City, 1880–1995." *Nevada Historical Society Quarterly,* Vol. 38, No. 2, Summer 1995.

Seagrave, Kerry. *Jukeboxes, An American Social History.* Jefferson, NC: McFarland, 2002.

Shepherd, Thomas B., and Cheryn L. Netz. "Mississippi." In *International Casino Law.* 3rd ed. Anthony N. Cabot et al., eds. Reno, NV: Institute for Studying of Gambling and Commercial Gaming, 1999.

Skolnick, Jerome H. *House of Cards, the Legalization and Control of Casino Gaming.* Boston: Little, Brown, 1978.

Smith, John L. "To the End, Preacher's Son Kept Faith in Gospel of Legalized Gambling." *LVRJ,* 10/15/2003.

Stevens, Joseph E. *Hoover Dam: An American Adventure.* Norman: University of Oklahoma Press, 1988.

Stevenson, Richard W. "Slot Machine Maker Hits Jackpot," *New York Times,* 09/12/1989.

Stubbs, Steven H. *Mississippi's Giant Houseparty: The History of the Neshoba County Fair.* Philadelphia, MS: Dancing Rabbit Press, 2005.

Thompson, Gary. "A Si of Relief: Slot Machine Pioneer Si Redd Retires." *LVS,* 10/16/1996.

Thompson, William N. *Legalized Gambling: A Reference Handbook.* 2nd ed. Santa Barbara, CA: ABC-Clio, 1997.

Time. "Las Vegas: 'It Just Couldn't Happen.'" 11/23/1953, http://www.time.com/time/magazine/article/0,9171,860113,00.html, accessed 06/26/2009).

Toledano, Ben C. "Mississippi Gambles: The Carpetbaggers Are Back." Rep. from *National Review,* Apr. 7, 1997. BNET Business Network.

http://findarticles.com/p/articles/mi_m1282/is_/ai_19298055.

United States Federal Census, 1900, 1910, 1930. Ancestry.com. http://search.ancestry.com/cgi-bin/sse.dll?rank=1&gsfn=William&gsln=Red&gsby=18.

Von Herrmann, Denise, ed. *Resorting to Casinos, the Mississippi Gambling Industry.* Jackson: University Press of Mississippi, 2006.

Voyles, Susan. "Judge Tells Bally to Leave Market." *REG,* 07/13/1982.

———. "Slot Company's Prospects Bright," *NSJ,* 03/03/1982.

———. "'Slot king' Sells Control of Reno Gambling Business." *RGJ,* 12/19/1986.

Waddell, Lynn. "It's a Redd Letter Day for Slot King." *LVS,* 11/15/1991.

Walton-Buchanan, Holly. *Historic Houses and Buildings of Reno, Nevada.* Reno, NV: Black Rock Press, 2007.

Weiss, Clyde. "Redd Completes Purchase of Sy's." *LVRJ,* 08/29/1980.

Welty, Eudora. *One Time, One Place: Mississippi in the Depression.* New York: Random House, 1971.

Works Progress Administration, Federal Writers' Project. *Massachusetts: A Guide to Its Places and People.* Boston: Houghton Mifflin, 1937.

World War I Draft Registration Cards, 1917–1918. Ancestry.com. http://search.ancestry.com/cgi-bin/sse.dll?rank=1&gsfn=Red&gsby=18, accessed 05/27/2008.

Yagoda, Marvin. "Marvin's Marvelous Mechanical Museum." http://www.marvin3m.com.

Yates, Jenelle B., and Theresa T. Ridout, eds. *Red Clay Hills of Neshoba: Roots–Reflections–Ramblings, The Early History of Neshoba County, Mississippi.* Philadelphia, MS: Neshoba County Historical Society, 1992.

Zilker v. Klein et al., (1981). Fred ZILKER, etc. Plaintiff, v. Sam W. KLEIN et al., Defendants. UNITED STATES DISTRICT COURT FOR THE NORTHERN DISTRICT OF ILLINOIS, EASTERN DIVISION. Case No. 77C1672. April 6, 1981.

SIGNIFICANT PERSONAL INTERVIEWS OR COMMUNICATIONS

(Audio tape recordings of all interviews in the possession of author, unless otherwise noted.)

Boyd, William S. Interview by author, 01/21/2009.
Bryan, Richard. Interview by author, 02/19/2009.
Carter, Rick. Interview by author, 01/08/2009.
Cashell, Robert "Bob." Interview by author, 11/17/2008.
Frey, Dale. Interview by author, 09/14/2008 and 04/01/2009 (no audio tapes on second interview).

Green, Alan. Interviews by author, 08/2008–03/2009; e-mails in possession of author.

Green, Sherry. Interview by author, 08/14/2008 (no audio tape).

Hughes, Jimmie. Interview by author, 01/31/2009.

Humm, David. Interview by author, 02/11/2009.

Jones, Robert M. Interviews by author, 06/28/2008, 07/01/2008, 09/28/2008, 11/03/2008, and 11/07/2008.

Keating, Hugh. Interview by author, 12/16/2008.

Kling, Dwayne. Interview by author, 10/27/2008.

Long, Rhett. Interview by author, 02/04/2009.

Mandas, Peter "Pete." Interview by author, 10/23/2008.

Mathewson, Charles "Chuck." Interview by author, 04/02/2009.

McClanathan, Jonnie. Interview by author, 07/25/2008.

Mills, Tony. Interview by author, 10/22/2008.

Olsen, Richard. Interview by author, 08/14/2008.

Rich, Barbara. Interview by author, 03/12/2009.

Risinger, Cindy. Interview by author, 02/10/2009; e-mail in possession of author.

Rodesch, Dale. Interview by author, 09/06/2008; e-mails in possession of author.

Roemer, Mickey. Interview by author, 11/11/2008.

Rothermel, Brad. Interview by author. 01/30/2009.

Sciotto, Tyler. Conversation with author, 08/22/2008. (No audiotape available.)

Studebaker, Elwin. Interview by author, 03/03/09.

Swetman, Chevis. Interview by author, 01/12/2009.

INDEX

Note: Page references ending in "i" (e.g., 8i) indicate a photograph; those ending in "t" indicate a table.

Redd, William Silas "Si"
  (*continued*)
as chief executive,
  shortcomings/strengths of,
  173–177
Circus Circus hotel-casino (Las
  Vegas, NV), lends money
  to, 103–104
Cocoanut Grove nightclub fire
  (Boston, MA), avoids,
  44–45
college, drops out of, 29–30
Colombia, South America, debt
  collection in, 211
competitors, treatment of, 176
as cotton picker, 15
craps (dice) shoots as youth,
  20, 27
and customer service, 48,
  222–223
and Dale Associates, 159–160
Dale Electronics, hires engineers
  from, 112
daughters, birth of, 37–38
death of, 225
  testimonials at, 225
and Desert Inn Country Club
  mansion, 135, 167–168
and Drama Club, 18
and Drews, George
  differences with, 157–158
  hires as president of Sircoma,
  153
dry cleaners job, 15, 256
East Central Junior College
  (Decatur, MS), enrolls
  in, 19
Electronic Display Technology,
  purchases, 160–162
employees, treatment of,
  102–103, 171–173
farm work, 9
first job of, 14–15
as fisherman, 212i

and food vending business,
  55–56, 59
Fortune Coin Co.
  adopts color video poker plat-
  form of, 137
  hires chief engineer away
  from, 136
  purchases, 136–137
Freeport, Illinois, visits, 32
friends of, 168–169
as gambler and sports fan, 20,
  27, 49, 71, 167–168
and Gaming Hall of Fame, 200
gray-area market slot machines,
  visits in Utah, 118–119
and *Guinness Book of World
  Records*, 114
health of, begins to takes
  seriously, 93
high school graduation, 17i
hobo life of, as youth, 18–19
horse racing game, considers
  purchasing, 160
Hughes, Jimmie, hires, 210
Hyatt Corp., oversells, 97–98
IGT
  board of directors, withdraws
  from, 200
  as chairman emeritus of, 190
  concerns about flagging
  fortunes of, 178–179, 185,
  187–188
  as proudest accomplishment
  of, 226
  sells controlling interest in,
  190
and International Technical Systems, 202–204
jukebox business, Illinois
  avoids costly business mistake
  in, 37
  hires brother-in-law, 39–40
  hires Jones, Bob, 36–37
  problems in, 35–36

About the Author

JACK HARPSTER, a resident of Nevada for twenty-four years, retired in 2002, following a forty-three-year career on the business management side of the newspaper industry. A graduate of the University of Wisconsin with a degree in journalism, Harpster first began writing following his retirement. This is his sixth nonfiction book, all in the biography genre. His other books are: *The Railroad Tycoon Who Built Chicago: A Biography of William B. Ogden* (2009); *John Ogden, the Pilgrim (1609–1682): A Man of More Than Ordinary Mark* (2006); *100 Years in the Nevada Governor's Mansion* (2009); *Helping Hands, Helping Hearts: The Story of Opportunity Village* (2007); and *Captive! The Story of David Ogden and the Iroquois* to be published by Praeger in 2010.

Harpster has also had a number of articles published in leading periodicals, including *The Writer, Travel & Leisure, Nevada,* and *Kiwanis* magazines.